2016年广东省初中英语骨干教师跟岗学习

新一轮广东省名教师工作室主持人宗建老师

宗健老师送课广西南宁

宗建老师参加外信委员会成立大会

宗健老师送课江西南昌

宗建老师送课广西桂林

宗建老师在2016年青岛召开的全国教育信息化应用展上做主旨讲座

宗健老师送课兰州为国培学员上示范课

宗健老师送课安徽淮南

广东省中小学名教师宗健工作室开班领导、导师及成员

广东省初中英语2017年骨干教师跟岗学习

宗健老师送课贵州遵义

名师名校名校长

凝聚名师共识
固定名师关怀
打造名师品牌
培育名师群体

程明道题

初中英语话题整合及话题下教学的实践与思考

宗健 ● 著

民主与建设出版社
·北京·

图书在版编目（CIP）数据

初中英语话题整合及话题下教学的实践与思考 / 宗健著. — 北京 : 民主与建设出版社, 2019.5

ISBN 978-7-5139-2473-3

Ⅰ. ①初… Ⅱ. ①宗… Ⅲ. ①英语课—教学研究—初中 Ⅳ. ①G633.412

中国版本图书馆CIP数据核字（2019）第076158号

初中英语话题整合及话题下教学的实践与思考

CHUZHONG YINGYU HUATI ZHENGHE JI HUATI XIA JIAOXUE DE SHIJIAN YU SIKAO

出 版 人　李声笑
著　　者　宗　健
责任编辑　刘　芳
封面设计　姜　龙
出版发行　民主与建设出版社有限责任公司
电　　话　（010）59417747　59419778
社　　址　北京市海淀区西三环中路10号望海楼E座7层
邮　　编　100142
印　　刷　北京虎彩文化传播有限公司
版　　次　2022年6月第1版
印　　次　2022年6月第1次印刷
开　　本　710 毫米 × 1000 毫米　1/16
印　　张　17.75
字　　数　320千字
书　　号　ISBN 978-7-5139-2473-3
定　　价　45.00 元

目录

CONTENTS

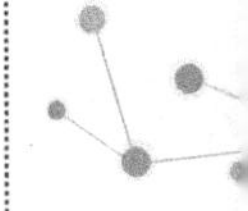

绪 论

中山市小榄镇华侨中学宗健老师撰写的《初中英语话题整合及话题下教学的实践与思考》是以话题为中心的教材整合及英语教学模式为主要内容，是基于建构主义学习理论以及与建构主义学习环境相适应的教学模式探索的一本专著。

本专著阐述了话题整合下适切教研、整合教材和实践话题教学的背景；同时提出话题整合的支撑理论及目前初中英语教学现实与目标的差距；以《义务教育教科书英语（Go for it!）》（简称人教版GFI）为例，初三复习话题整合、教材单元整合及话题下英语教学案例，突出初中英语教材整合及话题下教学的必要性和实效性。

《初中英语话题整合及话题下教学的实践与思考》，很好地促进了初中英语学科的深度探究、英语教师专业的发展及学生英语核心素养的培养，使一所生源中下的学校，在初中毕业时取得了优异成绩，彰显了话题整合及话题下教学的显著成效。

本专著的研究方向是以话题为中心的教材整合下英语教学探索。建构主义理论认为："以学生为中心，在整个教学过程中由教师起组织者、指导者、帮助者和促进者的作用，利用情境、协作、会话等学习环境要素充分发挥学生的主动性、积极性和首创精神，最终达到使学生有效地实现对当前所学知识的意义建构的目的。"在这种教学模式中，学生是知识意义的主动建构者；教师是教学过程的组织者、指导者，意义建构的帮助者、促进者。以话题为中心的教学模式是以学生为中心，以培养学生核心素养为目标，探索适合学生的教学模式。本研究是宗健老师二十多年的教学沉淀和教学智慧的结晶，具有原创性，有很强的操作性，因而有一定的推广价值。尤其是初三复习教材整合和各种课型在话题下教学，对当前的教与学，促进初中英语教师专业能力的发展，有较好的借鉴、推广作用。

第一章

话题整合能够为适切教研展现典范

教研，指总结教学经验，发现教学问题，研究教学方法，其目的是促进教师的专业发展，以便更好地促进教育教学工作。做教研一方面可以丰富教育教学手段和提高教育教学质量，另外一方面有利于教师突破职业发展的“瓶颈”，促进教师的专业发展，消除教师的职业倦怠，提升教师的职业幸福感。

一、适切教研的背景

1. 英语语言教学的发展

自从《新课程标准》实施以来，中学英语的课堂教学主要经历了或正在经历着以下几种模式：任务型教学法（Task-based Language Teaching）、五指教学法RPCPP［即复习（Review）—呈现（Presentation）—巩固（Consolidation）—练习（Practice）—表现（Project）］、3P教学法［即演示（Presentation）—操练（Practice）—运用（Production）］等。不管在课堂上使用哪种教学方法或者教学途径，能够达到语言教学的目的就是最好的。所以，当前语言教学界达成的共识就是：坚持交际语言教学的基本理念和基本原则，因地制宜，创造性地运用各种教学方法开展教学。适切教研是教师帮助学生全面了解、把握知识，灵活运用知识来解决问题，培养学生创新能力的一种研究途径。

2. 教育教研能力是英语教师教学职责

刘道义在《试论中小学英语教师的专业发展》一文中提出教师专业发展的五个点，即学科专业水平、通识文化知识、育人能力、教学能力以及科研能力。对于教师来说，教研是将教学实践与研究密切结合的探究性、反思性、合作性的学习和工作方式。教研能力是教师专业发展的重要方面，反之，教师的专业发展能够促进教师提高教研能力。适切教研反映了教师专业发展的水平，也为教师的专业发展保驾护航。

3. 学校及学生的现状

中山市小榄镇华侨中学是一所镇区农村公办学校，学生的来源以片区招生为主，片区招生的学生经过其他学校的层层选拔，留在本校的学生英语水平普遍不高。而珠三角外来务工人员符合条件的积分入学的学生，来自不同的民办学校，甚至有部分学生来自于外地，小学阶段根本没有学过英语，英语水平参差不齐。学生的英语基础摆在面前，没有抱怨，只能想办法；学生的状况无从改变，只有改变教师，通过教师的教研，并且是适切的教研，才能走出困境，带领学生学好英语，完成义务教育的教学目标。

二、适切教研背景下的校本教研

1. 初中毕业学生的英语水平目标

教师的主导作用、学生的主体作用在很大程度上决定教学效果的优劣。根据《新课程标准》的规定，其总体目标是激发和培养学生学习英语的兴趣，使学生树立自信心，养成良好的学习习惯和形成有效的学习策略，发展自主学习的能力和合作精神；培养学生掌握一定的英语基础知识和听、说、读、写的技能，形成一定的综合语言运用能力；培养学生的观察、记忆、思维、想象能力和创新精神；帮助学生了解世界和中西方文化的差异，拓展视野，培养爱国主义精神，形成健康的人生观，为学生的终身学习和发展打下良好的基础。初中学生毕业时要达到五级目标，其词汇量要求是学会使用1500～1600个的单词和200～300个习惯用语或固定搭配语；功能语方面要熟悉和运用24个话题；能够达到一定的语言认知能力和综合运用能力。

2. 现实与目标的差距

《新课程标准》明确规定了初中毕业学生的五级目标，但是在比较短的复习时间内，从语言知识上要达成规定目标不是容易的事情。首先，语言知识的容量非常大，而学生所储备的语言知识相对匮乏。其次，学生在初中三年里所学习的知识都是碎片化的，每册教材每个单元的知识都是独立的、分散的。再次，在重交际、轻语法的教学理念影响下，初三学生的综合知识运用是比较薄弱的。可以说《新课程标准》规定的目标很理想，但是现实很残酷。面对现状，教师要积极探索，充分考虑本校以及教师个人的教学背景因素，因地制宜，创造性地开展适切教研，寻求行之有效的教学方法，从而保障教学目标的实现。

3. 实现目标的途径与方法

为了达成教学目标，结合本校的特点，适切教研应运而生。

（1）请进来、走出去，夯实教师的教学理论，学习名家教学风格，更新教师的教学观念，为适切教研提供必要条件。为了让教研组成员树立“以学生发展为本，以创新精神和实践能力培养为重点，结合情感、态度、价值观”的新课程理念，教研组制订了三级全员培训计划。

① 校级培训，定期安排教师骨干进行专题讲座；选购教育专著，让教师研习；邀请北师大、广东教育学院的知名教授、人教社专家等来校指导；对新教师、教学基础薄弱的教师、老教师和骨干教师分别制订不同的培训计划，提出不同的要求，分层培训、分类推进。制定教师专业发展“三、四、五、七”方案，即三年内成为合格教师：我们采用“一对一”师徒，“捆绑式”帮带教学，要求老师理解《新课程标准》，读通教材，结合学校实际，精准地把握课堂进行有效教学。四年内成为校级骨干教师：要求教师能够活用教材，重组教，具有一定的教研能力。五年内成为镇级骨干教师：通过全员培训，培养其分析了解学生、设计教学方案、实施教学策略、教育管理学生的意识和能力。七年内成为个性鲜明，具有名师风范的市级优秀教师：要求教师更新观念，多交流、多听课，通过学习和研讨，树立先进的教学理念，形成自己独特的教学风格。

② 全员参加市、镇举行的继续教育培训、各种研讨活动。组织英语教师积极参加市、镇举行的各种研讨活动、教育培训，使教师在活动过程中，其实践能力、调整能力得到提高；促使教师进行思考与反思。教师学会对自己的教育实践进行反思，寻找理论支撑，在观察、反思中发现问题，从大量的教育现象、案例中归纳出理性的观点，努力寻找解决问题的途径。

③ 选派骨干教师参加各种省级、国家级的教研活动；选送教师参加国培学习以及到英美国家学习。新课程改革要求教师必须具有高素质、专业化水平，而现阶段达到这个要求的教师还不多。那么如何提高现有教师的专业化水平

呢？根据教师专业发展的方向以及学校实际，我们认为选派骨干教师参加各种省级、国家级的教研活动；选送教师参加国培学习以及到英美国家学习，是我校英语教师专业化发展的主要途径和切入口。

通过不同层次的培训，全体教师的教学理论得到了夯实，教育教学知识得以更新，教学理念得以转变。

（2）规范教研组的教研活动，实施有效备课，开展具有学校特色的适切教研。英语教师的个人素质虽然较高，但是如果缺少了团结协作、资源共享，就只是闭门造车。因此，英语教研组规范各备课组教研活动，实施有效备课，实行公开课常态化，重视听课、评课环节和专题研讨。

精简教研组的管理梯队，由“学科组长—备课长—教师”的三层管理，改为“学科组长—教师”的两层管理；将英语教研组按年级分成三个科组。科组长可上可下，给想干事、能干事的教师提供更多施展才华的平台，从而激发科组长加强教研组里教师沟通、团结凝聚教研组教师，致力于提高教学质量。

规范集体备课模式。教研组下属的三个年级科组，要求每周四进行一次三个课时的有效集体备课，互相交流、切磋教育经验，达到共同提高、共同进步的目的。在集体备课时要求做到：

① 定时间、定地点、定内容、定中心发言人。

② 共同研讨教学大纲、教材、教学计划以及教学方法。

③ 反馈教学中存在的问题，集体探究解决方案，分享个人的成功。

④ 创新形成行之有效的“三模块”“四流程”“五设计”的集体备课策略模式。

所谓“三模块”，即创新备课模式，包括学期模块备课法、单元模块备课法、课时模块备课法。

学期（年）模块备课法是指以一个学期的教材内容为备课单位进行备课的方法，它要求教师在开学前初步完成整学期的备课。单元模块备课法又称为主题单元模块备课法或章节模块备课法，它是指以一个相同主题的单元内容或一个章节的内容为备课单位进行整合设计的备课方法。课时模块备课法是指以一节课的上课内容为备课单位进行备课的方法，它要求教师把导入、授课、练习和作业等环节作为模块进行教学设计。

所谓“四流程”，即优化集体备课流程。

所谓“五设计”，即明确集体备课内容。

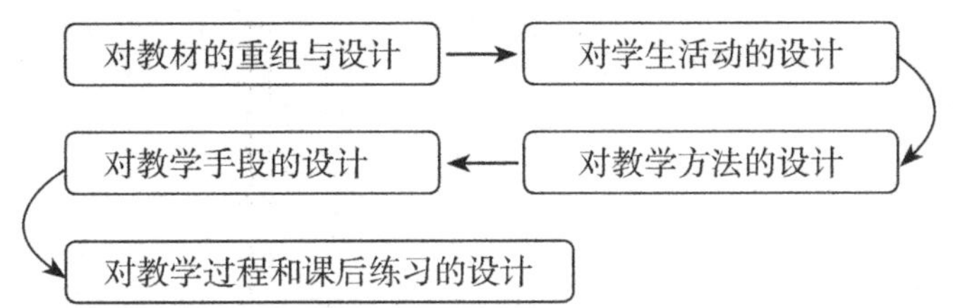

（3）实行推门听课制度。实行推门听课制度，教师开门上课；实施课堂比武，组织教师听优质课、示范课、观摩课。实行推门听课制度，教师开门上课，教师之间随时互相听课，通过认真细致的说课、评课、专题研讨，深入交流，以集体的智慧解决教学中的难点问题、共性问题，从而提高教师的教育教学基本技能和能力，实现高效课堂。

每一学期伊始，教研组就制订多层次的课堂大比武方案，以检验教师的教学能力。

校内公开课评比常态化，要求人人参加，个个听课，课后参与评课。

开展“教学开放周”活动，选派优质课获奖教师参加大文科公开课；选派青年教师、骨干教师参加国家、省、市、镇范围的教学比赛，为适切教研展现典范。

第二章

探索整合教材、实践话题教学

一、初中英语教材与小学英语教学衔接性不强

中山市初中英语教材使用的是人教版“Go for it”教材。该教材使用范围广，覆盖面大，认可度较高。但是教材编写以零基础的学生为起点，与中山市英语教学的历史发展和目标定位不相符。我市从1996年开始在全市一、二年级开设英语课程，迄今已有20年历史。当前，全市小学英语课程开设规范，教学基础扎实，教学质量和社会认可度高，家长和学生对初中英语学习的要求和期望更高。显然，以零基础学生为起点的人教版初中英语教材与我市小学英语教学缺乏衔接性，难以满足教学需求和社会期盼。

1. 初中英语教材话题与小学教材话题大量重复

从课程标准层面来看，小学和初中阶段的话题界定清晰，不存在重复问题。但是由于人教社初中英语教材以零基础学生为编写起点，因此初中教材必然覆盖课程标准中二级和五级目标规定的所有话题，这是导致初中教材很多话题与小学话题重复的主因，也是造成初一教学“炒生饭”、初中与小学教学不衔接的主要因素。

2. 初一与初二教材难度和跨度过大

由于教材编写以零基础学生为起点，初一教材必然要兼顾二级目标达成，即覆盖小学阶段的话题和内容，教材难度自然降低，内容简单、话题重复现象则不可避免。从初二开始，教材着眼于五级目标的达成，难度和梯度自然加大，学习难度自然提高，初二教材与初一教材缺乏有效衔接，部分学生难以适应，掉队和两极分化现象持续出现，教学效果难以保证。

二、话题整合和材料补充能有效地弥补教材内容重复和语料不足的缺陷

教材是学生重要的语言输入材料，是教学的主要材料，是教师组织、设计和实施教学的重要指引。由于各种主客观条件的限制，地级市难以编写适合本地英语发展的教材，因此很多地市选择使用省级出版社或国家级出版社的教材。但是由于各个地方的经济、社会发展程度不同，对教育的定位和需求差异较大，省级或国家级教材难以满足不同地方的实际需要。在实践中，出版社由于人力、物力等主客观因素限制，无法专为某一个地方编写或修改教材。在这样的背景下，地级市则需要根据本地教育发展的实际需求，采取具体措施，弥补教材不足，补充和提高教材的适切性。在当前背景下，话题整合和材料补充是弥补教材缺陷、提高教材适切性的主要手段。

1. 话题整合能有效地避免初中与小学教材话题重复的缺陷

话题整合意味着对小学和初中话题进行重新梳理，或合并，或删减，或增加，规避话题重复教学。在话题整合中，首先，初中教师需要对小学阶段所学话题进行梳理，确定小学话题所涉及的概念。然后，教师要对教材中初中的话题进行列表式整理，确定其概念归属。最后，教师要对小学和初中话题进行对比分析，确定初中教材中哪些话题是小学阶段已经学过、哪些话题是还没有学过的。在全面对比和分析的基础上，合并整理小学阶段已经学过的话题，整理的基本思路是建立上位概念，提高话题的综合性。比如，对于小学阶段学过的姓名、年龄、爱好等话题可以在上位概念“人物介绍”的框架下进行整合。小学阶段没有学过的话题则单列并作为教学重点。通过话题整合，对重复的话题或合并，或删减，有效地规避了初中和小学教材话题重复、初一教学“炒生饭”的问题。

2. 材料补充能够有效地避免初一教材语料不足的缺陷

由于人教版初一英语教材以零基础学生为起点，受制于话题的局限，教材的语料也较为单薄，语言输入明显不足，学生接触的语言广度和深度都极为有限，不利于学生的语言学习。在这样的背景下，补充与话题相关的语言材料是弥补教材缺陷的主要方式之一。教师可以结合单元话题和基本语言知识，选择或者改

编一定长度和深度的文本供学生阅读，增加学生接触和使用语言的机会。

三、话题整合和材料补充能有效地提高学生的语言运用能力等核心素养

当前，初中英语教学受限于教材，内容仍局限于语言、词汇、语法知识等碎片化处理，体系构建不彻底。低效、枯燥乏味的课堂使“学科育人”的理念很难落实，更与英语学科核心素养的培养背道而驰。因此，基于英语学科核心素养的要求，在行文中致力于初中英语话题教学的实践与研究，利用思维导图整合教材，话题整合，提高学生的语言应用能力、文化品格、思维品质以及学习能力。英语是一门外语语言学科。一门语言的背后是一种文化和一种思维，学生学习英语，不能仅仅停留在运用这门外语进行交流对话，还要理解英语国家的文化背景，渗透他们的思维方式。英语学科离不开语言、文化和思维，修订中的《高中英语课程标准》（以下简称《修订课标》）为此提出了语言能力、文化品格、思维品质和学习能力四大学科核心素养。四大核心素养是互相影响、互相促进的整体，其中语言能力是基础要素，文化品格是价值取向，思维品质是心智保障，学习能力是发展条件。话题整合和材料补充最终的目的是提高学生的语言运用能力等核心素养，为高中阶段的学习打下基础，这是中小学英语教学衔接的应有之意。话题在本质上是一个概念，概念既有上位概念又有下位概念。每一个概念下面又有子概念，每一个概念都涉及具体的词汇、句型等语言。在概念的框架下学习英语，既能有效建构学生的语言知识，又能提高学生的语言运用能力。具体和地道的语言材料能为学生提供接触和使用真实语言的机会，学生接触和使用的语言材料越多，语言素养的提高则越快。

1. 话题整合提高了概念的综合性，能有效地提高学生使用语言的广度和深度

在话题整合的背景下，学生需要产出更多的语言才能完成话题任务，因此学生需要使用更多的词汇、句法和概念组织和表达意义。在这个过程中，学生的思维能力和语言产出能力会随之提高。更重要的是，在话题整合的概念下，话题的下位概念通常已经是学生知识和能力系统的一部分，学生在表达的过程中遇到的障碍和困难相对较小，话题的概念表述更加顺畅，产出效果更佳，有利于提升学生的自信心。

2. 补充材料拓展了教材语料，能增加学生接触和使用语言的机会

语言学习的主要途径是大量接触和使用语言。补充材料意味着给学生提供更多真实、地道、生动的语言材料，这些语言材料是学生知识系统重要的语言输入。学生在接触这些语料的过程中，能有效习得文本语言知识、提高获取信息的能力。更重要的是，这些语言材料是学生进行类似语言产出的重要模板和素材。学生在表达类似话题和主题的时候，材料中的概念、语言等都是学生重要的信息支架和结构支架，能有效地帮助学生提高语言综合运用能力。

四、整合教材基于英语教学方法论原理考虑

教师是课程改革成败的关键，而课堂教学是重点。加德纳的多元智能理论启示我们要以丰富的形式激发学生的兴趣，培养智能，跨越学科本身带来的局限，整合学科的内部，深化研究，着力提升教学效果。教学效果的好坏很大程度是受多种因素制约的，但很大程度上取决于能否充分发挥教师的主导作用和学生的主体作用。因此，教师应想方设法让学生做课堂的主人，让学生尽可能地参与全过程，每一个问题尽量让学生自主探究完成，给学生成功的机会。此外，教师还应该创设富有挑战性的问题情境，激发学生学习的兴趣。

第三章

初中英语话题教学的支撑理论

一、建构主义

建构主义认为，知识不是通过教师传授得到，而是学生在一定的情境即社会文化背景下，借助他人（包括教师和学习伙伴）的帮助，利用必要的学习资料，通过意义建构的方式而获得。在本专著中，学生利用教材的单元学习，在话题整合的指引下进行听、说、读、写训练，和同伴同时学习，与同伴横向、纵向产生比较，得到师生的帮助，完成教师精心挑选的听、说、读、写训练任务，包括和课文相关的词、句、文的朗读训练、英文电影、英文歌曲、英文配音等学生感兴趣的补充资源的学习，让学生能够找到适合自己的学习方式，不断调整其学习目标，形成自主学习的习惯，达到建构自身认知的最佳方法。

建构主义代表人物皮亚杰(J.Piaget)认为，儿童是在与周围环境相互作用的过程中，逐步建构关于外部世界的知识，从而使自身认知结构得到发展。我们通过话题教学的方式来进行听、说、读、写教学，正是给身体和心理尚在发育生长的初中学生创设一种让他们比较感兴趣的、易操作的、长期反复的学习环境，使其在更真实的语言环境中得到语言学习的刺激，并整合到其原有认知结构内，实现“同化”与“顺应”，找到自己在知识结构中的“平衡”，再到“不平衡”，再找到“新的平衡”，在这种循环中不断地丰富、提高和发展，并且建构适合自己的学习方式，如图3–1所示。

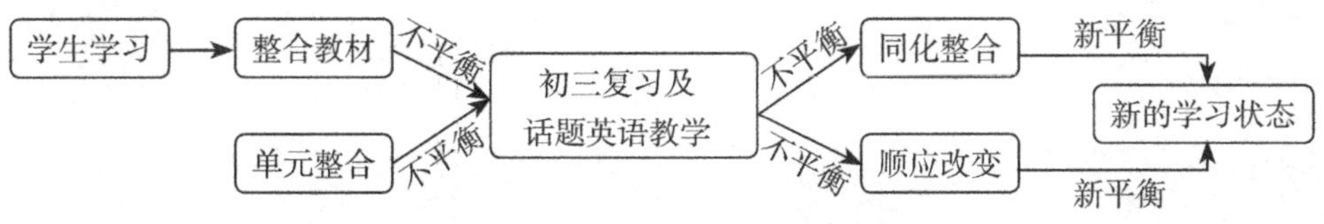

图3–1　初三复习及话题英语教学策略

二、语言习得机制（Language Acquisition Device，LAD）

美国语言学家乔姆斯基认为，语言是人类的某种天赋，儿童天生就具有一种学习语言的能力，他把这种天生的学习叫作“语言习得机制（LAD）”。本专著中，正是重视初中学生的这种语言学习能力，本着以学生为中心、培养学生的学习兴趣、挖掘学生自我学习的潜力、提升学生的英语听、说、读、写综合运用语言的能力的宗旨，相信每一个学生都有能力去学习并学好一门语言，我们遵循学生天生的好奇心和语言学习的能力，将听、说、读、写教学不仅仅是放置于课堂进行，更是结合当前信息技术的发展，引导学生对各种资源整合使用，使学生积极主动投入学习，并通过教师、学生和家长三方面的跟踪和评价，充分发挥学生的自我能动性，通过教学中的反馈，促使学生在教师的指引下能进行自我调整、反思和改进，在家长的鼓励与支持下，能够继续学习，走上自觉、自主学习的道路，更好地体现出语言习得机制的实用价值，并最终使这种话题教学和学习变为学生喜爱的学习方式，成为有实效的教学实践。如图3-2所示。

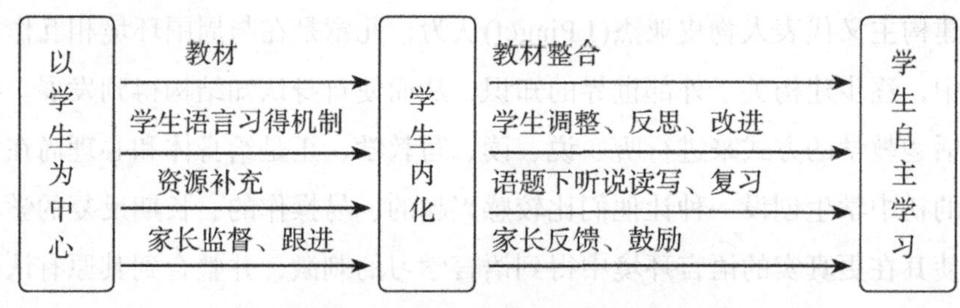

图3-2 语言习得机制的实用价值

三、Anderson认知目标分类学（2001年）

1. 认知过程维度（见表3–1）

表3–1　认知过程维度

水平层次	内 容
回忆	包括记忆、识别
理解	包括解释、举例、分类、总结、推断、比较、说明
应用	包括执行、实施
分析	包括区分、组织、归因
评价	包括核查、判断
创造	包括生成、计划、设计、贯彻

2. 分析的概念界定

《现代汉语词典》对“分析”的解释是“把一件事物、一种现象、一个概念分成较简单的组成部分，找出这些部分的本质属性和彼此之间的关系（跟‘综合’相对）”。布鲁姆教学目标分类法中把“分析”界定为“把复杂的知识、整体材料分解成部分，并理解各部分之间联系的能力”。本专著给出的界定是：将学习对象分解为不同的组成部分，并确定各个组成部分之间的关系以及部分与总体结构的关系的能力。

3. 评价的概念界定

《现代汉语词典》对“评价”的解释是“评定价值高低”。布鲁姆教学目标分类法中把“评价”界定为“对用来达到特定目标和学习内容、材料和方法给予价值判断的能力”。本专著给出的界定是：根据准则和标准进行判断。其中，准则是指做出评价根据的原则，标准是评价对象在每一条准则上的好坏程度。

4. 创造的概念界定

《现代汉语词典》中“创造”的解释是“想出新方法、建立新理论、做出新的成绩或东西。”布鲁姆教学目标分类法中把“创造”界定为“将不同的要素整合到一起，形成一致的或有功能的整体，它要求学生通过思维将某些要素，尤其是不同来源的要素，重新组织形成以前没有呈现过的模型或结构，从而产生一个新的结果”。本专著给出的界定是：将不同的要素整合到一起，形成一致的或有功能的整体，它要求学生通过思维将某些要素，尤其是不同来源的要素，重新组织形成以前没有呈现过的模型或结构，从而产生一个新的结果。

话题下的教与学充分体现了高阶思维教学。高阶思维，是发生在较高认知水平层次上的心智活动或较高层次的认知能力，主要表现为问题求解、决策、批判性思维、创造性思维等能力构成，促进学生创新素养提升的高阶思维教学。

第四章

英语教学现实与目标的差距

英语教学的核心理念与固有教学常规冲突，多数老师疲于应对考试，在日常教学中仍以考试为主线，主要体现在两个方面：一方面英语课程目标在实施过程中存在难以把握教学的难度；另一方面《新课程标准》对教师的要求与教师的教学行为很难有机统一。另外，不容忽视的一点就是，新课程的课堂教学与大班级授课学生的英语水平参差不齐的现象，造成了英语教学的核心理念在英语教学过程中难以贯彻与实践。

一、21世纪教育观及教学观

教育部提出各学段学生发展的核心素养体系，明确学生应具备的适应终身发展和社会发展需要的必备品格和关键能力，突出强调个人修养、社会关爱、家国情怀，更加注重自主发展、合作参与、创新实践。

1. 强调了从单一课本向多元课程资源转移

（1）使用单本教材和多元课程资源——韵诗、歌曲、戏剧、墙报。

（2）统一国家课程要求和校本课程设计。

（3）满足各种需求——社会、学校和个人的需求。

2. 从语言与文化向社会文化知识转移

（1）语言知识系统与能力和核心素养的内容——交流能力不仅是语言技能。

（2）行为规范与伦理美德，社会知识与学科，多元文化与国际意识的融合。

（3）多层次的思维能力得以发展。

3. 从结构—功能向多元任务大纲转移

（1）以语言结构、话题为主线和以多元任务为主线，每个单元各有语言重点。

（2）固定大纲（Fixed Syllabus) 和过程性大纲（Process Syllabus) ——教师提供资源和学生贡献与自主选择。

（3）语境与内容涉及“三个世界”（内心世界、知识世界与未来世界）。

4.“双基”变“四基”

（1）“双基”（基础知识、基本技能）。

（2）“四基”（基础知识、基本技能、基本思想、基本活动经验）。

5.“双能”变“四能”

（1）“双能”（分析问题、解决问题）。

（2）“四能”（发现问题、提出问题、分析问题、解决问题）。

二、目前初中英语教学现状

在教师方面，使用单本教材，缺乏多元课程资源；以单一的课堂教学模式施教。重语言结构、以话题为主线、轻多元任务；重固定大纲（Fixed Syllabus)、轻过程性大纲；重教师提供资源、轻学生贡献与自主选择；重语境、轻内容涉及“三个世界”（内心世界、知识世界与未来世界）。在“问题情境”设置上，往往满堂问、明知故问、一问即答、抢答或齐答等，都是常见的不当提问；有的教师提出问题之后，要求学生抢答，看谁先举手，就让谁回答。结果课堂成了智力超常的学生锻炼思维的场所，大部分学生思考的权利被剥夺；有的教师比较喜欢提问之后，学生一齐作答，课堂气氛显得十分活跃。然而，一齐作答很难做到答案一致，结果造成对问题的理解模糊不清，甚至有部分学生滥竽充数，缺乏理性思考，这也间接地剥夺了学生的思考权。在关注知识生成过程中，预设与生成是课堂教学面临的一对矛盾，教师上课没有预设，没有准备，有时预设与实际不一致，这些都需要教师在课堂里随时进行调整。然而，在实际教学中，教师忙于完成教材内容。教师上课拘泥于预设性的教学设计，没有根据课堂教学的实际情况活用教学设计及教材。

学生方面，存在着学习行为的被动化问题；缺乏品格、思维方式与语言。认知也出现偏差，认为英语不过是一种交流的工具；英语学习就是背英语单词、词组和重点句型；英语学习只是了解一些英语国家文化；在英语学习中认为功能意念大纲代表交际语言教学。

因此，目前初中课堂存在的问题：

（1）注重结果，缺乏英语的实用性。目前，我国初中英语课堂，普遍注重学生的学习成绩和升学率，以成绩的高低来衡量学生学习的好坏，往往忽略了英语这门语言的交际和实用性，使学生在还没有了解英语这门语言时就进行强制的学习。学生在课堂的学习中变得机械化，为了成绩而学习，没有从根源上认识英语学习的重要性。教师在英语教学中，注重成绩，注重理论教学，严重缺乏教学中的实践性，导致学生在使用语言时单一死板，缺乏灵活变通，使课堂的教学氛围变得枯燥乏味，教学质量无法得到提高。

（2）英语逻辑表达结构不完善。传统的课堂学，部分教师采用填鸭式的教育方式，即教师讲，学生听，教师注重学生的书写规范，却往往忽略了学生在交流、书面上的表达能力，导致学生在运用语句时，每一个句子看起来都是独立的，缺乏语言的逻辑性，内容松散，语句之间连贯性差。如果学生在初中阶段没有打下良好的基础，在以后的英语学习中就容易走弯路。

（3）忽略学生的综合表达能力。教师在英语课堂教学中，注重学生学习英语的技能，却往往忽略了学生的综合表达能力。也有一部分学生片面地认为英语的表达，就是将语言表面的信息原文不动地进行翻译，没有意识到在翻译的过程中语句之间的连贯性，语言表达之间没有层次感，英语学习过于片面、机械化。

（4）缺乏语言表达的流畅性。教师在向学生传输英语知识的过程中，只是注重学生的英语语法、技巧等方面，使学生的学习变得机械化，失去了语言的紧密性和连接性，语句中的单词组合运用生硬，语句和语句之间存在割裂现象，段落之间融合不到一起，缺乏流畅性和起承转合，语言表达不够规范、严谨。

第五章

教与学拓展需要

英语话题教学，即开展以话题为中心的英语教学。首先，要求教师对教材有系统性的认知，高度的概括能力，分析教材，精确定位，即定位教学观；其次，以话题为指引，教师应明确课型，根据课型改变教学目标；再次，教师应该研究学情，做到有的放矢，即改变学生的学习观；最后，教师应该立足现实，根据不同的课型，采用不同的教学方式，即巧用教与学的有效途径。

对教师来说，英语核心素养下的英语教学以及核心素养在英语教学中如何实现，对英语教师的教学都具有较强的指导作用和现实意义。核心素养的形成并不能仅靠单纯的课堂教学实现，而需要学生参与其中，丰富多彩的教学活动贯穿始终，通过学生的实践和思考日积月累逐步形成的。因此，核心素养的培养需要教师有目的地培养，在学生的学习过程中落实。教师需要整体设计目标，充分考虑语言学习的渐进性和持续性；要面向全体学生，关注语言学习者的不同特点和个体差异，以及丰富课程资源，拓展英语学习渠道；要更加注重素质教育，体现语言学习对学生发展的价值。

《义务教育英语课程标准》（2011年版）提出，英语课程，就其工具性而言，应当使学生通过英语课程掌握基本的英语语言知识，发展基本的英语听、说、读、写、看的技能，初步形成用英语与他人交流的能力，进一步促进学生思维能力的发展，为学生今后继续学习英语和用英语学习其他相关科学文化知识奠定基础。当然，英语课堂教学是英语教学中不可或缺的一部分，然而随着世界多极化和经济全球化以及信息化的发展，如何培养学生交际能力？英国学者威多森（Widdowson）说："真实性交际要把学生的兴趣、态度和行为方式考虑进去，必须与他们自己熟悉的文化环境以及他们关心的事情建立起联系，而不是与他们生疏的外国社区环境相连。交际语言教学如果真要讲求语用，就要遵从学习者的现实，就要创造出适合当地环境条件的话语，按照学习者的真实情况使用语言。认为交际语言教学的目标就是要学生仿照英语为母语的人的规范去发展交际能力，这是一种误解。”

从英语学习的角度来看，英语学习不是一蹴而就的事情，需要学生长期浸润，寻找技巧，形成习惯，培养语感。如果仅仅是针对考试而进行训练，由于时间短，训练不足，教学实际效果大打折扣，不仅无法满足考试的要求，也无法满足学生对学习的需要和未来学习对他们的要求。话题整合教学充分利用多元资源，可以每天进行，且时代性强，选择接近学生生活及社会性的语料材料，学生不仅喜欢，而且可以弥补课本教学中文本偏单一及材料不足的缺陷。

从目前的考试制度来看，在中考的指挥棒下，人文性比例逐步加重，既表达了当前社会对英语学习早已不仅仅满足其工具性，又显露出当前形势下对英语学习要求的拔高，更加凸显了英语教学对文化传承的重要性。因此，将国家英语课程的课堂教学与校本下话题整合的学生自主学习结合起来，以期取得良好的学习效果，十分迎合当前形势的需求。需要强调的是，我们进行的是初中英语话题教学实践，是以英语国家语境、文化、语言能力为参照的“英本主义”（Native Speakerism）理念，转为基于学生成长的角度去审视课程目标、教学内容的理念；从跨文化交际到人的文化素养、品格与关键能力的培养。而班级授课制下的学校教学依据的文体载体主要是教材，英语课程作为国家课程的重要组成部分，其教材的编制者自然不乏权威，他们由学科专家、课程专家，以及部分一线资深教师组成，因此在逻辑结构、专业体系及知识整合上显示了应有的科学性。但是，作为国家课程的通用教材有着根本性的缺陷，那便是制定教材的参照系相对农村英语的实施环境来说有所脱节。另外，学科专家的学科痕迹往往束缚了学科间的整合与融洽。作为教师，我们不能一味地依赖于教材，因为再好的教材都有其局限性。我们应当树立新的教材观，使有限的教材发挥出无限的育人功能和无限的价值。新的教材观倡导教师活用教材，我们明白教材只是实施教学的一种载体，是促使师生互动的一种文本载体，教师在运用这一载体时完全可以依据其个性化教学行为，在遵循课标的要求下，重整并拓展教材。为此，教师要在平时的教学实践中努力尝试整合与拓展教材，使教材更好地服务学生的学与教师的教。

总之，教材是相对固定的，但教学情境是不断变化的。这就要求教师在具体的教学情境下根据不同的教学对象对教材进行修正、开发和创造。现在的课堂要成为——动态，发展，富有创造性的课堂，课堂不能仅限于教材上的知识，还应有教师个人的知识和师生互动产生的知识。著名教育家苏格拉底说“教育不是灌输，而是点燃火焰。（ Education is the kindling of a flame, not the filling of a vessel.）”因此，教师在教学过程中，应充分发挥创造性，成为学生学习生活的激活者，激活教材、激活学生，使学生能够积极主动地投入学习生活中，实现《新课程标准》的要求。

话题下初中英语教学是既符合新课改精神，又符合探究性课程的设计要求，对话题下教学模式的探索和设计是十分必要的。一是目前探究性课程没有统一的话题课程教材，要求教师根据新课程改革的大纲灵活设计，设计各类话题的教学活动；二是话题下初中英语教学既适应跨学科教学，也可渗入到学科教学中。无论采用哪类教学形式，都需要广泛的教学资源作为支持资源。

综上所述，新课改对英语教学提出了更高要求，有针对性地整合教材，设立情境和话题，在情景模式中围绕特定的话题发挥自己的创造力，更深入地体会语言，在实践中运用语言。教师不断加强多元化的教学措施，注重培养学生在学习中的创造性和自主性，激发学生的学习兴趣，培养学生良好的学习习惯，加强实践教学，注重英语的实用性，从而提高英语课堂的教学质量，为学生的发展打下坚实的基础。

总之，教材是相对固定的，但教学活动是不断变化的。这就要求教师在具体的教学情境下根据不同的教学对象对教材进行修正。正是由此，现在的课堂要成为一种动态、多变、富有创造性的课堂，课堂不能仅限于教材上的知识，还应有教师个人的知识和师生互动产生的知识。著名教育家苏格拉底说"教育不是灌输，而是点燃火焰。（Education is the kindling of a flame, not the filling of a vessel.）"因此，教师在教学过程中，应充分发挥创造性，成为学生学习生活的激励者，激活教材，激活学生，使学生能够积极主动地投入学习生活中，实现《新课程标准》的要求。

语境下初中英语教学是贯彻新课改精神、又符合学生性格课程的设计要求，对语境下教学模式的探索和设计是十分必要的。一是目前探究性课程没有统一的活动课程教材，要求教师根据新课程改革的大纲灵活设计，设计各类教学活动；二是语境下初中英语已经超越了学科教学，由于涉入到学科教学中，无论采用哪类教学形式，都需要广泛的教学资源作为支持资源。

综上所述，新课改对英语教学提出了更高要求，有针对性地整合教材，设立情境和话题，在情境模式中围绕特定的话题发挥自己的创造力，更深入地体会语言，在实践中运用语言。教师不断加强多元化的教学措施，注重培养学生在学习中的创造性和自主性，激发学生的学习兴趣，培养学生良好的学习习惯，加强实践教学，注重英语的实用性，从而提高英语课堂的教学质量，为学生的发展打下坚实的基础。

第六章
途径与策略

话题带动词汇，词汇带动功能语，功能语带动结构语言，结构语言带动综合运用。如何有效整合教材？如何高效实施话题下的课堂教学？教师必须高度整合教材，对话题材料具有高度的敏感性，因材施教制订教学计划以及相关的教学计划。此外，话题带动语法、话题带动听说、话题带动阅读、话题带动写作、话题带动复习等一系列的教学都围绕话题展开相关的教学活动。

一、通过教材内容的拓展与重整，培养学生学习英语的能力，激发学生的学习兴趣

在字母教学中，我们看到学生在初学英语的过程中，常有这样的困惑。那就是字母单个是一种音，在单词中又是一种音。针对这一问题，在字母教学中，教师可以有意识地把辅音字母的发音与其在单词中的发音结合起来教学，即在学生掌握了辅音字母名称音的发音后，口头把字母的名称音分解出辅音字母所包含的音素。例如，字母B的名称音是由〔b〕+〔i:〕构成的，要求学生能够读出字母并能分解读出构成名称的两部分音时，利用掐头法、去尾法、英汉对比法，使字母音与其在单词中的发音建立联系。这样，使学生对字母的发音有了一个初步的认识，有利于学生的可持续发展，更好地开启学生的心智，活跃学生的英语思维，为学生日后的学习打下了基础。

在字母教学中，为便于学生有意义地学习字母，使字母与实际生活建立联系，培养学生的兴趣，扩展各类与现实生活密切相关的缩写词，特别是生活中的热点，如KFC，CCTV，PRC，a.m.，p.m.，WTO，IC，MTV等；在教学过程中，学生不仅练习了字母的发音，又扩展了学生的知识面，活跃了思维，课下积极搜寻周边发现的英语缩略词，英语学习的积极性也大大增强。另外，

在词汇教学中，适当扩展词汇的内涵与外延，增强英语与现实生活的联系，架起词汇学习与跨文化交际的桥梁，从而激活学生思维。词汇是构成英语大厦的基石,教材只给出了词汇的基本含义，对其他的用法没有解释。而词汇的使用在一定程度上也反映了一个国家的文化。因此，在教学中，当学生充分掌握词汇的基本含义后，教师可以适当拓展词汇的外延，比较词汇在中西文化中的不同，培养学生跨文化交际的意识。例如，在动物词汇教学中，适当拓展在中西文化中，人们对dog与dragon、sheep与 goat等的不同看法和用法。“dog”在西方国家被视为与人一样尊贵的动物；因而有“love me，love my dog.”之说，而“dragon”在中国虽被认为是吉祥之物，但在西方国家却是邪恶的化身；“sheep”在英语中表示好人、能干的人，而“goat”表示坏人和能力差的人。另外，在词汇教学中，增强英语与现实生活的联系。在学了left，right后，告诉学生这是体育口令的“一、二、一”；在学east，west，south，north后，让学生说“East，west，north，south，home is best.”（金窝，银窝，不如自己的狗窝。）；在学习了player, team后，让学生说：“One player doesn’t make a team.”意思是一个球员组不成一个球队，言外之意是团队不是靠一个人来取胜的，教育学生要有集体主义思想；在学了before，after后，扩展“the day before yesterday”“the day after tomorrow”，然后让值日生每天汇报，加强了before、after的重现率，增强了英语与现实生活的联系。通过此类教学，既增强了学生学习的积极性和兴趣性，活跃了学生的思维，又增强了学生的英语思维能力，为学生以后的英语学习打下了基础。

此外，由于初中起始阶段学生学习音标有较大难度，而音标的学习对于学生记忆单词很有用。如何解决这一问题？这就更加需要教师在词汇的音、形上进行拓展教学。在教学中，教师可通过由旧单词拼读引入类似的新单词（如增、减、改动一个字母为新单词），可正反单词同时记忆，对于一些有规律的字母或字母组合，让学生通过说绕口令和儿歌的方式来记忆拼读规律。例如，“A good cook cooks good food for students”；而通过“Two black rats catch that fat cat”来练习“a”在单词中的发音，通过“Thirty-six thinkers think”来练习“th”的发音等，然后教师可写出很多类似的单词活跃学生的思维，让学生在观察、思考中加以归纳总结。在此教学过程中，使学生懂得记忆单词有一定的规律可循，活跃了学生的思维，如形象思维、对比思维和联想推理能力，学会获得知识的方法和本领，从而消除学生记忆单词的恐惧心理。在具体教学中，我们还要根据学生的实际情况来调整教学的顺序，重新调整和组合教学内容，创造性地使用教材。

二、通过学科间的课程整合，提升学生逻辑思维与综合分析能力，使学生掌握方法，学会学习

课程整合的最基本特征，就是它的学科交叉性和立足于能力的培养。它注重事物联系的整体性和能力培养的重要性。

例如，在英语的任务型教学中，有意识地开展英语与其他学科（甚至多学科）相联系的横向综合的教学。这些任务可以是具体学科的任务，也可以是真实性的问题情境（学科任务包含其中），使学生置身于提出问题、思考问题、解决问题的动态过程中进行学习。通过一个或几个任务，把相关的各学科知识和能力要求作为一个整体有机地结合在一起。学生在完成任务的同时，也就完成了所需要掌握的学习目标的学习。

另外，在创设语境的过程中，我们也应该关注学科整合。比如在施教《贝多芬》一课时，我们不妨将音乐学科中有关贝多芬的生平简介引入英语课堂，让学生在了解贝多芬坚持不懈的抗争精神的基础上感悟《月光曲》给小女孩带来的力量，符合语言课本应遵循的情境性原则，更有利于学生在思想上重视本课的学习。

三、通过学科内容与学校传统文化的整合，培养学生的人文素养

学科教学与学校传统文化的整合是符合国民教育基本原则的一大举措，学校教育本就是基于“教书且育人”的。为此，将英语教学与育人目标整合，充分利用教材中的相关素材，适当拓展，寓思想教育于日常教学之中。例如，人教版 GFI B 5 Unit 6 When was it invented? 话题是Inventions。在教学中，我们进行了整合与拓展，围绕汽车的发展这一话题展开，考虑到设计的话题既要源于教材，又要超越教材，于是就着手解剖教材，发现其主要由两个部分组成，一部分谈论汽车发展的价格趋势，另一部分谈论当前汽车的价格：How much does the car cost？于是我们就在这两部分内容的基础上分别进行了拓展，在拓展汽车发展的价格趋势时，就拓展了几个与德育建设有关的问题，设计了汽车发展所带来的环保问题及汽车消费中的攀比观、民族观问题的辩论。

首先，把班级学生分成“正、反”两方进行辩论。

Task: Debate

People’s lives get better, more and more people want to buy cars, do you think it is good or bad? Why?

学生们进行了热烈的讨论，有的学生说到小汽车给人类带来的好处：

We can use it to travel, I think it makes our lives become more convenient. It’s can save us a lot of time. It can also keep off rain and wind for us.

有的学生谈到了小汽车给人类带来的问题：

It’s can pollute our environment. It’s can bring oil problem.

针对这一观点，教师趁热打铁，继续拓展：

汽车的发展是势不可挡的，但会给人类带来许多的负面影响，那我们应如何去解决汽车发展所带来的负面影响？很多学生纷纷提出了宝贵的意见，有的学生提到了发明太阳能汽车，有的学生提到发明风能汽车，教师对这些学生的回答均给予了充分的肯定并激励。同时，教师也发现学生的发散性思维很强，希望通过这个任务的拓展来增强学生的环保意识，紧接着，教师又设计以下问题进行拓展：

Task: Discussion

If you want to buy a car, will you buy a Chinese car or a foreign car? Why?

当谈论到这个问题时，学生们的兴致很高，纷纷发表意见，把整个英语课堂推向了高潮，有的学生说：

If I have much money, I want to buy the most expensive car in the world—the Rolls Royce. Because it’s very beautiful and comfortable, it can also show that I have a lot of money.

有的同学说：

The more expensive, the better.

有的同学说：

The foreign moon is always rounder than Chinese moon. So foreign cars are always better than Chinese cars , too.

在言谈中，发现现在的学生中存在着比阔气、爱炫耀的思想，崇洋媚外的思想，作为一名教师，有必要及时指出，对学生进行思想教育。因此，教师因势利导，陈述自己的观点与学生共勉。

Ok. I agree with you. We Chinese should buy Chinese cars, we should support Chinese business. Especially after China enters into WTO, many foreign products enter into Chinese markets. It will affect our business, so we all should buy Chinese products. For example, we should buy Zhonghua toothpaste. Do you agree with me?

此时，学生们都领会地点了点头，学生们陷入沉思，此时，可能他们会想到我们中国的现状，想到了……

从上面的论述中，我们发现，有关教材拓展与文化品格内容整合的尝试许多情况下都是在教学过程中生成的。

四、探索出义务教育阶段英语教材话题整合方案

1. 探索出广东版小学教材话题整合方案

对广东版小学英语教材三年级至六年级的教材话题进行了分析、研究和整合，形成了广东版小学英语教材话题项目方案。整合方案把小学阶段的56个单元整合为37个话题，每个项目后面标注常用表达结构以及涉及的单元。比如，在第一个话题问候与道别的话题下，常用的表达句式有4项，如Hello/Hi! How are you? Fine, thank you. Good morning! Goodbye/Bye. 涉及的单元主要是三年级的Unit 1，Unit 5，Unit 6。话题整合方案提高了话题的系统性和关联性，有利于学生概念的系统性建立，避免知识的碎片化。教师在教学时可以前后联系，根据话题调整教学顺序。

2. 探索出初中英语教材话题整合方案

对人教版GFI教材七年级至九年级的教材话题进行了分析、研究和整合，形成了具体的整合方案。根据整合方案，人教版GFI教材55个单元话题可以整合在20个话题概念下。每个话题下列举了关联单元、相关语言结构、功能用语等。以第一个话题 Personal Information为例，关联的单元有七年级第一、

第八单元以及七年级下册第一单元。相关的语言结构有："Be"的一般现在时，"What"引导的特殊疑问句，形容词性物主代词"my，your，his，her，When"引导的特殊疑问句，"'s"所有格形式，询问年龄，"Where...from"引导的特殊疑问句，"Where"引导的特殊疑问句、序数词等。功能用语涉及介绍自己，问候别人，电话号码问答，讨论日期，讨论国籍、民族、住处等。整合有利于建立单元话题之间的内在逻辑，提高概念的系统性，避免碎片化学习，有利于学生知识的系统性构建。

3. 开发话题下九年级复习材料

话题整合遵循关联性、拓展性、生活性、程序性的四项基本原则。关联性是指开发的补充阅读、策略及写作、策略与话题有关。拓展性是指材料相比教材材料在内容与语言层面有一定的提升与拓展。生活性是指材料内容应具有时代性，贴近学生生活。程序性是指在编写过程中充分考虑学生认知过程及思维发展，不仅仅局限知识的陈述。材料的开发以选择、改编杂志、网络平台等媒体的文章为主，一般不改编文章的原貌，除非文本长、生词过多，结构过于复杂。

4. 开发基于人教版GFI中的55个单元话题影视材料

根据课程标准话题和中考考纲24个话题，开发了基于初中英语三个年级教材单元话题的影视材料248个，平均每个话题下有2～27个影视材料，初步建立了基于话题的初中英语影视材料资源库（见表6-1）。

表6-1　初中英语影视材料资源库

话 题	话题名称	视频数量	备 注
T1	个人情况	11	
T2	家庭、朋友与周围的人	8	
T3	居住环境	13	
T4	日常活动	11	
T5	学校生活	14	
T6	兴趣与爱好	4	
T7	个人情况	7	
T8	人际关系	13	

续 表

话 题	话题名称	视频数量	备 注
T9	计划与愿望	9	
T10	节假日活动	21	
T11	购物	6	
T12	饮食	10	
T13	卫生与健康	2	身体部分、体育健康、个人卫生
T14	安全与救护	4	安全守则、意外与救急
T15	天气	4	
T16	文娱与体育	27	
T17	旅游与交通	9	
T18	通信	4	写信、打电话、使用互联网
T19	语言与文化	8	
T20	自然	9	
T21	世界与环境	12	
T22	科普知识与现代技术	23	
T23	历史与社会	9	
T24	故事与诗歌	10	
	合计	248	

影视材料的整合开发主要采取整理的方式，这些影视材料来自各种媒介，如翼课网、优酷视频、TED、各类优课、英语周报、英语双语报、China Daily、21st Century网站等。影视材料时长一般为2～5分钟，视频短小、精炼、形象、直观，趣味性强。可以在不同课型中的不同课堂阶段使用。例如，在听说教学中，教师可以选用与话题相关的影视材料作为输入材料，也可以作为拓展训练材料等。在阅读教学中，可以选用相关影视材料拓展学生的思维，如在八年级上册Unit 7　Will people have robots? 中，教师可以播放话题22科普知识与现代技术中“AI前沿地球首位机器人公民Sophia采访实录”视频，扩大学生知识面，帮助学生系统地建构知识体系。当然，学校学情不同，教师选择的影视材料的内容、长度等有所差异。

广东版小学英语教材话题整合方案（见表6-2）：

表6-2　小学英语教材话题整合方案

要求	序号	功能与话题	常用表达句式	单元
3级	1	问候与道别	1. Hello!/ Hi! 2. How are you? Fine, thank you. 3. Good morning! 4. Goodbye! / Bye	U1, U5，U6, B1
3级	2	相互介绍（自己、家庭成员、朋友等）	1. I'm Gogo . What's your name? I'm Tony. 2. This is my sister / Mary / my friend. 3. Nice to meet you. 4. Who's she ? She 's my mother	U1, U5，U6, B1U5, B1
3级	3	询问姓名、年龄等	1. What's your (his / her) name? 2. How old are you ? I'm ten. 3. How old is he / your brother (sister)? He (she) is seven	U6, B1 U10, B1
3级	4	询问能力	1. Can you read ? Yes,I can . What about you? No, I can't . But I can fly	U3, B1
3级	5	谈论职业	1. What do you do? I'm a nurse. 2. What does she do? She's a doctor. 3. What do they do? They are teachers. 4. What do you want to be? I want to be a teacher	U11, B4
3级	6	谈论喜好	1. What do you like, Tony? I like cake / cheese. Yum! 2. Do you like tennis? Yes, I do/ No, I want to be a teacher	U11, B1 U3, B2 U5, B3 U7, B4

续 表

要求	序号	功能与话题	常用表达句式	单元
3级	7	表请求	1. Can I have a peach? Sure. Here you are. / No, sorry. 2. Can you take out the trash, please? Sure. I'll take it out. / Sorry, I' m busy now	U3, B3 U11, B6
3级	8	表需求	1. Do you want a guitar? Yes, please. 2. Does she want a computer game? No, she doesn't. 3. What do they want? Do they want a guitar? No, they want a car	U6, B3 U3, B5
3级	9	描述人或动物	1. I'm big. She is small. You are … It's … 2. We are happy . They are cold	U2, B2
3级	10	询问物品	1. What's this? It's a desk. And this? Oh, it's an eraser. 2. What's that? It's a pink lamp. 3. Is this a panda? Yes, it is./ No, it isn't. 4. Is that a black pillow? Yes, it is./No it isn't. 5. What are these/those? They're pears. 6. Are these/those grapes? Yes, they are./ No they aren't	U2, U7, B1 U5, U6, B2
3级	11	谈论颜色	1. What colour is this? It's red. 2. Is it blue? Yes, it is. / No, it isn't	U9, B1
3级	12	询问数量	1. How many cherries are there? There are twenty. 2. Look , there are 12 books	U10, B2

续 表

要 求	序 号	功能与话题	常用表达句式	单 元
3级	13	询问所有	1. Do you have forks? Yes, we do. / No, we don' t. 2. Does he have glasses? Yes, she does. / No, she doesn't. 3. Do you have any stamps (salt)? Yes, I do. / No, I don't	U11, B2 U2, B5
3级	14	询问物品位置	1. Where's my skirt? It's on the bed. 2. Where are my socks? They're under the pillow	U7, B2 U7, B3
3级	15	询问所属	1. Whose bag is this? It's my (your / her / his / our / their) bag. It's mine (yours / hers / his / ours / theirs). 2. Is this money yours? Yes, it is. / No, it isn't. 3. Are these Mom's keys? Yes, they are. / sorry, I don't know	U11, B3 U9, B4
3级	16	询问价格	1. How much is the guitar? It's $85. Wow! That's expensive! 2. How much are those socks? They're $1. Hey! That's cheap	U5, B7
3级	17	询问时间	1. What time is it? It's eleven o'clock. 2. Is it twelve o'clock? Yes, it is. 3. It's time to go to school	U9, B2 U6, B4
3级	18	谈论月份	1. When's winter holiday? It's in January and February. 2. Is January after February? No, January is before February	U6, B5

续 表

要 求	序 号	功能与话题	常用表达句式	单 元
3级	19	谈论日期	1. What's the date today? It's October 20th. 2. When is your birthday? My birthday is (It's) on May lst	U7, B5
3级	20	谈论天气与季节	1. What's the weather like today? It's sunny. 2. What's the weather like in spring? It's rainy in spring	U5, B5 U9, B6
3级	20	谈论天气与季节	3. Is it rainy in fall? Yes, it is. / No, it's windy. 4. What's the weather like in Guangzhou? It's hot. 5. What was the weather like yesterday? It was fine . 6. What will the weather be like tomorrow	U5, B5 U9, B6
3级	21	询问星期与活动	1. What day is it today? It's Monday. 2. What do you do on Monday? I play the violin on Monday	U2, B3
3级	22	询问活动频度	How often do you go fishing? Very often. I often go fishing once a week. Not very often. I go fishing about once a year	U3, B7
3级	23	谈论现在进行的活动	1. What are you doing? I'm swimming. 2. What are they doing? They're painting. 3. What is she doing? She's writing. 4. Are you (they) sleeping? Yes, I am. (we are) / No, I am not. 5. Is she doing the dishes? No, she's washing the clothes	U9, B3 U2, U3, B4

续 表

要求	序号	功能与话题	常用表达句式	单元
3级	24	谈论打算与计划	1. What do you want to do? I want to see a movie. 2. Do you want to take a walk? Yes, I do. / Sure. Not really. I want to go to the park. 3. What are you going to do today? 4. Are you going to …	U10, B4 U5, B6
3级	25	谈论去何地	1. Where are you going? I'm going to the bank. 2. Is she going to park? No, she isn't. 3. Are they going to the beach? Yes, they are	U5, B8
3级	26	谈论旅游计划	1. How are you going to get to Guangzhou? We're going by bus. 2. Where are you going to stay? We're going to stay in a hotel	U10, B8
3级	27	谈论过去的状况（与现在对比）	1. Your bedroom was dirty this morning. 2. Is it tidy now? Yes, it is	U9, B5 U5, B5
3级	28	谈论过去的活动	1. Did you study yesterday? Yes, I did. / No, I didn't. 2. What did you do the day before yesterday? I planted trees yesterday. 3. What did Tony do last week? He visited Shanghai	U10, U11, B5 U2, U3, B6 U5, B8
3级	29	询问原因	Why did you stay up later? Because I watched TV	U3, B8
3级	30	谈论过去正在进行的动作	1. Where were you at 3:30? I was at the subway station. / I was waiting for my friend. 2. Were you at the bookstore at 7:00? No, I was looking for a game. 3. Hey, you are late. What were you doing? I was digging a new hole	U5, U6, B8

续 表

要求	序号	功能与话题	常用表达句式	单元
3级	31	谈论过去一系列的活动	1. What happened? First, I woke up late. Next, I missed the bus. Then, 1 forgot my homework	U7, B8
3级	32	谈论身体部位	1. This is his body. This is his head / nose / mouth. … 2. These are his arms/legs / eyes … 3. Touch your nose . Open / Close your mouth	U10, B3
3级	33	询问身体情况（看医生）	1. What's the matter with you? I have a cold . You should stay in bed. 2. What's wrong with you, Gogo? I had too much Cola. That's bad for you. 3. What's good / bad for me? 4. Get plenty of exercise, eat plenty of vegetables and drink a lot of water. That will make you healthy	U7, B6 U9, B8
3级	34	问路、指路	Excuse me. / Pardon me. Where's the bank? Turn left at the comer. It's next to the grocery store. / Go straight. It's across from the park	U2, B8
3级	35	询问交通方式	1. How do you get to school? I usually take the bus. 2. Do you ever take a taxi to school? No, I never take a taxi to school	U2, B7
3级	36	抱怨与劝解	1. Oh no! I lost my bag! Don't worry. I can help you. 2. Oh no! We can't get out! Don't push, You have to pull	U11, B8
3级	37	询问未来情况（存在）	Will there be a living room in your new apartment? Yes, there will. / No, there won't	U10, B6

续表

[illegible]	[illegible]	[illegible]	常用表达形式	单元
[illegible]		[illegible]	1. What happened? First, I woke up late. Next, I missed the bus. Then, I forgot my homework.	U7, B5
[illegible]	32	[illegible]	1. This is his body. This is his head / nose / mouth. 2. These are his arms / legs / eyes. Touch your nose. Open / Close your mouth.	U16, B5
[illegible]	33	[illegible]	1. What's the matter with you? I have a cold. You should stay in bed. 2. What's wrong with your Gogo? I had too much cake. That's bad for you. 3. What's good / bad for me? 4. Get plenty of exercise, eat plenty of vegetables and drink a lot of water. That will make you healthy.	U7, B6 U9, B8
[illegible]	34	[illegible]	Excuse me. / Pardon me. Where's the bank? Turn left at the corner. It's next to the grocery store. / Go straight. It's across from the park.	U2, B8
[illegible]	35	[illegible]	1. How do you get to school? I usually take the bus. 2. Do you ever take a taxi to school? No, I never take a taxi to school.	U2, B7
[illegible]	36	[illegible]	1. Oh no! I lost my bag! Don't worry. I can help you. 2. Oh no! We can't get out. Don't push. You have to pull.	U11, B8
[illegible]	37	[illegible]	Will there be a living room in your future apartment? Yes, there will. / No, there won't.	U10, [illegible]

第七章
实践案例分析

本专著所研究的教材话题整合和材料补充主要以中山市使用的人教版教材Go for it为依据。话题整合主要指的是在初三复习中对于教材七、八、九年级话题的整合；新课呈现中对教材中单元的整合，包括删减和增加，在整合的过程中充分利用小学阶段学生所学的话题以及话题之间的关系；在不同课型中如何基于话题整合教材及材料补充，旨在丰富教材话题材料，为学生提供更多与话题有关的材料。

第一部分　初三复习教材整合

（一）整合教材的诱因

1. 内容

复习的范围是全日制义务教育阶段七年级至九年级应该完成的教学内容，5本教材，48个Unit，跨度大，语言知识繁多，语言运用能力要求高。内容涉及《新课程标准》中所列教学目标的五个组成部分，其中，语言知识包括语音、1600个词汇、十八项语法（62点语法)、十一块功能意念（72条功能）、二十四个话题（涉及106个方面）、语言技能（听、说、读、写）；文化意识包括文化知识、文化理解、跨文化交际意识和能力；情感态度包括动机兴趣、自信意志、合作精神、祖国意识、国际视野；学习策略包括认知策略、调控策略、交际策略与资源策略；语篇中的西方文化。所以，初三复习任务重。GFI全方位55个单元所涉及的话题、结构语、功能语见表7–1：

表7-1　GFI涉及话题、结构语、功能语

序号	话 题	GFI相关单元	相关的语言结构（语法项目）	相关的功能用语
1	Personal information	Unit 1　My name is Gina. (B1)	1. Be的一般现在时； 2. What引导的特殊疑问句； 3. 形容词型物主代词：My, your, his, her	1. 介绍自己； 2. 问候某人； 3. 电话号码问答
		Unit 8　When is your birthday? (B1)	1. When引导的特殊疑问句； 2. 's所有格形式； 3. 询问年龄； 4. 序数词	谈论日期（月份）
		Unit 1　Where is your pen pal from? (B2)	1. Where ... from引导的特殊疑问句； 2. Where ... live 引导的特殊疑问句； 3. What引导的特殊疑问句（重复）	1. 谈论国籍、民族及其语言； 2. 询问并回答人们的住处
2	People around you	Unit 3　This is my sister. (B1)	1. 指示代词：this, that, these, those； 2. 主格代词：I, He, she； 3. Yes/No问句及回答； 4. 名词单复数	1. 介绍人物； 2. 辨别人物
		Unit 6　I am more outing than my sister. (B3)	1. 比较级：-er, -ier, more的使用； 2. Both的用法	1. 表述个人特征； 2. 对人物进行比较
		Unit 9　When was he born? (B3)	1. 被动语态； 2. When引导的状语从句； 3. How long/when引导的特殊疑问句	描述成功人士
3	Home life	Unit 5　I am watching TV. (B2)	1. 现在进行时； 2. 一般疑问句及其简单答语	谈论人们在干什么
		Unit 9　How was your weekend? (B2)	1. 规则和不规则动词的一般过去时； 2. What引导的特殊疑问句（重复）； 3. 惯用语How was your weekend?	谈论最近发生的事

续 表

序号	话题	GFI相关单元	相关的语言结构（语法项目）	相关的功能用语
3	Home life	Unit 1 How often do you exercise? (B3)	1. Wh-引导的特殊疑问句：What do...? How often...? 2. 表示频率的副词：all, most, none	谈论某项活动或行为的频率
		Unit 11 Could you please clean your room? (B3)	1. 用Could委婉地表示请求； 2. 用Could委婉地请求许可； 3. Make 与do的区别	1. 礼貌地提出请求； 2. 礼貌地请求允许做某事
4	School life	Unit 2 Is this your pencil? (B1)	1. 指示代词：this, that； 2. What引导的特殊疑问句； 3. Yes/No问答句	1. 辨认物品的所有者； 2. 询问物品的所属，及对应表达法
		Unit 4 Where's my backpack? (B1)	1. Where引导的特殊疑问句； 2. 基本方位介词	归纳学具名词
		Unit 12 Don't eat in class. (B2)	1. 祈使句； 2. 情态动词can 表示许可； 3. 情态动词have	谈论规则
		Unit 11 What time do you go to school? (B1)	1. When/what time 引导的特殊疑问句； 2. 表示频率的副词； 3. 询问时间（重复）	1. 谈论日常作息时间； 2. 询问和表达时间
		Unit 12 My favourite subject is science. (B1)	1. What（重复），why, who引导的特殊疑问句； 2. 表示品质的形容词（重复）	谈论自己喜欢的学科并给出理由
		Unit 5 It must belong to Carla. (B5)	Must, might, could 和 can't的用法及区别	根据提供的信息进行合理的推论
		Unit 10 By the time I get outside, the bus had already left. (B5)	过去完成时（不要求）	叙述过去发生的事情
5	Interests and hobbies	Unit 12 What's the best radio station? (B3)	1. 用-(i)est, the most 表示最高级； 2. 不规则的形容词的比较级和最高级形式	谈论喜好，对两种（或以上）事物进行比较

续 表

序号	话题	GFI相关单元	相关的语言结构（语法项目）	相关的功能用语
5	Interests and hobbies	Unit 6　How long have you been collecting shells? (B4)	1. 一般过去时（重复）； 2. 现在进行时（重复）	谈论人们做某事持续多长时间
6	Plans and hope	Unit 4　I want to be an actor. (B2)	1. What, where引导的特殊疑问句（重复）； 2. Want, work的一般现在时和肯定与否定陈述句（重复）	谈论工作
		Unit 5　Can you come to my party? (B3)	1. 用can 发出邀请； 2. 情态动词have to； 3. 现在进行时表示将来的计划或行动	1. 发出、接收、拒绝邀请； 2. 谈论已有的计划或安排
		Unit 1　Will people have robots? (B4)	1. 一般将来时，will 的一般疑问句和Yes/No回答； 2. 用more, less, fewer表达数量	1. 对未来进行预测； 2. 陈述表达各自的观点
		Unit 10　I'm going to be a basketball player. (B3)	1. Be going to表示将来； 2. Want to be表达想要； 3. What, where, when, how 引导的特殊疑问句	描述将来的打算
		Unit 5　If you go to the party, you'll have a good time! (B4)	1. 第一条件句 if+will； 2. 现在进行时表将来（重复）； 3. 情态动词should的用法（重复）	谈论因果关系
		Unit 8　I will help clean up the city parks. (B5)	建议和请求结构 I'd like to … /I'll …/You could … / Let's …	
		Unit 10　You are supposed to shake hands. (B5)	…be supposed to …/You should... 表示应该，被期望	1. 描述自己和他人在不同场合应该做什么； 2. 谈论不同国家的风俗习惯

续表

序号	话题	GFI相关单元	相关的语言结构（语法项目）	相关的功能用语
7	Holidays and celebrations	Unit 10 Where did you go on vacation? (B2)	1. 规则和不规则动词的过去式，was/were 的结构； 2. How引导的特殊疑问句（重复）	谈论过去的事件
		Unit 8 How was your school trip? (B3)	1. 规则和不规则动词的过去式； 2. 一般过去时的肯定句与否定句； 3. Did you...? Were you...?引导的一般疑问句	描述过去发生的事情
8	Shopping	Unit 7 How much are these pants? (B1)	1. How much ...?问句； 2. 指示代词：this, that, these, those（重复）	1. 询问价格； 2. 谈论服装； 3. 感谢某人
9	Food and drink	Unit 6 Do you like bananas? (B1)	1. 动词的肯定和否定用法； 2. 动词一般疑问句和肯定与否定回答	谈论喜欢和不喜欢的食物
		Unit 7 How do you make a banana milk shake? (B3)	1. 祈使句； 2. 可数和不可数名词； 3. How much/ How many 引导的特殊疑问句	1. 描述程序； 2. 遵照指令
10	Health	Unit 2 What's the matter? (B3)	1. 用have来描述身体不适； 2. 情态动词should/shouldn't	1. 描述身体不适； 2. 提出建议
11	Weather	Unit 6 It's raining. (B2)	1. How引导的特殊疑问句； 2. Yes/No问句及其简单回答；现在进行式（重复）	1. 描述天气； 2. 描述正在发生的动作
12	Sports	Unit 5 Do you have a soccer ball? (B1)	1. 动词have的一般现在时； 2. Let引导的祈使句； 3. 形容词	1. 物品所属问答； 2. 提建议

续 表

序号	话题	GFI相关单元	相关的语言结构（语法项目）	相关的功能用语
13	Movies and music	Unit 9 Do you want to go to a movie? (B1)	1. 一般现在时肯定句、疑问句及肯定和否定回答； 2. 连词and 和but； 3. 表示品质的形容词； 4. What...like 引导的特殊疑问句	1. 谈论爱好； 2. 制订计划
		Unit 11 What do you think of game show? (B2)	1. Wh-引导的特殊疑问句； 2. 惯用语：What do you think of ...? I do, too. / I don't either	1. 表达看法； 2. 谈论喜欢和不喜欢的事物
		Unit 6 I like music that I can dance. (B5)	1. That引导的定语从句； 2. Who引导的定语从句	谈论自己和他人的爱好
14	Travel and Transport	Unit 4 How do you get to school? (B3)	1. How引导的特殊疑问句（重复）； 2.肯定句与否定句	谈论出行方式
		Unit 9 Have you ever been to an amusement park? (B4)	1. 现在完成时（重复）； 2. 一般过去时（重复）； 3. 现在进行时表将来（重复）	谈论过去的经历
		Unit 7 Where would you like to visit? (B5)	1. If引导的条件从句； 2. Hope to 引导表示愿望的句型	谈论想去的地方
		Unit 14 Have you packed yet? (B5)	含already, yet 的现在完成时	谈论近期发生的事情
15	Study	Unit 2 Is this your pencil? (B1)	指示代词this, that, these, those在一般疑问句中	How do you spell pencil?
		Unit 4 He said I was hard-working. (B4)	1. 间接引语； 2. 一般过去时（重复）； 3. 情态动词can 表能力（重复）	转述他人的话语
		Unit 1 How do you study for a test? (B5)	动词+by/with + 动名词（不要求掌握）	谈论怎样学习

续 表

序号	话题	GFI相关单元	相关的语言结构（语法项目）	相关的功能用语
16	Animals	Unit 3 Why do you like koalas? (B2)	1. Why, what, where 引导的特殊疑问句； 2. 用Because表示原因； 3. 表示性质和品质的形容词	1. 描述动物； 2. 表示喜好
17	Environment	Unit 13 We are trying to save the manatees! (B5)	被动语态	就某个议题展开讨论
18	Position and direction	Unit 4 Where's my backpack? (B1)	1. Where引导问句； 2. Yes/No及答语； 3. 介绍on, in, under的用法； 4. 人称代词they	谈论物品所在地点
		Unit 2 Where is the post office? (B2)	1. Where引导的特殊疑问句及其回答； 2. 表示方位的介词	1. 问路； 2. 指路
		Unit 4 Could you please tell me where the restrooms are? (B5)	1. 情态动词：Could you please...? 表礼貌提问； 2. Where, how, if 引导的间接疑问句	1. 礼貌地向他人询问信息； 2. 描述地理位置； 3. 给他人指路
19	Problem and suggestions	Unit 2 What should I do? (B4)	1. 情态动词could, should的用法； 2. Why don't you ...结构	1. 谈论遇到问题； 2. 提出建议
		Unit 3 What were you doing when the UFO arrived? (B4)	1. When, while 引导的时间状语从句； 2. 过去进行时	谈论过去发生的事情
		Unit 7 Would you mind turning down the music? (B4)	1. Would you mind + 动名词结构； 2. 情态动词could 表请求	1. 提出请求； 2. 表示歉意
		Unit 8 Why don't you give her a scarf? (B4)	1. 情态动词should的用法； 2. How about结构； 3. 现在完成时	1. 对比物品质量； 2. 提出建议

续 表

序号	话 题	GFI相关单元	相关的语言结构（语法项目）	相关的功能用语
19	Problem and suggestions	Unit 7 Teenagers should be allowed to choose their own clothes. (B5)	1. 情态动词should的被动结构； 2. Should + be allowed to do	1. 谈论规章制度； 2. 表达同意和不同意
		Unit 4 What would you do? (B5)	情态动词should表示为他人提供建议	谈论一些假设的和虚拟的情况
		Unit 12 Rainy days make me sad. (B5)	1. Make 的用法； 2. Wish条件句（不要求）	1. 询问食物对自己和别人的影响； 2. 比较和选择对自己有影响的事物，并能正确处理一些实际问题
20	Science	Unit 6 When was it invented? (B5)	被动语态的肯定句和疑问句	谈论发明历史

（2）问题：要不要过教材？怎样过教材？时间够不够？怎样复习语法专项？怎样在复习中贯彻《新课程标准》的精神？

（3）原则："一纲多本"；话题、功能、结构和任务。

（4）对策：我们决定对教材进行重新整合；用话题来带动语法的专项复习。

因此，适切、高效地上好初中英语总复习课是英语教学中的一个重要环节，它是对初中阶段英语学科知识进行的一次系统地、全面地回顾与整理，力求完善学生英语认知结构，并提高学生综合运用知识分析问题、解决问题的能力。若能把握好英语学科的基本规律和特点，巧用复习方法，便能提高复习效率。

（二）整合的具体措施与举例

复习课是课堂教学的重要课型之一，在英语教学中占有重要的地位。复习课既不同于新授课，又不同于练习课，新授课目标集中在解决知识上的一个或几个"语法点"；练习课是将某一点或一部分知识转化为技能技巧；复习课不是旧知识的简单再现和机械重复，而是通过学生的再认识、再实践，进一步提高学生的学习能力和运用知识解决问题的能力，具有查漏补缺、系统整理和巩固发展的作用。结合我校实际，我们在初三复习课中，以课程标准的话题项目为依据，对初中阶段的5本教材的内容进行重组，把24个话题浓缩成12个话题项目：My school，Animals and environment，Introduction，Holidays and celebrations，Countries and people，A visit to Hongkong，Numbers in our lives，Health，Shopping，Sports and entertainment，Weather，Science，每一话题为一章，每章中的内容可能分布在不同年级的教材中，所涉及的话题内容是基本相同的。实施了校本化的"话题、功能、结构、任务"八字的复习教学策略。整合后的GFI全方位话题复习整合目录见表7-2：

表7-2 GFI全方位话题复习整合目录

序号	话题	语法	小话题及课时分配
1	My school	名词	people around you, school subjects, school life, interests and hobbies, daily routines, jobs (5节)
2	Animals and environment	形容词	animals, habitats, getting along with animals, disasters （3节）
3	Health	情态动词	body parts, rules to keep healthy, emotions, illness（2节）
4	Introduction	代词与冠词	getting to know you, interpersonal relationships, introducing a product（4节）
5	Numbers in our lives	数词	dates of festivals, holidays and celebrations, numbers in our daily life（2节）
6	Countries and people	介词	countries and languages, history and geography, society, personal environment（2节）
7	Shopping	连词	things to shop, in a shop (size, color, price, material, service and quality), getting and asking directions（3节）
8	Sports and entertainment	不定式	sports, entertainment, plans, intentions（3节）
9	A visit to Hong Kong	动词和时态	kinds of transportation, distance, getting and asking directions, safety rules and warnings, international travel, inquiring and making reservations, travel activities（5节）
10	Science	被动语态	popular science and modern technology, literature and art（2 节）
11	Holidays and celebrations	句子种类	ways to celebrate festivals and holidays, food and drinks, expressing wishes and congratulations（2节）
12	Weather	复合句和主谓一致	describing weather, understanding weather reports dressing for the weather, activities in different weather conditions（3节）

现以Topic 2 "Animals and environment" 为例，阐述整合初三英语复习策略。

示例：

Topic 2 "Animals and environment"（动物和环境）的话题内容分布在教材七年级下和九年级中，详情见表7–3：

表7–3 Animals and environment

复习话题	GFI相关单元	相关的语言结构（语法项目）	相关的功能用语	备注
Animals and environment	Unit 3 Why do you like pandas? (B2)	1. Why, what, where 引导的特殊疑问句； 2. 用Because表示原因； 3. 表示性质和品质的形容词	1. 描述动物； 2. 表示喜好	2 课时
	Unit 13 We are trying to save the earth. (B5)	各种时态、语态的巩固复习	谈论环境保护	

1."话题"带出词汇复习，系统归类本话题需要掌握的词汇

根据本话题，我们整合了Book One Unit 3 Why do you like pandas? 和Book Five Unit 13 We are trying to save the earth. 进行系统归纳本话题需要掌握的词汇。例如，names of animals（动物的名称），以及description words（描述动物习性）的词汇：long / ugly / fat / tall / gray / small fast / short / cute / quiet / shy / kind slow / funny / smart / scary / gentle / noisy / clever / playful / friendly / unfriendly / beautiful / endangered / dangerous / enormous / aggressive，habits（动物的习性），disasters（灾难）和get along with animals and environment（人与动物、自然的相处）等五大词类进行归纳，共185个单词及短语。既复习了词汇，又为学生词汇量的输出奠定基础。由话题进行的头脑风暴、发散性思维，林林总总的知识碎片变得有逻辑性，让学生把书读薄，轻松地跨过词汇关。

2."功能"带出句型复习，主要包括完成任务所需的语言结构

这个话题的功能语是描述动物的喜好以及保护环境的问题，集中为描述动物和表达观点两个方面：一方面是完成任务所需的语言结构，如，What does a panda look like? / What's a panda like? / What can a panda do? / What does a panda like eating?/ Where is a panda from；另一方面是培养学生的表达能力，表达自己的观点，如What can we do to save the endangered? / What can we do to save the endangered animals / How can we protect the earth? I think (believe/ agree/ feel)/ We should

(shouldn't/ could) ...

3. "结构"带出语法复习，将语法分散在各个话题中

因为时态和语态在别的话题里面重点复习，所以本话题结合我校实际，着重复习形容词：一是形容词作定语的用法；二是形容词的比较等级，特别是其重要的句型结构；三是形容词作表语的用法。由点到面，全方位地对形容词的用法做一个全面的梳理。

4. "任务"带出综合复习，结合中考题型，突出用本话题所学语言去做事情

一切的教学策略都服务于学生对语言的综合运用，复习的最后检验就是实践。根据复习的需要，给学生设置相应的任务，让学生在做中真正掌握英语，也真正体现英语语言的工具性、人文性。设置本话题的任务如下：

（1）历年的中考真题详解与巩固练习。

（2）相关文段阅读填写信息表格。

（3）根据所读材料，模仿写作"关于我国国宝大熊猫"的短文，内容包括外貌、性格、习性等的介绍以及如何保护好大熊猫等。

我们设置的任务从简到繁，层层递进，让学生学有所获。

第二部分 Topic 1 My school ~ Topic 12 Weather

Topic 1 My school

一、能力目标

（一）听力

（1）能听懂说话对象之间的关系（如父子、师生、朋友等），对话发生的地点（如教室、餐馆、商场等）。

（2）能听懂所学科目的名称及其相关内容（如任课教师、上课时间等）。

（3）能听懂关于学习活动的描述。

（4）能听懂关于校园环境的描述。

（二）口语

（1）能说出和自己有关系的周围人的称呼并能指认。

（2）能简单描述自己的课程。

（3）能简单描述自己的学习活动。

（4）能简单描述自己的校园环境。

（三）阅读

（1）能读懂文段中的人物关系。

（2）能读懂关于教育类的文章，包括中西方学校教育的对比，特别是学期学制课程的安排和设置等。

（3）能读懂对一次学习活动的描述并抓住细节。

（4）能读懂关于校园环境介绍的文章。

（四）写作

（1）能写出相关的人的称呼，课程及学习活动。

（2）能简单写出自己的课程表。

（3）能清楚地描述一次学习活动。

（4）能简单介绍自己的校园环境。

二、思维导图

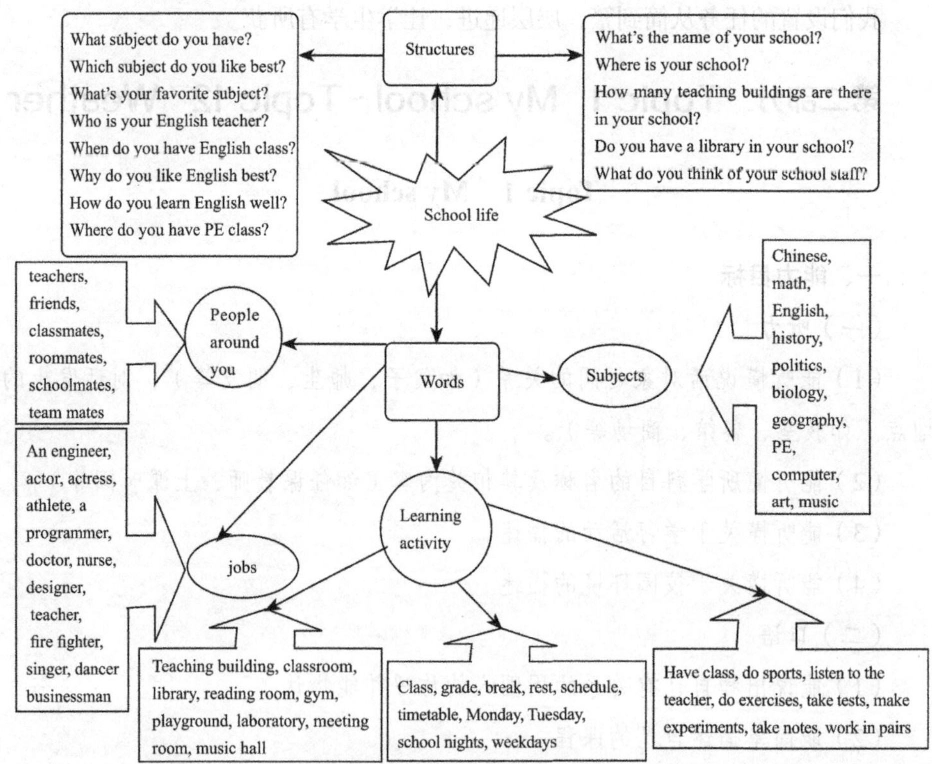

三、话题词语准备

（一）话题单词

1. 科目

Politics, History, Biology, Geography, Chemistry, Physics, Art, Spanish, Science, Mathematics, Music, Physical education, etc.

2. 人物称呼

teacher, classmate, schoolmate, roommate, desk mate, librarian, woman teacher, man teacher, team leader, the captain of the school basketball team, girl student, boy student, etc.

3. 学习场所

school, school gate, teaching building, teachers'office, library, reading room, meeting room, gym, playground, soccer field, laboratory, cafeteria, dormitory, music hall, etc.

4. 职业

Writer, reader, president, head master, scientist, policeman, soldier, lawyer, violinist, pianist, office worker, bank clerk, etc.

（二）话题词组

1. 学习活动

have a math class, take an English test, take notes, get the report card, pass the test, fail the test, practice conversation, finish homework, play baseball, be late for school, etc.

2. 根据情境编写对话

（1）同桌之间互相询问彼此最喜欢的科目的对话。

（2）请一名学生扮演一位新来的同学，询问学校基本情况的对话。

（3）你和你的小学同学毕业后不在同一学校上中学，互相了解对方学校情况的对话。

（4）自己设计情境，展开关于学校学习生活的对话。

四、功能句和语法聚焦

（一）话题功能句和语法准备

话题功能句和语法准备的目的是帮助学生整理、归纳与本话题相关的重要句型，并让学生能熟练地运用以“最喜欢的科目”为中心的功能句进行真实对话。同时，在实际对话过程中掌握名词的用法。

1. 与科目相关的常用句型

My favorite subject is history.

I like history best.

My history teacher is Mr. Wu.

I have history class on Monday and Thursday.

I study history by listening to the teacher carefully in class.

2. 学习方法常用句

I study English by listening to the teacher carefully in class.

I study English by doing more exercises.

I study English by asking the teachers for help.

I study English by taking notes.

I study English by working with a group.

I study English by doing homework.

3. 语法

名词的用法。

（二）中考语法聚焦

1. 名词分类

- 名词
  - 专有名词（China，Mary）
  - 普通名词
    - 可数名词
      - 个体名词（book）
      - 集体名词（family）
    - 不可数名词
      - 物质名词（water）
      - 抽象名词（love）

2. 名词所有格

（1）意义。表示人或物的所属和拥有关系，翻译为“的”。

（2）构成，见表7–4。

表7–4　名词的构成

分类	规则	词例
有生命的名词	一般情况，词尾+'s	Women's shoes
	以s结尾的，词尾+'	Teachers' office
无生命的名词	用“of+名词”	The gate of the school

五、话题语境运用

（1）目的：通过上节课的语句复习，本节课要求学生能将所复习的Topic words、phrases和sentences在语境中灵活运用。

（2）小组讨论介绍自己的学校。

（3）小组讨论自己最喜欢的科目并分享自己的学习方法。

【口语训练】

1. 根据图片，介绍自己的学校

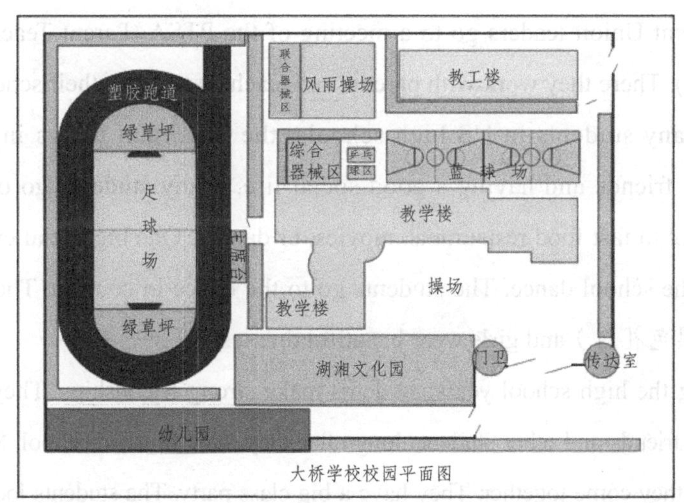

大桥学校校园平面图

2. 谈论自己最喜欢的科目的相关情况

Favorite subject：

Teacher：

Lesson periods：

Place:

Opinions:

Reasons:

Normal information:

Something related to future careers:

六、话题阅读

（一）篇章阅读

In US high schools, there is often as much interest in other students as there is in school subjects. You can see this when you look at a typical high school yearbook. There is a picture of every teacher and student. Other photos show teachers and students at football and basketball games, in class, at club meetings, or at school dances.

Choosing leaders is a large part of high school life. The children decide which students should help direct（指导）school business and lead them in the Student Union（学生会）. The union is usually a group of five or six students. They talk to the headmaster and teachers about what happens at school. About once a month, some of the Student Union leaders go to a meeting of the PTSA (Parent Teacher Student Association). There they work with parents and teachers to make their school better.

For many students in US high schools, the important things in their lives are making friends and having a good social life. Many students go out together after - school to fast food restaurants, movies, or dances. One big social event in high schools is the school dance. The students go to the dance in <u>couples</u>. The boys wear tuxedos（黑色礼服）and girls wear beautiful dresses.

During the high school years, students make strong friendships. They remember high school friends and other students long after they have finished school. So every ten years or so, they come together. They have a big class party. The students look at the old yearbook photos and talk about what happened at school and what has happened since then. They often remember the high school years as the best years of their lives.

Read the passage and choose the right answer according to the passage.（阅读文章内容，根据文章内容选择正确答案。）

1. In the school yearbook, you can see the photos of teachers and students in many places except ________. (　　)

A. classroom　　B. club meetings　　C. soccer field　　D. stations

2. Which of the following statements is not true according to the second paragraph? (　　)

A . The Student Union help direct school business.

B. The Student Union is usually made up of five or six students.

C. The Student Union can only talk with the teachers about the school.

D. The Student Union can take part in the school affairs.

3. What's the Chinese meaning of the underlined word in paragraph three? (　　)

A. 成双成对　　B. 成群结队　　C. 夫妻　　D. 小组

4. What can we learn from the last paragraph of the passage? (　　)

A. The students in the US don't mind their high school life.

B. The high school years don't play an important role in the students' life.

C. Nobody likes their high school years.

D. High school years affect the students a lot.

5. Why do they think the high school years as their best years of their lives? (　　)

A. Because they can make friends.

B. Because they can choose leaders.

C. Because there are many activities.

D. Because they can join the Student Union.

（二）阅读策略指导

通过阅读，我们可以看到这是一篇介绍美国高中生活的说明文。由每一段的开头我们知道这篇文章的主题是关于high school life 的，结合学生的生活实际，文章内容很容易理解。

第一题：细节加生活常识进行推理题。这道题只要看懂了第一段的最后一句话就可以找到正确答案，然后加上生活常识的判断，就可以确定正确答案是D选项。

第二题：判断正误题。像这种判断正误的题目，按常理说，为了考试时间一般放在最后做。但是本题有个条件是根据第二段来进行判断，就缩小了范围，降低了难度。通过读第二段就可以找到正确答案。本段主要介绍the Student Union的作用，对照选项，一一排除，就可以确定C选项是不对的，因为除了teachers,还有parents，所以答案非常明确。

第三题：猜测词意题。本题最容易混淆的答案是A选项和B选项。这道题要考虑本身的意义，是夫妇二人，结合文章最后的那句The boys... the girls...，综合考虑即可判断答案是A选项而不是B选项。

第四题：细节题。本题给出了寻找答案的具体文段，因为要通读整段并理解其文字意义，具有一定的难度，但是在理解的基础上也不难确定答案是D选项。

第五题：这是一道综合性比较强的题目。猛一看，哪个答案都正确。ABCD四个选项在文章中都有提到，这就有一个总与分的逻辑关系在里面。每个选项都正确，要求学生看到它们的所属关系，从而确定答案是C选项。

七、话题下综合运用

（一）话题句子

1. I can't work out these questions, can you work them out?

2.Whom does this book belong to?

3. She improves her english by joining an english club.

4. The teacher asked me to read aloud the text.

5. Good learners aren't afraid of making mistakes.

6. Your explanation sounds reasonable to me.

7. As he grew older, he lost interest in everything except music.

8. He usually does after-school activities after school.

（二）话题下读写综合运用

1. 信息归纳

下面是关于Li Dong对初中三年学校生活的回顾。请阅读短文，完成表格。

I started my junior high school life at the age of thirteen. At first the school for me, a boy, meant play, play and more play. However, I changed the way I used to behave at school with the help of my teachers. I tried my best to do well in my school work and follow the school rules. Growing and learning were great fun. Every year we had different kinds of school trips. Not only could we learn many things from them, but also we were given many projects as homework. They helped us know more. At the same time, we made many friends. In Grade 8, I won prizes in drawing and English speech competitions. When I was in Grade 9, I realized that I should give all my attention to my studies because I was going to take the exams to get into senior middle school. Whenever I think of my school life, I feel very happy and I think in everybody's school life there are many ups and downs（苦乐）that influence his life. School is a place where all of us learn to care and share. "School" is not just a place, but a large building made up of rules, knowledge and love. I can describe my school as "Three Ss". They are Small, Sweet and Simple. My school was the best, is the best and will always be the best.

Information Card

The persons who helped Li Dong change the way he used to behave at school	1.
Two things of great fun in his school life	2.
The competitions Li Dong won prizes in	3.
Things that influence everybody's life	4.
"Three Ss" Li Dong describes his school as	5.

2. 书面表达

升入高中的第一周，学校将组织一次以“Our New School Life”为主题的班会。根据个人的三年初中生活，你认为怎样才能成为一名合格的高中生？请用英语写一篇发言稿，可以从思想修养、学习生活、体育卫生等方面阐述自己的观点。

注意：

（1）词数：不少于80词。

（2）开头和结尾已给出（不计入总词数）。

【写作策略】

1. 审题，找要点（至少包括以下三点）

（1）从思想修养方面阐述个人观点。

（2）从学习生活方面阐述个人观点。

（3）从体育卫生等方面阐述个人观点。

2. 怎样写

开头：We are senior high school students now.（过渡句子：It's well-known that our school is very famous. As new members of this school, we must follow the school rules.）

第一点：First, we should respect（尊敬）______.

第二点：Second, we must ______.

第三点：Third, and it's our duty to keep it clean and tidy, so ______. To exercise and keep healthy is important for us all, so ______.（还可以从其他方面写来拓展。）

结尾：If everyone makes a contribution to our school, it will be more beautiful.

Good evening, everyone!

We are senior high school students now. It's well known that our school is very famous. As new members of this school, we must follow the school rules. We must study hard and do well in each subject. And it's our duty to keep it clean and tidy. Furthermore, we should respect our teachers and be polite to others. In this family, we also need to help and learn from each other. To exercise and keep healthy is important for us all. If everyone makes a contribution to our school, it will be more beautiful.

That's all. Thanks for your listening!

Topic 2 Animals and Environment

一、单元学习目标

（一）听力

（1）能听懂动物名称的简单介绍（如老虎、狮子、猴子、狼等）。

（2）能听懂常见的关于动物特征（如大的、高的、有毛皮的、有斑点的等），以及性格修饰词（如友好的、害羞的、聪明的、温顺的等）的简单描述。

（3）能听懂谈论保护动物、爱护环境和表达对动物喜好以及观点的简单对话。

（二）口语

（1）能简单描述动物，包括动物的名称、外形、习性。

（2）能简单谈论环境问题（如海啸、洪水、干旱等），并介绍常见的应对措施。

（3）能说出几点保护环境的建议和观点。

（三）阅读

（1）能读懂关于动物的名称（如海牛、海豚、豹子、北极熊等）。

（2）能读懂关于动物生活环境及习性简单介绍。

（3）能读懂对环境问题的讨论和观点。

（四）写作

（1）能写出动物的名称和习性的词语或短语。

（2）能简单描述动物。

（3）能写出爱护动物，保护环境的建议。

（4）能简单描述个人观点。

二、思维导图

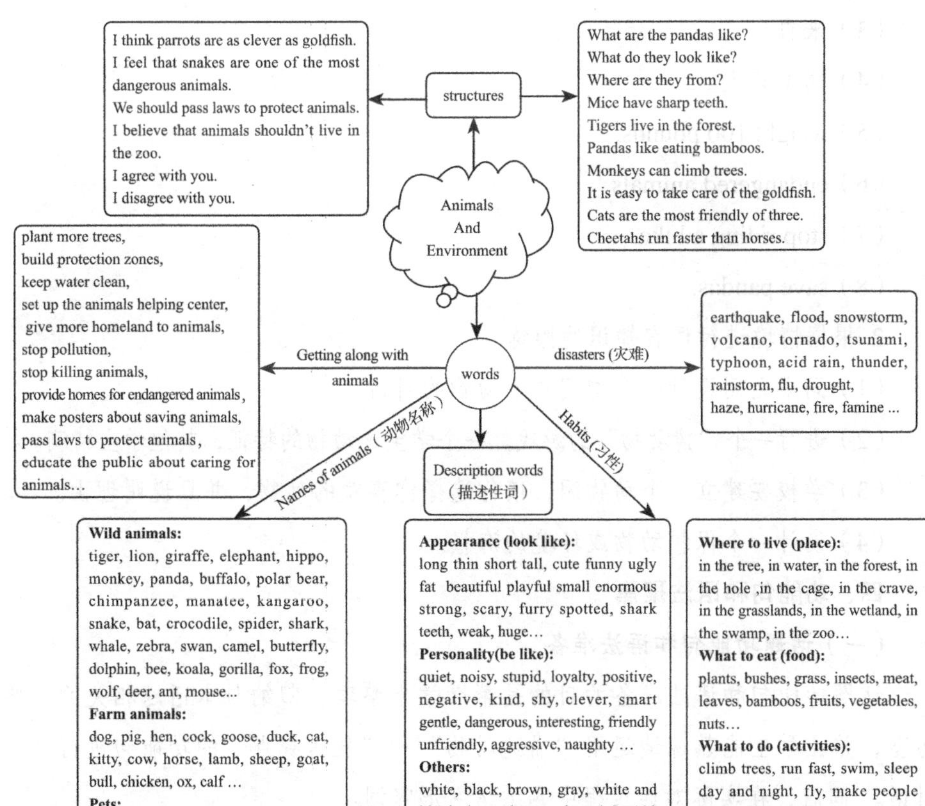

三、话题词语准备

（一）话题单词

1. 动物名称

giraffe, lion, wolf, snake, kangaroo, turtle, goose, shark, whale, fly, mouse, rabbit, kitty, parrot, spider, crocodile, deer, sheep, zebra, etc.

2. 描述性的词语

kind, enormous, dangerous, furry, noisy, quiet, weak, ugly, unfriendly, gentle, aggressive, etc.

（二）话题词组

1. 词组

（1）建立。

（2）有点吵闹。

（3）来自。

（4）同意某人。

（5）weight 100 pounds.

（6）endangered animals.

（7）stop riding a bike.

（8）save pandas.

2. 根据情境进行语言知识的操练。

（1）同桌之间设计一个询问关于动物的对话。

（2）进行一个“猜动物”的游戏。一个学生说动物的特征，其他学生猜测。

（3）学校要建立一个动物园，请你选择你喜欢的动物，并且说明理由。

（4）设计一个保护动物或环境的海报。

四、功能句和语法聚焦

（一）话题功能句和语法准备

话题功能句和语法准备的目的是帮助学生整理、归纳与本话题相关的重要句型，并让学生能熟练地运用“描述动物”和“表达观点”的功能句进行真实对话。同时，在实际对话过程中熟悉运用形容词。

1. 描述动物的常用句

The giraffes are very tall.

It has a long nose.

They are huge animals with a long tail.

They live in the forest.

It can climb trees.

It is kind of friendly.

2. 表达观点的常用句

I think that…

I believe that…

I feel that…

I agree that…

I agree with / disagree with you.

We should …

We shouldn't…

(二)语法概念与比较

1. 中考聚焦：形容词的用法（见表7-5）

表7-5 形容词的用法

概念	用法	位置
形容词是用来说明人或事物的特征、性质或状态的词	作定语	放在名词前，不定代词之后
	作表语	放在系动词之后
	作宾补	放在宾语后，常和make，leave，keep 等动词连用

2. 特别提醒

（1）复合不定代词（something, anything, nothing, nobody, anybody, everybody）的定语要放在形容词的后面。

eg. something important

（2）在形容词比较级前可用much，even，still，a bit，a lot 等修饰，以加强语气。

eg. Our garden is much more beautiful than theirs.

（3）enough作形容词时，常位于名词前，或放在被修饰词的后面。

eg. enough water; fast enough

五、话题语境运用

（1）目的：通过上节课的语句复习，本节课要求学生能将所复习的Topic words、phrases和sentences在语境中灵活运用。

（2）个人表述和小组讨论。

【口语训练】

口语案例1：

The students are visiting Guangzhou Zoo. Mary and Tony are talking about the animals while they are watching them.

Sample：

Mary: Tony, what animals do you like?

Tony: I like giraffes.

Mary: Why do you like them?

Tony: Because I think they are very beautiful and friendly.

Mary: Yes, I think so. Sometimes I feel they are kind of shy.

Tony: Well, do you know where they are from?

Mary: They are from the grasslands of Africa. They like eating leaves.

Tony: You are great. What animals do you like?

Mary: I like koalas.

Tony: ...

口语案例 2：

While visiting Guangzhou Zoo, the students are having a debate about "Do you think the animal should stay in the zoo or not? Why or why not" between Team A and Team B.

Sample:

Team A: I feel animals should live in the nature.

Team B: I don't think so. Animals can't live in the nature because it is very dangerous.

Team A: I disagree with you. Nature is their home.

Team B: Well. But now there is less and less food and the water has been polluted.You know many animals are dangerous for example pandas. So they must stay in the zoo. There people can take care of them.

Team A: ...

六、话题阅读

（一）篇章阅读

Britain is building the world's biggest butterfly house—Butterfly World. It is used to protect butterflies. The building will be 300 feet wide and will cost about 25 million pounds.

Butterfly World is planned to open before March 2011. And it will bring the most beautiful wildlife to people. There will be about 10,000 butterflies flying in the building at a time. Every child in the world has butterflies living near them, and most of them like butterflies. There will be a million visitors a year and 40% of them will be children.

But more and more butterflies can't find a place to live now, as people have destroyed their natural environment. It is said that there are fewer and fewer British butterflies over the past 20 years. During the 20th century, five of Britain's butterfly species and 60 moth species became extinct.

In Butterfly World, people will be taught that is bad for butterflies is bad for all species—including our own.

Read the passage and choose the right answer according to the passage.（阅读文章内容，根据文章内容选择正确答案。）

1. A Butterfly House will be built in ________. (　　)

A. China　　B. Asian country　　C. England　　D. a house

2. According to the passage, Butterfly World is built to ________. (　　)

A. stop butterflies from disappearing（灭绝）

B. show people all kinds of wildlife in danger

C. attract more and more butterflies

D. teach children to love the butterflies living near them

3. According to the passage, which of the following is true? (　　)

A. Butterfly World is the world's biggest butterfly house.

B. Butterfly World will have 25 million butterflies flying at a time.

C. There will be more and more butterflies in Butterfly World.

D. A million children will visit Butterfly World each year.

4. More and more butterflies cannot find a place to live because ________. (　　)

A. they are hunted and killed by people

B. there are a few flowers and plants

C. people are destroying their living environment

D. Butterfly World will open in 2011

5. What's the main idea of the passage? (　　)

A. Butterflies are very cute.

B. Butterfly World are nice.

C. People like butterflies very much.

D. Butterfly World give us a lesson about the nature.

（二）阅读策略指导

这是一篇介绍 butterfly building的文章。文章分为四段，段落的层次不断提高，由简单的描述到探讨问题的发生以及由此得到的感想，是用事例说理的说理性文。要求学生能读懂文字背后的寓意，有一定的难度。因此，学生可以采取“带问题阅读”，先看题目，大概了解文章的文化背景。

第一题：细节题。处理这类题目考生首先要仔细读懂题目，然后在原文中找到相似的内容。本题就是对语篇中的第一句话“Britain is building the world's biggest butterfly house—Butterfly World.”的提问，理解了Britain 和England 之间的联系，答案为C选项。

第二题：细节题。但是此题不是对原文中的某一句的问题，而是涉及整个篇章。要求考生抓住题目的关键词“is built to”，分析每个选项，找到相对应的原文。本题读懂了第一段第二句就可以找到答案。但是题目在意思的表达上设置了一定的难度，原文是be used to protect butterflies，意思是“用来保护蝴蝶”，但是本题的题干用了“stop... from doing”这个短语，从意思上理解答案是A选项。

第三题：判断正误题。关于 True，Not true or False之类的题目，要求考生先要理解题目，分清要回答的问题是True还是False；分析题干之间的相同和不同。例如本题题干之间都有数量的输入：25 million，more and more，A million，那么考生只要核实数量的准确性，就可以找到正确答案，即A选项。

第四题：细节题。读懂题目找到原文第三段第一句，理解 as 在此表达的意思就是because，判断C选项是正确答案。

第五题：综合题。一般题目会以 main idea, tell /teach you… learn… from… talk about…出现。这类题目是对篇章主旨的概括或是提升，一般会在篇章的开头或是结尾点出，所以考生要特别留意篇章中概括性的句子。同时，需要考生在读懂篇章的字面意思基础上，理解篇章的中心思想，结合话题的文化背景综合考虑。如本题的话题应该是：建立蝴蝶馆来保护蝴蝶。这是一个事件，但是事件背后的意思在篇章的最后做出总结：In Butterfly World,people will be taught that is bad for butterflies is bad for all species—including our own. 考生只需理解此句就可以推断出答案D选项和原文吻合。

七、话题下综合运用

（一）话题句子

1. Today, pollution has become a serious problem to us.

2. We cannot have fresh air because many factories have the poisonous smoke sent into the air.

3. It's said that strange diseases have appeared in some places because of

pollution.

4. We are looking forward to seeing the clear sky, clean rivers and beautiful parks again.

5. The sea covers nearly three-quarters of the world's surface.

6. Earth Hour aims to remind people of influence of global warming and to raise awareness of environmental protection.

7. The typhoon rainbow destroyed the whole village.

（二）话题下读写综合运用

1. 信息归纳：阅读下面的短文，完成信息卡

It was a bit cold one morning, but Li Ping quickly got out of his warm bed. He picked up two plastic buckets（水桶）and rushed to the center of the village, where a fire truck arrives once a day to provide water for residents（居民）. About 4,000 thirsty villagers come with their buckets and stand in line for water, because the only reservoir（水库）in the village has dried up. It hasn't rained for six months.

Li, a 14-year-old student, lives in LiGuan village—about 60km away from Kunming. He has risen early to get water in the last three months. "My family gets two or three buckets of water every day. We use them for drinking, washing and cooking," said Li. "If we save a little every day, then once a week we can take a shower." "My father planted two mu of beans last autumn, but now the field is so dry that he can't even plough（耕犁）it because of the drought（旱灾）," said Li.

"The rice is food for my family—my parents and younger brother. We have no money to buy rice from the market."

In Li's opinion, there are many ways to prevent a drought, such as planting more trees. "It has taught me that, if we make full use of water, two buckets of water a day should be enough for four family members. We can recycle the water for different kinds of uses," said Li. "Every drop of water is very important. I hope people can realize this."

Information Card

The number of the villagers who take water from the fire truck with their buckets.	1.
The food which Li's family have no money to buy.	2.
One way to prevent a drought	3.

续表

How to make full use of water	4.
The idea people should realize	5.

2. 书面表达

在我们身边，经常有自然灾害发生。2018年4月20日，四川省雅安市芦山发生强烈地震，造成巨大损失。为此，学校号召全体师生向灾区捐款。请你写一篇80词左右的发言稿，发言稿主要内容包括：

（1）对灾区情况的简单介绍（包括地震发生的时间、地点，造成的财产损失和人员伤亡等）。

（2）捐款的意义（帮助灾区人民渡过难关、帮助灾区重建）。

（3）如何捐款（自愿、多少不限、以班级为单位，收齐后交到学校红十字会）。

【写作策略】

1. 审题，找要点

（1）对灾区情况的简单介绍（包括地震发生的时间、地点，造成的财产损失和人员伤亡等）。

（2）捐款的意义。

（3）如何捐款。

要求至少写出上述三个要点。

2. 怎样写

开头：Dear teachers and students, As we all know,（已给出。）

第一点：a terrible earthquake happened ______（地震情况可以多写一点。）

第二点：In order to help ______________________.

第三点：This donation is voluntary. ______________________.

结尾：We hope that everyone will be kind enough to do what you can to help our fellowmen out of the difficulty.

As we all know, a terrible earthquake happened in Lushan, Sichuan Province on April 20. In the earthquake many buildings were destroyed and many people were injured. In order to help the earthquake victims（受害者）to go through the hard time and rebuild（重建）their hometown, the school has called on everyone in our school, including both teachers and students, to donate（捐赠）money to the earthquake-stricken（遭受）area. This donation is voluntary. You can give away however much you want to. The money will be collected by each class before it is handed to the Red Cross Society of our school. We hope that everyone will be kind enough to do what you can to help our fellowmen out of the difficulty.

Thank you.

Topic 3　Health

一、单元学习目标

（一）听力

（1）能听懂关于人体各部位的名称及其不适的简单介绍（如手、脚、眼睛、鼻子、耳朵、牙齿等）。

（2）能听懂常见疾病的名称及简单描述（如头痛、肚子痛、流感、着凉等）。

（3）能听懂关于意外事故以及急救的简单介绍。

（4）能听懂医生、护士与病人之间关于疾病及治疗的简单对话。

（二）口语

（1）能简单介绍个人饮食习惯，并能谈论饮食健康。

（2）能简单描述一些常见疾病（如肚子痛、头痛、流感、感冒等），并介绍常见的应对措施。

（3）能说出人体基本部位的名称（如胳膊、腿、手、脚、脸、眼睛、耳朵等），并能简单描述病情。

（三）阅读

（1）能读懂关于人体各部位的名称（如胳膊、腿、手、脚、脸、眼睛、耳朵等）。

（2）能读懂关于个人饮食和卫生、个人健康与锻炼方面的简单介绍和评论。

（3）能读懂对普通疾病的简单描述（如头痛、肚子痛、感冒等）。

（四）写作

（1）能写出人体各部位的名称和一般功能（如胳膊、腿、手、脸、眼睛、耳朵等）。

（2）能简单描述健身与锻炼方面的内容。

（3）能写出常见疾病（如头痛、肚子痛、感冒、流感等）的名称和简单的治疗方法。

（4）能简单描述个人饮食习惯。

二、思维导图

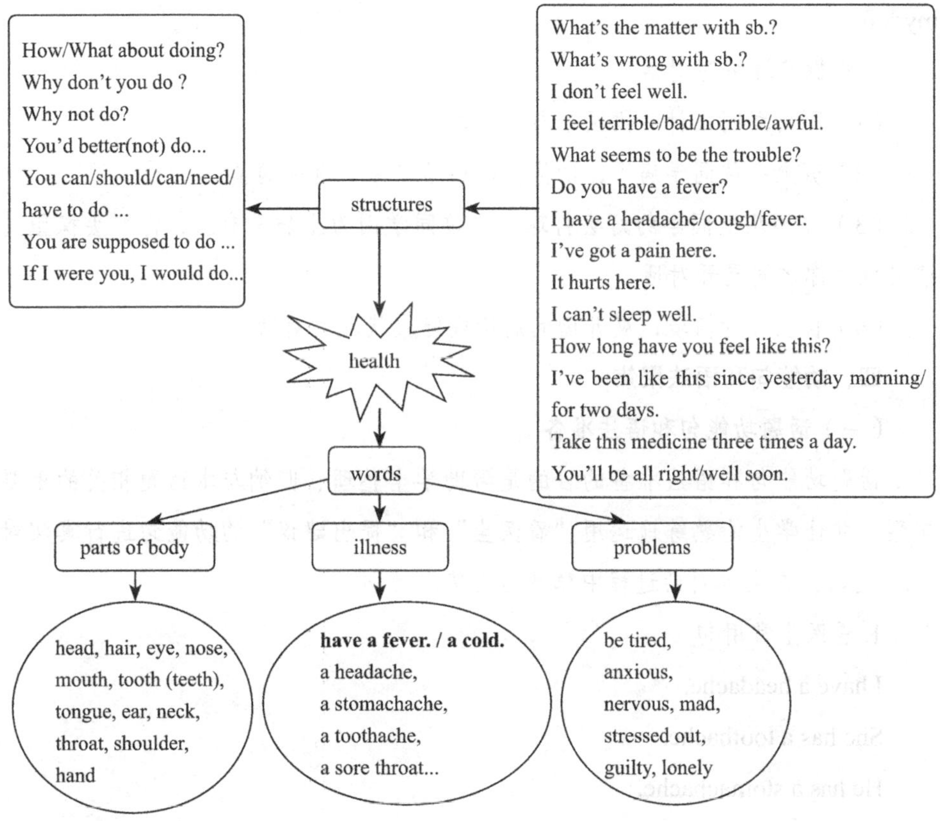

三、话题词语准备

（一）话题词语

1. 身体部位词

head, hair, forehead, eye, nose, mouth, tooth（teeth）, tongue, ear, neck, throat, shoulder, arm, elbow, wrist, hand, finger, chest, waist, back, leg, knee, ankle, foot, toe, heel, etc.

2. 疾病词

stomachache, headache, earache, broken arm, fever, cough, runny nose, etc.

（二）话题词组

1. 词组

have a cold, have a toothache, have a fever, have a sore throat, have a headache, have a backache, have a stomachache, have a sore neck, have a pain in the back, hurt my left.

2. 根据情境编写对话

（1）同桌之间设计一段医生与病人之间的对话。

（2）班上一位同学病了，请你打电话给其家里询问病情。

（3）你和几个同学约好去打球，一位同学因为生病没有来，你要去探望。请在他和你之间展开对话。

（4）自己设计情境，展开询问病情或健康状况的对话。

四、功能句和语法聚焦

（一）话题功能句和语法准备

话题功能句和语法准备的目的是帮助学生整理、归纳与本话题相关的重要句型，并让学生能熟练地运用“看医生”和“提出建议”的功能句进行真实对话。同时，在实际对话过程中熟悉运用情态动词。

1. 看医生常用句

I have a headache.

She has a toothache.

He has a stomachache.

I hurt my leg.

2. 提建议常用句

You should go to bed.

He shouldn’t go to bed.

You must drink more water.

You can do some exercises.

You'd better stay in bed.

3. 语法

情态动词表建议的用法。

（二）语法概念与比较

1. 中考聚焦

情态动词本身具有一定的词义，但词义不完整，不能单独作谓语，必须和一个动词原形一起构成谓语；没有人称和数的变化。

2. 特别提醒

（1）may表示“允许、可以”的意思时，否定回答是mustn't。

— May I take the newspaper away?

— No, you mustn't. You can read it only here.

（2）must表示“强制、一定”的意思时，否定回答是needn't 或don't have to。

— Must I hand in the weather report this morning?

— No, you needn't.

（3）need 引导的一般疑问句，肯定句要用 must; 否定回答要用 needn't。

— Need I come?

— Yes, you must./ No,you needn't.

（4）could, should, would, might等过去式有时不表示过去，而是表示更加委婉的语气。

Would you help me?

（5）情态动词表示猜测的用法。

把握很大：must

不太确定：may, might, could

一定不是：can't

五、话题语境运用

（1）目的：通过上节课的语句复习，本节课要求学生能将所复习的Topic words、phrases 和 sentences在语境中灵活运用。

（2）小组讨论并设计对话。

【口语训练】

口语案例1：

This is Zhu Peng. Read about his daily diet and exercise routine. What is he doing right and what is he doing wrong? In pairs, discuss the advice you would give him to improve his health.

Zhu Peng's

7 a.m. breakfast—none coffee very sweet

11 a.m. snack—chocolate bar

1 p.m. lunch—burger and fries and coke

7 p.m. dinner—fried noodles

10 p.m. supper—curry chicken and rice

Zhu peng's Daily Exercise

Walks to school.

Takes bus home.

Takes elevator to apartment.

Plays basketball every weekend for one hour with friends.

Useful expressions:

What's the matter with Zhu Peng?

I think he...

What do you think he should do?

He should/shouldn't...

I agree/disagree.

In my opinion, ...

exercise every day

eat a balanced diet

eat less fatty or fried food

eat three regular meals a day

drink more water

Sample:

A: What's the matter with Zhu Peng, in your opinion?

B: I think he doesn't exercise enough. He only exercises on the weekend for one hour.

A: Well, he also walks to school. But you're right. He should exercise every day.

B: Do you think he should eat a balanced diet?

A: Oh, yes, I do. I think he should eat less fatty and fried food.

B: I agree. And he shouldn't drink so many sweet drinks. In my opinion, He should drink more water.

A: Definitely! Do you think he should eat three regular meals a day?

B: Yes, he shouldn't miss meals.

A: And he shouldn't eat late at night.

六、话题阅读

（一）篇章阅读

Almost every day, we discuss the topic of health, especially for kids. But what is health? "Health" means eating well, getting enough exercise, and having a healthy weight. Let's read the following rules. They can help you stay healthy.

1. Eat <u>a variety of</u> foods, especially fruits and vegetables. We all know that eating fruits and vegetables can help us stay healthy, but many of us only eat our favorite foods. Remember that we can only get the nutrition we need by eating different kinds of food, especially fruits and vegetables.

2. Drink water and milk most often. Everyone knows that water is important. Besides that, kids need plenty of calcium（钙）to grow strong bones, and milk has a lot of it. Every day, you should drink at least three cups of milk (1300 milligrams of calcium), when you are 9 years old or older. You should also try to have less sugary drinks, like soda and coca. They include a lot of added sugar. Sugar just adds calories, not important nutrition.

3. Listen to your body. When you are eating, notice how you body feels. When

your stomach feels comfortably full, stop eating. Eating too much makes you feel uncomfortable. If you do it too often, it can make you unhealthy and fat.

4. Limit screen time. What's screen time? It's the amount of time you spend watching TV, movies, and playing computer games. The more time you spend on these sitting-down activities, the less time you spend playing sports, like basketball, and doing other activities like bike riding and swimming. Try to spend no more than 2 hours a day on screen time.

Read the passage and choose the right answer according to the Passage.（阅读文章，根据文章内容选择正确答案。）

1. According to the passage, "health" includes all of the following except ________. (　)

A. eating well　　B. doing more exercises

C. having a healthy weight　　D. wearing comfortably

2. The underlined phrase "a variety of " means ________. (　)

A. kinds of　　B. plenty of

C. several　　D. the rest of

3. Which of the following is NOT true? (　)

A. Eating more fruits and vegetables is difficult for some people.

B. We should eat and drink something with less sugar.

C. When we are full, we should stop eating, however delicious the food is.

D. We should spend the same time on both sitting-down activities and on sports.

4. As a kid, you should eat at least ________ to grow strong bones. (　)

A. four cups of milk　　B. three cups of milk

C. two cups of milk　　D. one cup of milk

5. What's the best title for the passage? (　)

A. How to Eat Healthily.

B. Eating and Playing are Both Important.

C. Tips for Staying Healthy.

D. Health is Very Important.

（二）阅读策略指导

这是一篇总分式的科技文章。由第一段知道它的话题是health，而下面的所有内容都是为这个话题做的解说，所以由Besides that, kids need plenty of calcium（钙）to grow strong bones, and milk has a lot of it. Every day, you should drink 可知这篇文章主要讲健康。

第一题：细节题。这道题是针对全文的，细节只用看第1、2、3、4段的第一句话就好了。这四段分别讲了吃、喝、锻炼，还有看电视，所以D选项正确。

第二题：猜测词意题。最主要的是找同义词a variety of foods 和different kinds of food，这明显就是很多种类的意思，所以A选项正确。

第三题：判断正误题。像这种判断正误、mention or not mention和选标题这种题，为了考试时间一定放在最后做。由于你做完所有的细节题对全文有掌握，更好做题。而且对于这种题，出现在篇幅较长的文章中，要从选项中找。可以从选项中看到，这道题从描写吃的和锻炼那一段中找。所以A选项正确。因为B选项所对应的句子You should also try to have less sugary drinks, like soda and coca. They include a lot of added sugar. Sugar just adds calories, not important nutrition. C选项所对应的句子是 When your stomach feels comfortably full, stop eating. Eating too much makes you feel uncomfortable. If you do it too often, it can make you unhealthy and fat. D选项的句子是The more time you spend on these sitting-down activities, the less time you spend playing sports, like basketball, and doing other activities like bike riding and swimming. Try to spend no more than 2 hours a day on screen time. 所以A选项正确。

第四题：细节题。从选项中可以看出都是讲牛奶。只要在第2段中找就好了。Besides that, kids need plenty of calcium（钙）to grow strong bones, and milk has a lot of it. Every day, you should drink at least three cups of milk(1300 milligrams of calcium), when you are 9 years old or older. 所以B选项正确。

第五题：就是所谓的标题，整篇文章都是讲健康，纵观全文，讲的是如何让你保持健康，所以选C选项。

七、话题下综合运用

（一）话题句子

1. My shoes are so tight that my feet hurt.

2. Take 2 pills and two more in 6 hours.

3. I advise you to give up smoking and not to drink too much.

4. The boy had a headache and had to see the doctor.

5. Drink plenty of water and have a good rest in bed.

6. I don't feel like eating anything.

（二）话题下读写综合运用

1. 信息归纳

请阅读下面短文，完成表格。

The generation gap（代沟）has become a serious problem. I read a report about it in the newspaper. Some children have killed themselves after quarrelling with parents. I think this is because they don't often have a talk with each other. Parents now spend more time in the office, so they don't have much time to stay with their children.

As time passes, they both feel that they don't have the same topics（话题） to talk about. I want to tell parents to be more with your children, get to know them and understand them. And for children, show your feelings to your parents. They are the people who love you. So tell them your thoughts（想法）. In this way, you can have a better understanding of each other.

Information Card

________ has become a serious problem .	1.
________ causes the generation gap.	2.
Parents and children feel ________.	3.
As for the problem, parents should ________.	4.
As for the problem, children should ________.	5.

2.书面表达

假设你们班要在下星期一举行题为“The Ways for Students to Relax”的班会，请结合报道的内容，用英语写一篇80词左右的发言稿。内容包括：

（1）简要介绍造成现在学生学习压力大的原因。

（2）你认为来自于English Online调查结果的放松方式是否有效？为什么？

（3）谈谈你个人自我放松的有效做法（至少三点）。

【写作策略】

1. 审题，找要点

（1）简要介绍造成现在学生学习压力大的原因。①

（2）你认为来自于English Online调查结果的放松方式是否有效②，为什么？③

（3）谈谈你个人自我放松的有效做法（至少三点）。④⑤⑥

必须要写出上述这六点。

2. 怎样写

第一点：Not only adults but also we students often feel stressed（已给出），because ________________.

第二、三点：From the result of the survey, I think ____________.

Because __________.

第四、五、六点：I also have three ways to relax. First, ___________. Second, __________. Third, ________.（接着还可以Fourth, ... Fifth, ... 来拓展。）

结尾：I hope my suggestions can help you.

Dear fellows,

Not only adults but also we students often feel stressed because we have too much homework to do, and we are very busy studying every day, we don't have our own time to do what we are interested in. We are very tired and sleepy all day, so we should learn to deal with it. What should we do to relax?

From the result of the survey, I think doing sports with classmates is a good way to relax. Because it's good for our health and it can make us relaxed.

I also have three ways to relax ourselves. First, we can listen to music. Second, we can go to the movies with our parents on weekends. Don't study at home all the weekend. Third, when we feel tired, we can think about something interesting.

I hope my suggestions can help you.

Thanks!

Topic 4 Introduction

一、能力目标

（一）听力

（1）能听懂简单有关家人、亲戚、朋友的词，以及相关描述的词，如职业、兴趣、性格等。

（2）能听懂常见打招呼及相互介绍的简单语句，并能做出相应的反应。

（3）能够通过有关介绍人或物的语段内容理解语篇大意，并记录简单的信息。

（二）口语

（1）能简单介绍有关家人、亲戚、朋友或者学生作品以及学校某个活动等。

（2）能进行一些有关介绍的简单交流，并能交流观点和意见。

（3）能够用英语询问简单信息、请求帮助、与他人沟通、合作完成任务。

（三）阅读

（1）能读懂有关家人、亲戚、朋友的词，以及相关描述的词，比如职业、兴趣、性格等。

（2）能读懂有关家人、亲戚、朋友或者学生作品以及学校某个活动等简单介绍和简单评论。

（3）能捕捉所介绍的人或物语篇的主题，理解细节，并推断语篇的深层含义。

（四）写作

（1）能写出有关家人、亲戚、朋友，以及相关描述的词，如职业、兴趣、性格等。

（2）能对学生作品以及学校各种活动等进行简单描述，并简单发表自己的看法或观点。

（3）能根据文字说明或图标提示，收集、筛选、整理有关的词语素材，写出合适的文段。

二、思维导图

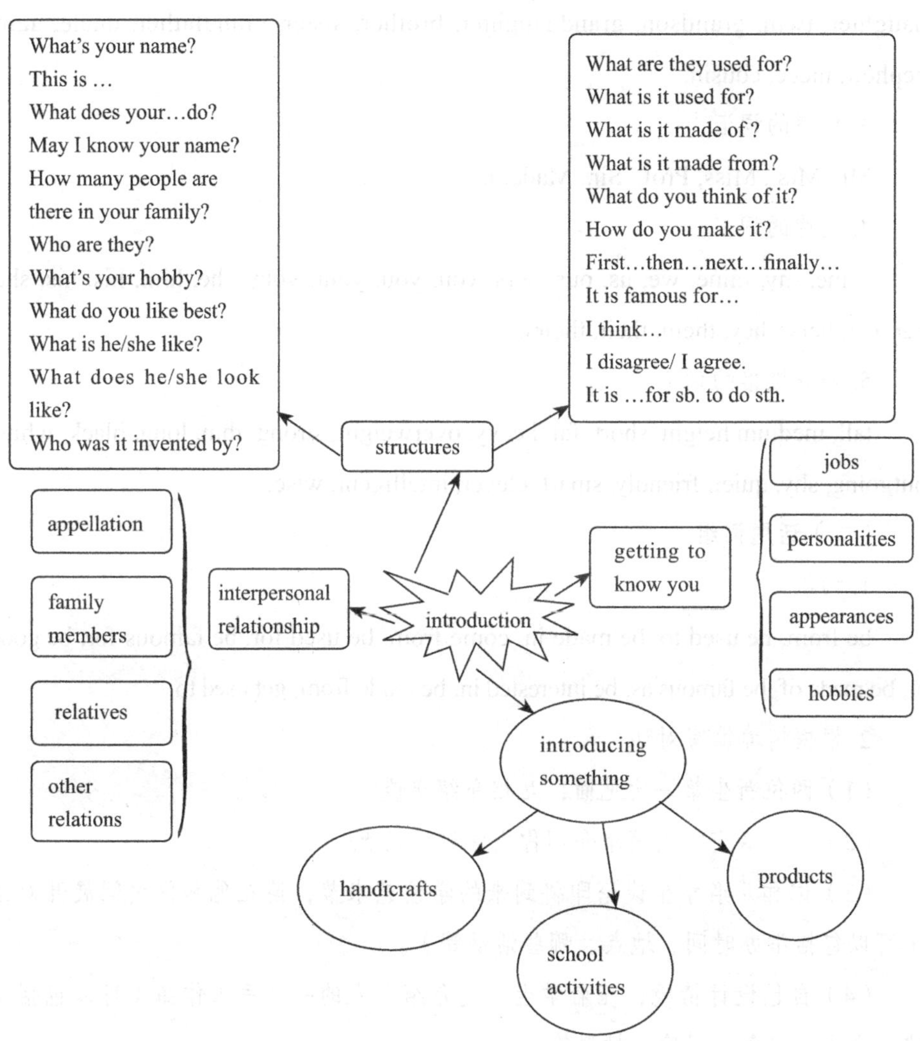

三、话题词语准备

（一）话题单词

1. 有关职业的词汇

actor, actress, artist, baseball player, teacher, tour guide, translator, typist, waiter, waitress, vet, writer, astronaut, chef, reporter, scientist, singer, soldier, policeman, postman, nurse, doctor, librarian, lawyer.

2. 家庭成员的词汇

family, couple, parents, child, male, female, husband, wife, father, mother, son, daughter, twin, grandson, granddaughter, brother, sister, grandfather, uncle, aunt, nephew, niece, cousin.

3. 称谓的词汇

Mr., Mrs., Miss, Prof., Sir., Madam.

4. 人称的词汇

I, me, my, mine, we, us, our, ours, you, you, your, yours, he, him, his, his, she, her, her, hers, they, them, their, theirs.

5. 外貌性格的词汇

tall, medium height, short, fat, heavy, overweight, strong, thin, long, black, white, outgoing, shy, quiet, friendly, smart, clever, intelligent, wise.

（二）话题词组

1. 词组

be from, be used to, be made in, come from, be used for, be famous for, be good at, be made of, be famous as, be interested in, be made from, get used to.

2. 根据情境编写对话

（1）两位新生第一次见面，互相介绍交谈。

（2）向一名交换生简单介绍你们学校的情况。

（3）你和几名学生谈论即将到来的学校艺术节，请在他和你之间展开对话（可以包括举办时间、地点、哪些活动等）。

（4）自己设计情境，几名学生一起介绍个人的一个手工作品（可以包括形状、大小、颜色、用途、材料等）。

Sample：

A：Hello！ My name is LiHua.

B：Hi! Nice to meet you, LiHua. I'm Tom.

A：Nice to meet you, too! Welcome to our school. Are you from America?

B：No. I'm from Canada…

四、功能句和语法聚焦

（一）话题功能句和语法准备

话题功能句和语法准备的目的是帮助学生整理、归纳与本话题相关的重要句型，并让学生能熟练地运用“介绍”的功能句进行真实对话。同时，在实际对话过程中熟悉并运用情态动词。

1. 介绍的常用句

May I introduce myself?

May I introduce Mr. Smith to you?

This is …

How do you do !

I'm glad to meet you!

Nice to meet you!

2. 综合训练

回答以下有关家庭成员的问题：

（1）Can you introduce something about your family to me?

（2）How many people are they in your family?

（3）Who are they?

（4） What does your father do?

（5）How old is your father?

（6） Does your mother work in a factory or a school?

（7）Is your mother as old as your father?

（8）What do you call your father's brother?

（9）Does your uncle have a son or a daughter?

（10）Is the man in that car your uncle?

（二）语法概念与比较

1. 中考聚焦：代词

中考在代词方面的考查主要有人称代词主格和宾格、物主代词、反身代词、指示代词、不定代词和疑问代词。

（1）人称代词的主格和宾格的形式和用法

主格：I, we, you, he, she, it, they

宾格：me, us, you, him, her, it, them

（2）物主代词

形容词性：my, our, your, his, her, its, their

名词性：mine, ours, yours, his, hers, its, theirs

（3）反身代词

myself, ourselves, yourself, yourselves, himself, herself, itself, themselves

（4）指示代词

this—these, that—those

（5）不定代词

中考要考查的不定代词如下：

someone, somebody, something, any, anyone, anybody, anything, none, nobody, nothing; everyone, everybody, everything, many, much, all, both, each, one, other, another, either, neither, etc.

2. 特别提醒

以下是学生需要引起注意并能运用自如的复习要点：

（1）形容词和不定代词连用时，形容词要放在不定代词的后面，即形容词后置。

eg. something different

（2）many和much的区别。

（3）all和both的区别。

（4）区别little和a little，few和a few。

（5）each和every的区别。

（6）some和any的用法。

（7）other和another的用法。

五、话题语境运用

（1）目的：通过上节课的语句复习，本节课要求学生能将所复习的Topic words、phrases 和 sentences在语境中灵活运用。

（2）小组讨论并设计对话。

【口语训练】

口语案例：

张华在英国留学，一天在等车时与一位陌生人Jack进行谈话。张华来自中国，学英语两年了，Jack很惊讶，他认为张华的英语说得很棒。

Useful expressions:

Lovely day, isn't it?

You are... are you?

What do you think of …

I agree/disagree.

How long have you …

Where are you from?

Where do you come from?

You are very…

It's really happy to talk with you.

Have a good day!

Sample：

A: Lovely day, isn't it?

B: Oh, yes. Beautiful!

A: You're not English, are you?

B: I'm from China.

A: How long have you been learning English?

B: For almost two years now.

A: Almost two years? Goodness me! Your English is very good indeed.

B: Thank you. You are very kind. There is still a lot for me to learn.

六、话题阅读

（一）篇章阅读

Many Americans find silence uncomfortable during a buffet（自助餐）or a formal dinner. So in US small talk is a popular way to kill the time in certain social situations. The topics of small talk are various, simply for keeping a talk going. The topics might include the weather, sports, school courses, clothing, food, etc.

Small talk is especially useful at social gatherings（社交场合）when you meet someone for the first time, or when polite conversation is expected but no serious topic is welcome. Usually you may join in a conversation if you know someone in a group before. However, at a party or other informal social gathering, a simple "May I join you?" is ok for joining in a conversation. In some places, such as the lobby（休息室）of a concert hall or theater, a waiting room or a classroom, strangers start a conversation even without an introduction.

People in the United States expect those whom they speak to put aside whatever they are doing and listen. As a rule, the conversation distance between two people is at least two or three feet. Standing at a close distance will make many Americans feel uneasy.

Read the passage and choose the right answer according to the passage.（阅读文章，根据文章内容选择正确答案。）

1. The meaning of the underlined word "various" in the passage is ______.（　　）

A. 自由的　　B. 愉快的　　C. 多种多样的　　D. 严肃的

2. Which small talk is not mentioned in this passage?（　　）

A. The weather.　　B. The sports.　　C. School test.　　D. Food.

3. What do people usually say if they want to join a conversation at an in formal social gathering?（　　）

A. I want to join you!　　B. Excuse me.

C. Could I join you?　　C. Nice to meet you!

4. Which of the following is not true?（　　）

A. In US small talk is a popular way to kill the time .

B. Small talk is the only way at social gatherings when you meet someone for the first time.

C. In some places, strangers start a conversation even without an introduction.

D. You need to stand at least two or three feet away when you have a conversation with others in American.

5. The best title for this passage is ________ . (　　)

A. small talks in The U.S.A.　　B. how to talk with others

C. the conversation distance　　D. how to be polite

（二）阅读策略指导

我们可以看到这是一篇总分式的说明文。由第一段知道它的话题是small topic，而下面的所有都是为这个话题做的解说，所以由每段的开头句可知这篇文章主要美国人如何交谈。

第一题：猜测词意题，主要通过上下文来分析various这个词所包含的意思，从后面给出的举例可以推出是很多种类的意思，所以C选项正确。

第二题：细节题，直接去原文找即可。细节只用看第1段的最后一句话就好了，当然要注意题目要求是not。所以C选项正确。

第三题：同样是细节题。只要通过看题目，从文中找到关键句“join a conversation at an in formal social gathering”，从选项中可以看出只有C选项的答案和原文中的“May I join you?” 的意思接近，所以C选项正确。

第四题：是判断正误题。像这种判断正误题,为了考试时间一定放在最后做。由于你做完所有的细节题对全文有掌握,更好做题。而且对于这种题，出现在篇幅较长的文章中，要从选项中找。特别要看清每句话的细节部分，认真对比原文，可以从选项中看到，A、C、D基本和原句一样或者相近，只有B选项答案中“the only way”这种表述与原句的“a popular way”意思不同，而且过于绝对，一般像这样过于绝对的词，一般情况下都是错误的，类似的还有像all，every，must等这类词，所以考生在做题时留意了。答案选B选项。

第五题：考的是所谓的标题，整篇文章都是small topic，纵观全文，写美国人是如何用small talk来打开话题的，所以选A选项。

七、话题综合运用

（一）翻译句子

1. Jack is three months past fifteen years old.

2. I will be graduating from No. 105 Middle School.

3. How many subjects do you have in your school?

4. The boys are good at singing and dancing.

5. My family are busy with their work.

6. Our head teacher doesn't allow us to talk in the class.

7. He is an able and honest player.

（二）话题下综合运用

1. 信息归纳：阅读一篇有关“感谢父母亲的最好途径”的短文，根据所提供的信息，完成下列表格

The Best Way to Show Gratitude（感谢）to Your Parents

Wherever we are today, whatever we are, we owe it to our parents who have given and taught us so much. We have only one set of parents, and we should show them how grateful（感激的）we are for everything that they have taught us. Whatever we do to express（表达）our thanks, the important thing is that they know how much we love them. Let's see how some people show their thanks to their parents.

Jett Pangan: I like making my mum proud of me. My mom is a widow（寡妇）and retired, so I'll always be around her. I won't make her feel lonely.

Miguel Mendoza: The best way I can show my gratitude is to write a song for them and sing it.

Nar Cabico: I will thank my parents by doing well in school in order not to make them worried.

Rajo Laurel: My parents taught me that the best to reward（回报）them is to help those in need. So I will become a man for others.

Yanan Laurel: By showing（给……一连串的）my parents with lots of hugs and kisses. By telling them I love them.

Information Card

Reasons	They have 1. ________ us so much.
	We have only one set of 2. ________ .
Different people's ways	Jett will be around his mother in order not to make her feel 3. ________.
	Nar will thank his parents by 4. ________.
	Yanah gives her parents lots by 5. ________.

2. 书面表达

假设你们班级即将召开以“感恩”为主题的班会，要求向大家介绍一下你最想向谁表达感恩之情，他或她为你做了什么，你又将怎样回报他或她的付出。请结合上文内容，以“Thank You, My…”为题写一篇发言稿。

要求：

（1）句子通顺，语意连贯。

（2）包括所有提示内容。

（3）不少于80词。

【写作策略】

1. 审题，找要点

（1）你最想向谁表达感恩之情？

（2）他或她为你做了什么？

（3）你又将怎样回报他或她的付出？

内容必须包括上述这三点！

2. 怎样写

Thank You, My Mother

第一点：开头：Wherever we are today, whatever we are, we owe it to our parents who have given and taught us so much（这是信息归纳的第一句），so we should thank them, especially, thank our mother. I think my mother is one of the best mothers in the world.

第二点：She is the busiest one in my family. She ____. She ____. She ____. She ____.（可以多写几件事情来拓展！）

第三点: How will I show my thanks to my mother.（信息归纳的第一段最后一句话改一下人称即可。）

First, ____. Second, ____. Third, ____.（可以参照信息归纳所提到的五个感谢方式。）

结尾：In a word, I love my mother.

Thank You, My Mother

Wherever we are today, whatever we are, we owe it to our parents who have given and taught us so much, so we should thank them, especially, thank our mother. I think my mother is one of the best mothers in the world.

She is the busiest one in my family. She does chores for the family and cares about my study. She has taught me a lot. She does lots of things for me. But she never wants anything in return.

How will I show my thanks to my mother? First, this year, I am going to give her a surprise birthday party and buy her a special present. Second, I'll do well in school. Third, I'll help her do housework when I'm free. I want to make her happy. In a word, I love my mother.

Topic 5　Numbers in Our Life

一、单元学习目标

（一）听力

（1）能听懂生活中的数字及其重要节日，如电话号码、月份等。

（2）能听懂事件发生的日期及对节日活动的简单描述，如春节、儿童节、愚人节、圣诞节等。

（二）口语

（1）能询问年龄、生日日期和庆祝活动的具体时间等。

（2）能简单描述一些常见的节日，并介绍其对应的庆祝活动（如端午节、中秋节、万圣节等）。

（三）阅读

（1）能读懂常见节日的日期及其生活中的其他数字，如电话号码、月份等。

（2）能读懂关于生日和节日以及庆祝活动的简单介绍和评论。

（四）写作

（1）能写出自己和家人的生日日期以及相关的庆祝活动。

（2）能简单描述重要节日（如春节、端午节、中秋节等）及其相关的庆祝活动。

二、思维导图

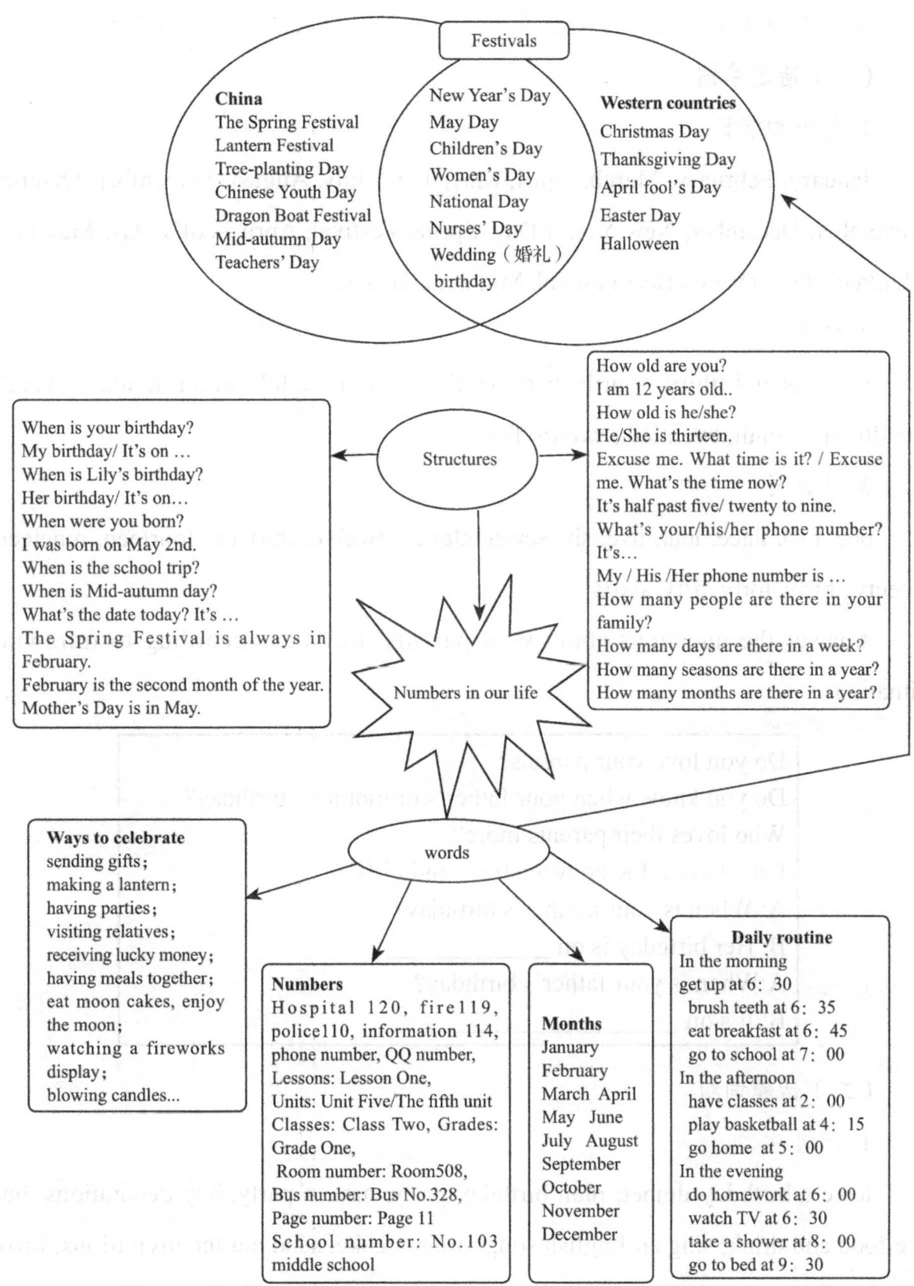
Festivals
China
The Spring Festival
Lantern Festival
Tree-planting Day
Chinese Youth Day
Dragon Boat Festival
Mid-autumn Day
Teachers' Day
New Year's Day
May Day
Children's Day
Women's Day
National Day
Nurses' Day
Wedding（婚礼）
birthday
Western countries
Christmas Day
Thanksgiving Day
April fool's Day
Easter Day
Halloween
Structures
When is your birthday?
My birthday/ It's on …
When is Lily's birthday?
Her birthday/ It's on…
When were you born?
I was born on May 2nd.
When is the school trip?
When is Mid-autumn day?
What's the date today? It's …
The Spring Festival is always in February.
February is the second month of the year.
Mother's Day is in May.
How old are you?
I am 12 years old..
How old is he/she?
He/She is thirteen.
Excuse me. What time is it? / Excuse me. What's the time now?
It's half past five/ twenty to nine.
What's your/his/her phone number?
It's…
My / His /Her phone number is …
How many people are there in your family?
How many days are there in a week?
How many seasons are there in a year?
How many months are there in a year?
Numbers in our life
words
Ways to celebrate
sending gifts;
making a lantern;
having parties;
visiting relatives;
receiving lucky money;
having meals together;
eat moon cakes, enjoy the moon;
watching a fireworks display;
blowing candles...
Numbers
Hospital 120, fire119, police110, information 114,
phone number, QQ number,
Lessons: Lesson One,
Units: Unit Five/The fifth unit
Classes: Class Two, Grades: Grade One,
Room number: Room508,
Bus number: Bus No.328,
Page number: Page 11
School number: No.103 middle school
Months
January
February
March April
May June
July August
September
October
November
December
Daily routine
In the morning
get up at 6：30
brush teeth at 6：35
eat breakfast at 6：45
go to school at 7：00
In the afternoon
have classes at 2：00
play basketball at 4：15
go home at 5：00
In the evening
do homework at 6：00
watch TV at 6：30
take a shower at 8：00
go to bed at 9：30

三、话题词语准备

自测单词，单词准备的目的是帮助学生回忆并复习与本话题相关的和课程标准词汇表中相关的词语，主要为生活中的数字以及重要的节日名称。

（一）话题单词

1. 月份和节日

January, February, March, April, May, June, July, August, September, October, November, December, New Year's Day, Spring Festival, April Fool's Day, May Day, Children's Day, Dragon Boat Festival, Mid-autumn Day.

2. 序数词

first, second, third, fourth, fifth, sixth, seventh, eighth, ninth, tenth, eleventh, twelfth, thirteenth, twentieth, twenty-first.

3. 基数词

one, two, three, four, five, six, seven, eleven, twelve, thirteen, fourteen, nineteen, twenty, thirty, forty, fifty, sixty.

Answer the questions about your parents' birthday according to following situation.

Do you love your parents?
Do you know when your father's or mother's birthday?
Who loves their parents more?
Let's have a PK between boys and girls!
A: When is your mother's birthday?
B: Her birthday is on ______________.
A:When is your father's birthday?
B: It's on ______________.

（二）话题词组

1. 词组

have a birthday dinner, plan birthday party, have a party, buy decorations, buy the food and drink, sing an English song, order a cake, send out the invitations, brow the candles, eat birthday cake, take photos, buy birthday gifts for.

2. 根据情境编写对话

（1）同桌之间设计一个生日当天的情景对话。

（2）假如你明天是你的生日，邀请几个同学参加你的生日。

（3）你和你的同学将在Jay的家里给他办一个生日聚会，请设计一个Jay生日当天活动的情境对话。

四、功能句和语法聚焦

（一）话题功能句和语法准备

话题功能句和语法准备的目的是帮助学生整理、归纳与本话题相关的重要句型，并让学生能熟练地运用“询问年龄和生日”和“祝愿与祝贺”的功能句进行真实对话。同时，在实际对话过程中熟练运用数词。

1. 询问年龄和生日

A: How old are you?

How old is he/she?

B: I'm twelve.

He/She is thirteen years old.

Uncle Wang is an old man.

A: When is your birthday?

B: It's on January 5th.

A: When is your father's birthday?

B: His birthday is on April 21st.

A: When is Sally's birthday party?

B: It's on October 5th.

2. 祝愿与祝贺常用句型

Have a good day/time!

Have a good journey/ trip!

Good luck!

Enjoy yourself!

Best wishes to you.

Happy New Year!

Merry Christmas!

Happy birthday!

Congratulations!

Well done!

Thank you.

You, too.

The same to you.

3. 语法

数词（基数词和序数词）的用法。

表示“多少”和“第几”的词叫作数词。

（二）语法概念与比较

1. 中考聚焦

（1）基数词的表示方法

基数词：表示数目的词是基数词。

提示：

hundred, thousand, million, dozen, score这些词前面如果有表示具体数字的词，它们不能加s;反之则要加s。

两组与数词有关的介词短语

① in+定冠词the+数词的复数形式，表示年代。

eg. in the 1870s/1870's（19世纪70年代）

② in+形容词性物主代词+数词的复数形式，表示某人的年龄。

eg. in his thirties（在他三十几岁的时候）

③ “数词+名词所有格”可作定语修饰名词，当所有格前的数词大于一时，要用复数名词的所有格。

eg. Don't worry. It's only about five minutes' walk.（不用着急，只有5分钟的路程。）

④ “数词+名词（+形容词）”构成复合形容词时，其中的名词要用单数形式。

eg. He is an eleven-year-old boy.（他是一个11岁的男孩。）

表示分数时，分子用基数词，分母用序数词；若分子大于一，表分母的序数词要用复数形式。

eg. one fifth（五分之一）

two fifths（五分之二）

（2）序数词的表示方法及用法。

序数词是表示数目顺序的词。

基数词变序数词助记歌
基变序，有规律，末尾加上th；一、二、三特殊记，八加h，九去e，ve要用f替；以y结尾变ie，后跟th莫忘记。若想表示几十几，只变个位就可以。

2. 特别提醒

（1）表示"次数"，一次是once，两次用twice表示，其他的用"基数词+times"表示。

（2）基数词可与表示度量衡量单位的词连用。

eg. ten meters deep（十米深）

五、话题语境运用

（1）目的：通过上节课的语句复习，本节课要求学生能将所复习的Topic words、phrases和sentences在语境中灵活运用。

（2）小组讨论并设计对话。

【口语训练】

口语案例：

Ann and Belle are preparing a surprise birthday party for Sarah. Make a dialogue between Ann and Belle, then act it out with your partners.

Useful expressions:

What shall we do for Sarah's birthday?

That's a great idea.

I can come to your house before the party to put them up.

Why don't you do that and I'll help your mom?

Let's just tell her that you're having a video night at your house.

She'll have a wonderful surprise when everyone jumps out and wishes her a happy birthday.

Sample:

Belle: Ann, what shall we do for Sarah's birthday? It's next week!

Ann: Yes, I know. I've been thinking about it and I'd like to plan a surprise birthday party for her.

Belle: That's a great idea. I never thought of that! But how do we do it without her knowing?

Ann: OK, let's plan it now. We can have it at my house. My mom has already said she would help with the food.

Belle: OK, that's good. I can buy some decorations to put up—you know, balloons and things. I can come to your house before the party to put them up. And I'll tell all our friends and get everyone to your house on time.

Ann: OK. But we need someone to bring Sarah to my house and a reason to get her there.

Belle: Well, Ann, why don't you do that and I'll help your mom? She's fun in the kitchen.

Ann: That'll work. But what shall we tell Sarah?

Belle: Let's just tell her that you're having a video night at your house. We won't mention her birthday. She'll think we've forgotten!

Ann: She'll have a wonderful surprise when everyone jumps out and wishes her a happy birthday.

六、话题阅读

（一）篇章阅读

Mr. Lee was in bed and was trying to go to sleep when he heard the bell ring. He turned on the light and looked at his clock. It was twelve o'clock. "Who can it be at this time of night?" He thought. He decided to go and find out. So he got up, put on his dressing gown（浴袍）and went to the door. When he opened the door, there was nobody there. "That is very strange." Then he went back to his bedroom, took off his dressing gown, got back into bed, turned off the light and tried to go to sleep.

A few minutes later he heard the bell ring again. Mr. Lee jumped out of bed very quickly and rushed to the door. He opened it, but again he found no one there. He closed the door and tried not to feel angry. Then he saw a piece of paper on the floor. He picked it up. There were some words on it："It is now after midnight（午夜）, so it is April Fool's Day（愚人节）. April fool to you!"

"Oh，it was the English boy next door!" Mr. Lee exclaimed（惊叫）and almost smiled. He went back to bed and felt asleep at once. The bell did not ring again.

Read the passage and choose the right answer according to the passage.（阅读文章，根据文章内容选择正确答案。）

1. When did Mr. Lee go to bed? (　　)

He went to bed ________.

A. before twelve o'clock

B. after twelve o'clock

C. when the bell rang

D. when he saw the boy

2. Why did he rush to the door when he heard the bell ring the second time? (　　)

A. He wanted to open the door for the visitor.

B. He wanted to find out who the visitor was.

C. He was afraid of the ring.

D. He was waiting for someone.

3. From this passage, we learn that we can ________ on April Fool's Day. (　　)

A. say "Hello" to each other

B. dance and sing at night

C. play jokes on each other

D. send presents to children

4. What did Mr. Lee think about the English boy? (　　)

He thought he ________.

A. was a good boy

B. was friendly with him

C. shouldn't ring the bell at midnight

D. did a dangerous thing just now

5. How about the English boy according to the passage? (　　)

A. He is friendly.

B. He is nervous.

C. He was handsome.

D. He was kind.

（二）阅读策略指导

我们可以看出这是一篇关于西方愚人节的记叙文。

第一题：细节题，直接去原文找即可。文章第一段的前三个句子就告诉了此题的答案。He turned on the light and looked at his clock. It was twelve o'clock. 所以A选项正确。

第二题：细节题，文中“Who can it be at this time of night?”，说明 Mr.Lee 很想知道是谁在午夜时来敲门。所以B选项正确。

第三题：判断正误题。像判断正误、mention or not mention和选标题这几种题，为了保证考试时间一定放在最后做。由于你做完所有的细节题对全文有掌握，更好做题。而且对于这几种题，出现在篇幅较长的文章中，要从选项中找，也可以用排除法来做。A选项的意思是互相打招呼，不符合全文大意。B选项晚上唱歌和跳舞，文章中没有提及，故而可以排除。C选项是说在愚人节这天，人们可相互开玩笑。跟文章第二段刚好相符。D选项是说给孩子送礼物文中也未提及。所以C选项正确。

第四题：判断正误题，判断李先生对英国男孩的看法。同样根据文章最后一段Mr. Lee对英国男孩跟他开玩笑的反应是 “Mr. Lee exclaimed and almost smiled.”可以看出英国男孩在和 Mr.Lee 开玩笑，说明他把 Mr.Lee 看成朋友，所以B选项正确。

第五题：就是所谓的推断题，根据第四题以及短文中男孩和 Mr.Lee 开玩笑，可以看出男孩很友好，所以选 A选项。

七、话题下综合运用

（一）话题下句子

1. What do you do at work?

2. For today's homework, you must do Exercise 2 on Page 40.

3. I'll go on an outing with some friends.

4. Smith lifted the box easily, without using much effort.

5. Yi Jianlian often travels in his own car.

6. Every night I watch TV for half an hour after dinner.

（二）话题下读写综合运用

1. 信息归纳：阅读下面校园论坛上关于过去和现在变化的帖子，完成信息卡

Chen Hua　　From Beijing
I have changed a lot in the last few years. For example, I used to be afraid of exams. But now, it doesn't bother me in the slightest, and I used to spend time watching TV every day. But now, I have no time, I study all day. They want me to become the top student in the class, and I don't want to let them down. So I can get good grades in exams, and I'm always happy.
Li Yun　　From Guangzhou
I have changed a lot over the years. I used to have lots of free time to play computer and watch TV. But now, I work harder on studies. I don't go to bed until 10：30 p.m. because of my homework. I used to love toys because they are so interesting. However, I prefer to play basketball now and it really gives me so much fun! Time goes by, it's amazing how I've changed and I am never a child.

Information Card

The number that students are mentioned	1.
The student who used to be afraid of exams.	2.
The student who love sports now.	3.
The reason why Li Yun used to love toys.	4.
The student whose parents want their child to be the top student.	5.

2.书面表达

你有没有发现你的家人或你身边的朋友也发生了变化？请你写一篇文章介绍你的一位家人或朋友这几年来的变化，包括外形、性格、喜好、生活方式等几个方面的变化。80词左右。

【写作策略】

（一）审题，找要点

1. 介绍你身边一位家人或者一位朋友现在的外形与过去对比。

2. 介绍他或她性格如何变化。

3. 他或她现在与过去喜好有何不一样。

4. 现在生活方式与过去对比。

内容必须包括上述四点！

开头总写：People sure change! My best friend, Mary has changed a lot in the last few years.

第一点：She used to be________, but now ______.

第二点：She used to be ________, but now ______.

第三点：She used to like ________, but now she likes _____.

第四点：She used to get up at 7：00 a.m., but now she gets up at 6：00 a.m. She used to ________________, but now she ______________.（在日常生活方面拓展。）

结尾：Time goes by, it's amazing how she's changed and she is never a child.

（二）怎样写

People sure change! My best friend, Mary has changed a lot in the last few years. She used to be fat but now she is thin. She used to have short hair but now she grows it long. She used to be really quiet but now she is outgoing. She used to spend a lot of time playing computer games, but now she has to study all day. She used to do morning exercises and some other activities every day, but now she is used to studying all the time and spend little time on her hobbies. In the evening, she used to watch TV with her family, but now she must go to bed early, because she has to get up early in the morning to read the text books.

Time goes by, it's amazing how she's changed and she is never a child.

Topic 6 Countries and People

一、单元学习目标

（一）听力

（1）能听懂常见国家的名字及其相对应的国籍、语言，如美国、美国人、英语等。

（2）能听懂常见国家的简单介绍，如首都、城市、著名景点、人文风俗等。

（3）能听懂身边的名人介绍，如国籍、所讲的语言、职业、出生地、出生时间、重要成就等。

（4）能听懂生活中的场所名称（如超市、银行、电影院等）及该场所位置的描述（如在书店的对面、在公园与图书馆中间等）。

（5）能听懂询问和回答具体路线的对话。

（二）口语

（1）能说出常见国家的名字，并能谈论它的文化、著名景点等。

（2）能简单介绍自己喜欢的名人，并描述名人的相关信息，如国籍、出生地、出生时间、重要成就等。

（3）能简单描述自己身边的环境，并能说出身边场所的具体位置。

（4）能问路并且回答具体路线。

（三）阅读

（1）能读懂国家的介绍，如首都、著名景点、官方语言、生活习惯等。

（2）能读懂名人的简单介绍和简单评论。

（3）能读懂对身边环境的简单描述，如生活场所及其他具体位置等。

（4）能看地图，并且能画出到达目的地的路线。

（四）写作

（1）能写出常见国家的名字，并能简单介绍该国家，如国名、首都、城市、官方语言、著名景点等。

（2）能简单描述名人的相关信息，如名字、年龄、出生地、出生时间、国籍、重要成就等。

（3）能简单描述身边的环境及各场所的具体位置。

（4）能根据地图，描述出从出发点到目的地的路线。

二、思维导图

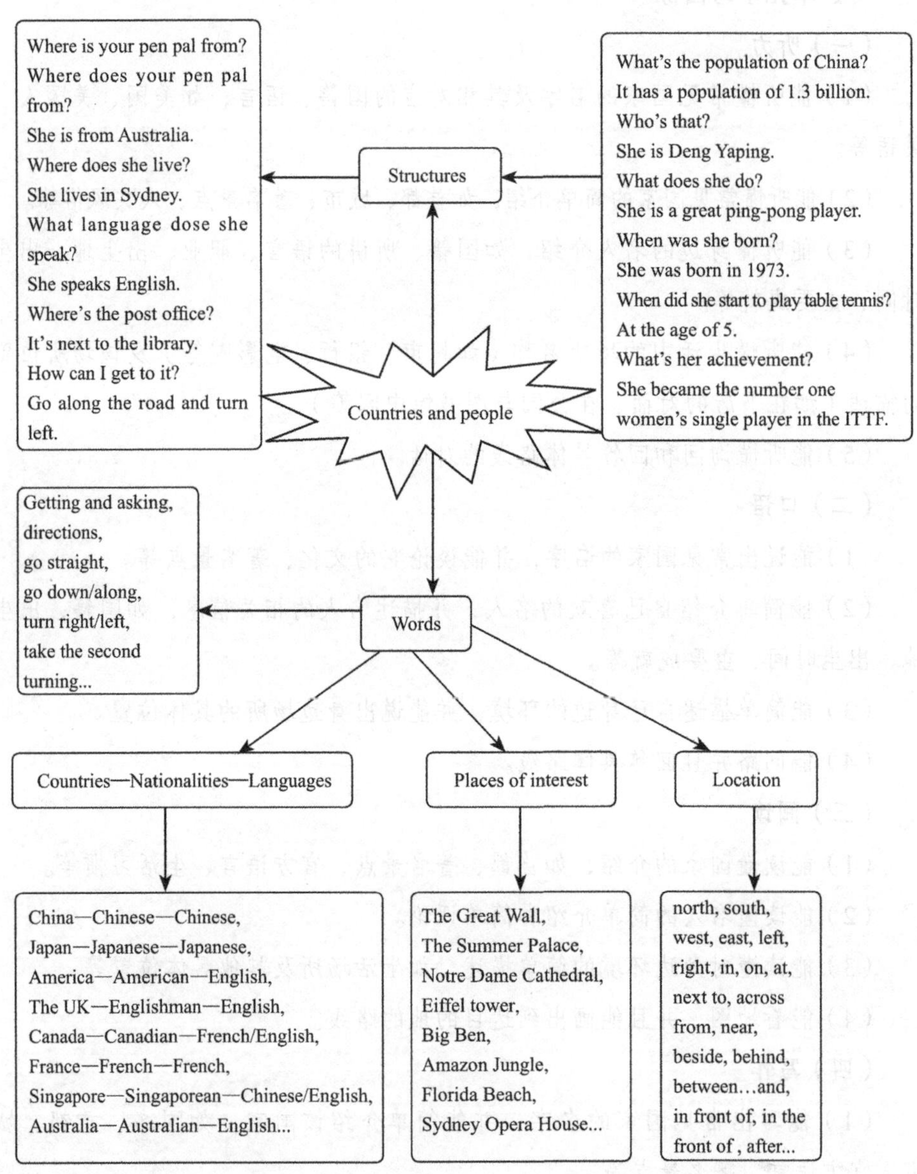

三、话题词语准备

（一）话题词汇

1. 城市名字

Sydney, New York, Paris, Toronto, Tokyo, Beijing.

2. 国家名字

China, Japan, the United States, the United Kingdom, Canada, France, Australia, Singapore, Spain, Brazil, Russia, Germany, Italy, India, New Zealand, Egypt, Cuba.

3. 国籍

Chinese, Japanese, American, Englishman, Canadian, French, Australian, Russian, Spanish, Italian, Brazilian, German, Indian.

4. 语言

Chinese, Japanese, English, French, Russian, Italian, Spanish.

5. 名胜古迹

The Great Wall, the Summer Palace, the Palace Museum, Eiffel Tower, Notre Dame Cathedral, Big Ben, London Bridge Sydney Opera House, Amazon Jungle.

6. 方位词

east, west, north, south, left, right, at, in, on, over, above, below, under, in front of, in the front of, before, behind, at the back of, by, beside, near, next to, between, among, along.

（二）词组

1. 词组示例

be from, come from, speak English, be born, live in, at the age of, take part in, start to do sth./doing sth., begin to do sth./doing sth., go along, turn left, turn right, take the second turning.

2. 根据情境编写对话

（1）同桌之间设计关于以下名人信息的对话。

Chinese name: Zhou Xingchi
English name: Stephen Chou
Job: an actor, a director
Age: 56
Birthday: June 22nd, 1962
Country: China
City: Hong Kong
Language: Chinese, a little English
Favorite sport: swimming
Hobby:singing

（2）看下图，对比下面两幅图的不同之处。请使用恰当的介词。

Tell the differences between the two maps.

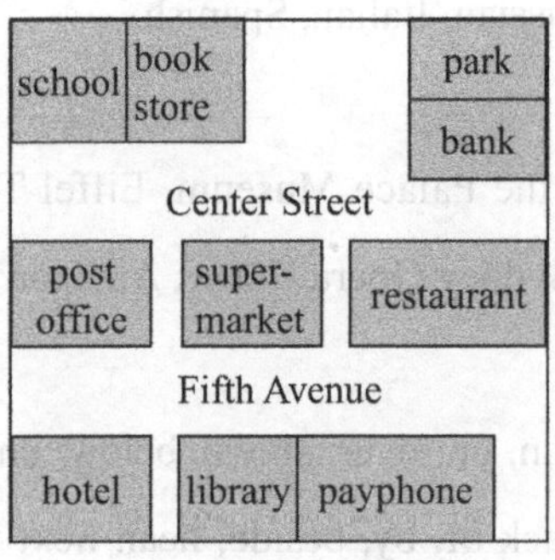

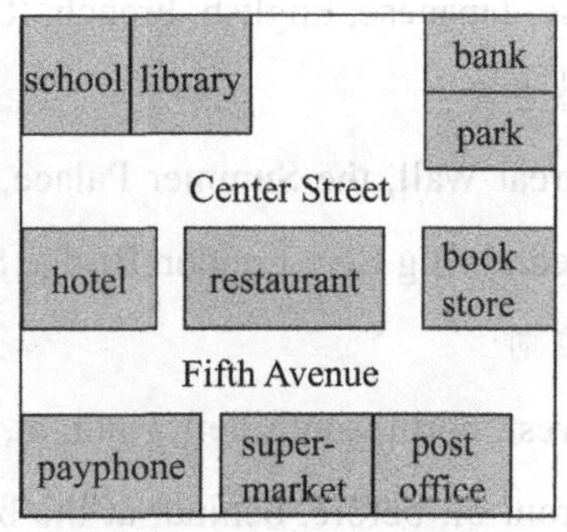

（3）同桌之间根据以下地图设计询问具体路线和回答具体路线的对话。

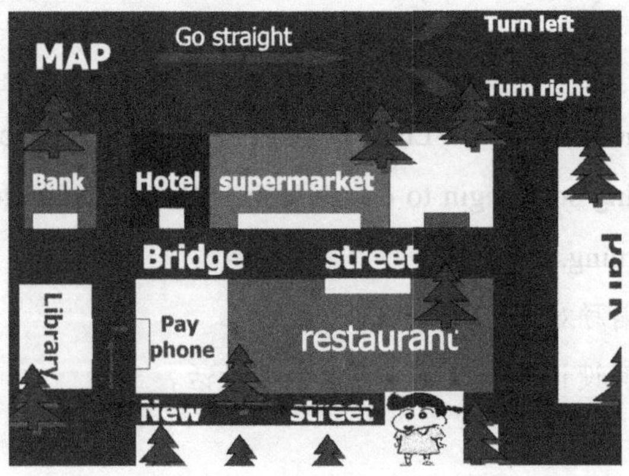

四、功能句和语法聚焦

（一）话题功能句和语法准备

话题功能句和语法准备的目的是帮助学生整理、归纳与本话题相关的重要句型，并让学生能熟练地运用“国家”和“名人”的功能句进行真实对话。同时，在实际对话过程中熟练运用介词。

1. 询问国籍、居住地、地方、语言及回答

Where are/is ...from?

Where do/does ...come from?

Where do/does...live?

What’s ...address?

I am/come from...

He/she is/comes from...

What languages do/does...speak?

2. 询问名人的相关信息及回答

Who’s that? He/she is …

What does he/she do? He/she is a …

When was he/she born? He/she was born in/on…

Where was he/she born? He/she was born in…

When did he/she start to … He/she started to …at the age of …/in …

What’s his/her achievement?

3. 询问周边环境及场所的具体位置的对话及回答

Excuse me, where is the…

Excuse me, is there a …near here/in the neighborhood?

It’s in Fifth street.

It’s near/next to/behind/after/in front of/on the right/left of …

It’s about … meters/kilometers/miles away.

Yes, there is. It’s not far from here. It’s only five meters’ walk.

4. 询问具体路线及回答

Excuse me, can you tell /show me the way to…

Excuse me, which is the way to…

Excuse me, how can I get to …

Excuse me, can you tell me how I can get to…

Go down/ along this street/road to the end.

It's at the end of the road.

Walk down/along the road/street.

Turn right at the first crossing.

Turn left at the second traffic lights.

Take the first turning on the right.

5. 询问距离及回答

How far is it from here?

It's about … meters/kilometers/miles away.

It's about five minutes' walk.

6. 语法

介词的用法。

（二）语法概念与比较

中考聚焦：

介词是一种用来表示词与词、词与句之间的关系的虚词，不能单独充当句子成分。基本分类为：

（1）时间介词。

（2）地点介词。

（3）方式介词。

（4）介词短语。

五、话题语境运用

（1）目的：通过上节课的语句复习，本节课要求学生能将所复习的Topic words、phrases 和 sentences在语境中灵活运用。

（2）小组讨论并设计对话。

【口语训练】

口语案例：

This is an introduction to a famous star. Talk about him with your partner.

Name: Justin Bibier

Nationality: Canadian

Languages: English, French

Sex: Female

Date of birth: March

Live in: Atlanta

Hobby: sing, dance, go skateboarding, play basketball

Famous songs: Baby, Never say never

Achievement:

2007 uploaded videos of his show on YouTube

2008 won the Stella local singing competition third place

2009 First song One Time came cut

2010 won MTV Europe music awards

From 2011 to now performed all over the world

Useful expressions:

Who's that? He is …

What does he come from? He comes from…

What does he do? He is …

When was he born? He was born …

Where was he born? He was born…

What language does he speak?

Where does he live?

What does he like doing? He like …

When did he …

What do you think of him?

Sample:

A: Who's that?

B: He is Justin Bibier.

A: Justin Bibier? What's he?

B: He's a famous singer and actor.

A: Oh, I know. He is the singer who sang the famous song Baby.

B: Yes, the song made him became world famous. I really admire him.

A: He is so young. I wonder how he becomes famous as a teenager.

B: He uploaded his video shows on YouTube. You can't believe it. The click on his video shows could increase to 15 million in a month.

A: How amazing! I think he must have lots of fans around the world.

B: Absolutely.

A: When did he upload his videos on YouTube?

B: He uploaded them in 2007.

六、话题阅读

（一）篇章阅读

Millions of people all over the world use the word OK. In fact, some people say the word is used more often than any other word in the world. OK means all right. If someone asks you to do something, you might say, "Okay, I will." Still, language experts do not agree about where the word came from.

Some people say it came from the Native American Indian tribe（部落）known as the Choctaw. The Choctaw word "okeh" means the same as the American word okay. Experts say early people in the American West spoke the Choctaw language in the 19th century. The language spread across the country. But many language experts don't believe this. Language expert Allen Walker Read wrote about the word OK in reports published in the 1960s. He said the word began being used in the 1830s and it was a short way of writing a different spelling of the words "all correct". Some foreign-born people wrote "all correct" as "o-l-l k-o-r-r-e-c-t," and used OK for short. Other people say a railroad worker named Obadiah Kelly invented the word long ago. They said he put the first letters of his name — O and K — on each thing people gave him to send on the train.

Still others say a political（政治的）organization invented the word. The organization supported Martin Buren for president in 1840. They called their group, the O.K. Club. The letters were taken from the name of the town where Martin Buren was born — Old Kinderhook, New York. Not everyone agrees with this explanation, either. But experts do agree that the word is purely American. And it has spread to almost every country on Earth.

Read the passage and choose the right answer according to the passage.（阅读文章，根据文章内容选择正确答案。）

1. What does OK mean? (　　)

A. All right.　　B. Old Kinderhook.

C. Obadiah Kelly.　　D. Okeh.

2. The underline word "the word" refers to ________. (　　)

A. all correct　　B. OK

C. Okeh　　D. reports

3. Which is not Allen Walker Read's opinion? (　　)

A. OK began being used in the 1830s.

B. It was a abbreviation of a different spelling of the word "all correct".

C. Some native Americans wrote "all correct" as "o-l-l k-o-r-r-e-c-t".

D. OK is a short way of writing "o-l-l k-o-r-r-e-c-t".

4. What do expects agree? (　　)

A. OK comes from the Choctaw word "Okeh".

B. OK is purely American.

C. OK is from a railway worker named Obadiah Kelly.

D. OK is the O.K. club that supported Martin Buren.

5. The passage mainly talks about ________. (　　)

A. the meaning of OK

B. where OK may come from

C. OK is known as Choctaw

D. a political organization invented OK

(二) 阅读策略指导

我们可以看出这是一篇总分式的说明文。由第一段知道文章的话题是关于OK，在讲解了OK的含义后，"Still, language experts do not agree about where the word came from." 预示着接下来要讲关于OK的来源。

第一题：细节题，直接去原文找即可。看第一段第三句，所以A选项正确。

第二题：猜测词意题，遇到这种题型，一般在前一句或者后一句找答案。根据前一句的"Language expert Allen Walker Read wrote about the word OK in reports published in the 1960s."可以推测出"the word"指代的是前面的OK，所以B选项正确。

第三题：判断正误题。根据题目的关键词"Allen Walker Read's opinions"，所以应该从第二段的后半部分"Language expert Allen Walker Read wrote about the word OK in reports published in the 1960s.He said the word began being used in the 1830s and it was a short way of writing a different spelling of the words "all correct". Some foreign-born people wrote "all correct" as "o-l-l k-o-r-r-e-c-t," and used OK for short."可以看出A、B、D选项都与原文一致，C选项错在"Some native Americans"，应该是"Some foreign-born people"，所以选C选项。

第四题：细节题。对于OK的来源，很多专家都有不同的意见，但是都一致同意OK是纯美国英语，后来才发展到全世界。可以从文中第三段的最后两句找出答案，所以B选项正确。

第五题：主旨题。纵观全文，可以发现都是在讲解OK是如何发展而来的几种猜测，所以选B选项，其他选项都是片面之词，概括不了全文。

七、话题下综合运用

(一) 话题句子

1. Practice makes perfect .

2. Keeping a diary in English is an effective way to improve English writing skills.

3. It must be noted that learning must be done by a person himself.

4. Bad news gets around more quickly than good news.

5. Einstein said: “Anyone who reads more and thinks less will form the habit of lazy thought.”

6. We have to respect our cultural differences, in order to keep any possible from misunderstanding.

7. With the help of the Internet，I have also got information about customs in different countries.

（二）话题下综合运用

1. 信息归纳：请阅读下面短文，完成表格

Christmas or the Spring Festival?

I believe that many people may have such a question in mind—Will Christmas replace the Spring Festival soon? Christmas arouses（引起）increasing attention year by year in China. On Dec. 25th each year, Christmas cards become extremely popular with students. People hold Christmas parties and exchange Christmas gifts. A lot of TV and radio programs about Christmas are on. It seems that this is also an important festival of our own. But the Spring Festival is less appealing（吸引人的）to young people. So, some people are worried whether Christmas will replace the Spring Festival. Some people think this worry is fairly unnecessary. Why? One reason lies that Christmas only affects Christians（基督教徒）, college students and foreign company workers. Another reason is that Christmas is mostly celebrated in cities. Few people in countryside show interest in this exotic（外来的）festival. By contrast, the Spring Festival is the most influential（有影响的）traditional festival in every family of China. I think it is natural that increasing exchanges and western holidays have been gradually introduced into China. For us Chinese, we should never give up Chinese traditional festivals. For centuries Chinese have been using this traditional holiday to welcome the beginning of a new year. Let’s love the Spring Festival forever.

Information Card

The date of Christmas every year.	1.
The people that Christmas cards are popular with.	2.
The places where Christmas is mostly celebrated in China.	3.
The most influential festival in China.	4.
The things that we should never give up.	5.

2.书面表达

不同的国家具有不同的风俗文化，在庆祝节日方式上也是不同的。在今天的班会课上，你班全体同学就"我们该如何看待外国节日对中国的影响"这个话题展开了激烈的辩论。请结合短文内容，用英语写一篇题为"How Should We Treat Foreign Festivals?"的作文，80词左右。

内容包括：

（1）现在有哪些外来节日？（至少列举3个）

（2）它们对我们有哪些影响？我们是否该庆祝它们？为什么？

（3）我们该如何看待外来节日？

【写作策略】

（一）审题，找要点

1. 界定外来节日。

2. 庆祝与否？

3. 你对外来节日的看法。

（二）怎样写

How Should We Treat the Foreign Festivals

Nowadays, more and more foreign festivals are coming into China, such as Christmas Day, Valentine's Day and April Fool's Day.

Some of them are arousing increasing attention yearly in China. So some people are worried whether these foreign festivals will replace the Chinese traditional festivals.

In my opinion, we should celebrate some meaningful foreign festivals because these festivals help us Chinese to know more about the culture of different countries.

I think we should love our own traditional festivals and never give them up. At the same time, why not try to introduce them to foreign countries?

Topic 7 Shopping

一、单元学习目标

(一)听力

(1)能听懂为他人提供帮助或对别人的帮助做出礼貌应答的交际用语。

(2)能听懂售货员与顾客关于买卖东西的简单对话。

(二)口语

(1)能简单介绍物品的价格、颜色和大小。

(2)能够为他人提供帮助或对别人的帮助做出礼貌的应答。

(3)能够表达感谢或对别人的感谢做出礼貌的应答。

(三)阅读

(1)能读懂日常用品的价格、颜色和大小。

(2)能读懂关于日常用品的简单介绍和简单评论。

(3)能读懂售货员与顾客之间买卖东西的对话。

(四)写作

(1)能写出日常用品的价格、颜色和大小。

(2)能简单描述自己想要的物品。

(3)能写出售货员与顾客关于买卖东西的简单对话。

(4)能够表达感谢或对别人的感谢做出礼貌的应答。

二、思维导图

A: Can / May I help you?
What can I do for you?
How many/much would you like?
What color/size/kind/ would you like?
What about this one?
Here's your change.
B: I want /I'd like a pair of shoes.
How much is it/are they?
May I try it on?
It's too big/small.
That's fine. I'll take it.
Well, I will think about it.
I will take it. / I will take them.

A: Excuse me. Where is the washroom?
Can you tell me how to get to the post office?
Excuse me. Which bus goes to the World Park?
Excuse me. Which is the way to the Bank of China?
Excuse me. Could you tell me the way to the station, please?
How can I get to No. 4 Middle School?
B: It's over there.
It's about 400 meters from here.
Go down this street until you see the tall red building.
Turn right /left at the first /second crossing /corner.

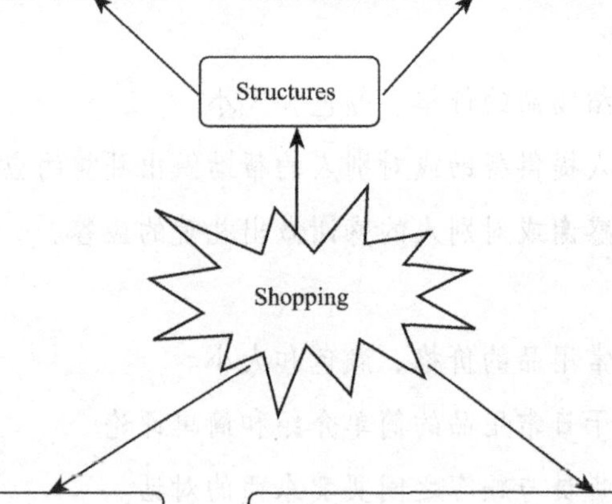

(shopping plan)Things to shop
Shopping list:
Money, Keys, Membership card, Basket, etc.

In a shop
Size: big, middle, small, long, short.
Color: black, white, green, red, blue, yellow, purple, brown.
Price: 5 yuan(¥), 10 dollars($).
Material: cotton, silk, cloth.
Service and quality: inexpensive, fine, high quality.
Personal items: purse, watch, cup, clock, slipper, Make-up, sweater, tooth paste, tooth brush, hair brush, tissue, soap, slipper, shampoo.
jeans; shoes; socks; coats; tooth paste; tooth brush; hair brush; tissue; soap; slipper; shampoo...

三、话题词语

（一）话题单词

1. 日常用品词汇

purse, bag, watch, cup, clock, slipper, make-up, sweater, jeans, shoes, socks, coat, tooth paste, tooth brush, soap, shampoo.

2. 颜色词汇

white, black, brown, purple, pink, red, yellow, green, blue, orange.

（二）话题词组

1. 学习活动

how much, pay for, try on, take off, put on, a pair of jeans, a blue cap, dress up, dress oneself, sell out.

2. 根据情境编写对话

同桌之间设计一个顾客和售货员之间的对话。

四、功能句和语法聚焦

（一）话题功能句和语法准备

话题功能句和语法准备的目的是帮助学生整理、归纳与本话题相关的重要句型，并让学生能熟练地运用句型，并让学生能熟练运用“选择商品”和“付款”的功能句进行真实对话。同时，在实际对话过程中熟练运用连词。

1. 选择商品常用句

Do you have a green skirt?

I'd like the pink one.

Can I try the brown shoes on?

2. 付款常用句

I will take it.

Here is the money.

3. 语法

并列连词和从属连词的用法。

（二）语法概念与比较

中考聚焦：

连词属于虚词，是用来连接词与词、短语与短语、句子与句子，在句子中起辅助作用。分为并列连词和从属连词。

1. 并列连词

（1）并列连词的作用是用来连接具有并列关系的词、短语或句子。

（2）表示并列的并列连词有：and, both...and, neither...nor..., not等。

（3）表示转折的并列连词有：but, however, while, yet等。

（4）表示因果的并列连词有：so, for, because等。

（5）表示选择的并列连词有：or, either…or等。

特别提醒：

（1）在否定句和疑问句中，常用or表示并列关系，而不用and。

（2）not only A but also B结构中，强调的对象是B；而在A as well as B中强调的对象是A。

（3）neither...nor, either...or, not only...but also...连接并列主语时，谓语动词要和靠它最近的主语保持一致。

2. 从属连词

特别提醒：

（1）though/ although 和but不能同时使用，但是though/although 可以和still / yet连用；because和so也不能同时使用。

（2）when, while和as的用法区别。when 可以表示时间上的一点或一段时间，主句和从句的动作可同时发生，也可先后发生，从句中的谓语动词可以是延续性动词，也可以是非延续性动词；while表示时间段，主句和从句的动作同时发生，常对同类的动作进行对比，从句中的谓语动词必须是延续性动词；as意为“一边……一边……”，主句和从句的动作同时发生。

（3）so…that和such…that 的用法区别。so 修饰形容词或副词；such 主要用来修饰名词。当名词前有many，much，few或little修饰时，要用so。

such + a/an + adj. + 单数名词+that从句

such + adj. + 不可数名词/可数名词复数+that从句

so + adj./adv. + that 从句

so many / much / few/little + 名词 + that从句

（4）if 和whether都可以引导宾语从句，大多数情况下，两者可以互换，但以下情况只能用whether。见表7–6。

表7–6 if 和whether的用法区别

与 or not 连用时	We don't know whether Tom will attend the meeting or not.
和不定式连用时	I don't know whether to go.
前面有介词时	He is thinking about whether he should tell her the truth.

五、话题语境运用

（1）目的：通过上节课的语句复习，本节课要求学生能将所复习的Topic words、phrases 和 sentences在语境中灵活运用。

（2）小组讨论并设计对话。

【口语训练】

口语案例：

Zhang Ming and his wife are talking about what they are going to buy for their fridge.

Role-play the dialogue with your partner.

Useful expressions:

What about vegetables?

Are there any carrots?

We don't need any more till those are gone.

There's lots of fruit and we don't need any more rice or noodles.

OK, is there anything else that we do need?

So is that all?

Yes, that's all.

Sample:

A: Zhang Ming, while you're in the kitchen can you just check and tell me what we need to buy at the supermarket this afternoon?

B: Sure. Now, let's see. There isn't much milk, so we should get some more. There are plenty of eggs and there's enough cheese. OK, there aren't any tomatoes so we need some of those. And some butter.

A: What about vegetables? Are there any carrots?

B: Yes, there are and some potatoes. We don't need any more till those are gone. There's lots of fruit and we don't need any more rice or noodles.

A: OK, is there anything else that we do need?

B: I don't think so. Oh, there isn't any coffee; I had to have tea this morning.

A: Ah yes, and I need to get some sugar too.

B: Good thinking. So is that all?

A: Yes, that's all.

六、话题阅读

(一)篇章阅读

Mary picked up a pencil and a piece of paper, saying, " Now, you want to earn money for the autumn camping trip, right? " Tom, her brother, nodded. He wasn't able to go last year because hadn't earned enough money during the summer. This year he came up with a plan.

He made a necklace for his mother that everyone admired. They were surprised to learn that Tom had made it for her. Why not make more necklaces and sell them?

"OK", said Mary, "The first thing you need to do is to figure out (计算) how much you have now."

"I have $20.00 in the bank and $7.25 in my room," explained Tom.

"That gives you a total of $27.25." said Mary. "That is called your capital. The next thing you need to know is how much it will cost you to make each necklace."

"Well, the pet shop will give me all the feathers the birds lose. I'll have to buy the beads (小珠子) and string," said Tom.

Mary wrote on the piece of paper:		
Capital	$27.25	
Expenses	Feathers	no cost
String for 10 necklaces		$ 2.50
Beads for necklaces		+ $ 15.00
Total		$ 17.50

" How much do you think you can sell such a necklace for? " asked Mary.

" Hmm," Tom looked thoughtfully and said, "There's a shop in town that sells almost the same kind of necklace for $7.50. If I charge $6.00, people will think that's a bargain."

"OK. If you sell each necklace for $6.00, you'll make a good profit（利润）on each then," said Mary.

"Hurry!" Tom cried, "If I sell 20 necklaces, I'll have enough from the profit for the camping trip and $10.00 left over."

Read the passage and choose the right answer according to the passage.（阅读文章内容，根据文章内容选择正确答案。）

1. According to the passage, Mary is ________. (　　)

A. beautiful　　B. useful

C. big　　D. helpful

2. The underlined word "bargain" in this story means "________" . (　　)

A. 价格　　B. 利润

C. 便宜　　D. 讨价还价

3. The best title for this story is ________. (　　)

A. How to Earn Money for a Trip　　B. How to Bargain

C. How to Save Money　　D. How to plan a trip

4. Tom would have to spend ________ on the camping trip. (　　)

A. $75　　B. $17.5

C. $85.00　　D. $35

5. How did Tom know how much he would have left over paying for the camping trip? (　　)

A. He took the cost of the trip from the profit he would make on 20 necklaces.

B. He added the cost of the trip to the profit he would make on 20 necklaces.

C. He asked Mary for this story.

D. He took the cost of each necklace from the amount of money he had to begin with.

(二)阅读策略指导

第一题：推断题。根据短文中的内容可知，Mary 是一个很有爱心的人，所以D选项正确。

第二题：猜测词意题。根据短文中“There’s a shop in town that sells almost the same kind of necklace for $7.50. If I charge $6.00，”的内容，可以推断是bargain是“便宜”的意思。所以C选项正确。

第三题：就是所谓的标题，整篇文章都是讲Mary如何给Tom出主意怎样为旅游赚钱。纵观全文，我们发现整篇文章是讲如何赚钱旅游的，所以选A选项。

第四题：细节题。$75 根据短文内容可知，Tom 买十条项链的资金是 $17.5，那么 20 条就是 $35，每条卖 $6.00，销售完可以得到 $85.00 的利润，确定旅游要花 $75.00。所以A选项正确。

第五题：根据短文内容可知，Tom 旅游的费用是来自20条项链，卖完这20条项链就有钱旅游了，所以选 A选项。

七、话题综合运用

(一)话题句子

1. I would like to have a look at the latest Apple iPhone.

2. If you buy the bike today, there will be a fifteen percent discount for you.

3. Something wrong with the MP4 I bought here yesterday. Can I ask my money back?

4. I don’t like the color, a little too bright.

5. What about this one? Short skirts are in fashion now.

6. How would you like to pay for these?

7. Will you be paying by cash, check or credit card?

（二）话题下读写综合运用

1.请阅读下面短文，完成表格

More and more advertisements appear on the website. You have to be careful not to be fooled or treated by the advertisements on the Internet. Something is said to be a bargain（便宜）, but it isn't always cheap. And some so-called new things just have a new outside.

However, shopping online is a kind of fashionable thing today. I live to buy things of everyday use, so I often get lots of information about them on websites online. For example, if I want an MP3 player, I can choose my favorite one, and look for what the users like or don't like about it, then decide whether to buy or not. And at the same time, you don't have to go to a shop or walk around a crowded shopping area, so you don't have to waste much time. The Internet is really useful for shopping, but be careful not to spend too much.

Information Card

The things that appear more and more on the website.	1.
The things that you have to be careful on the Internet.	2.
A kind of fashionable thing today.	3.
The things you don't have to do when you shop on the Internet.	4.
	5.

2. 书面表达

人们的生活节奏越来越快，网上购物已经成为大众生活中不可缺少的一部分。

请你用“Shopping Online”为题写一篇文章（80词左右），说说人们为什么喜欢网上购物？网上购物有哪些优点和缺点？

【写作策略】

（一）审题，找要点

1. 网上购物已经成为大众生活中不可缺少的一部分。

2. 人们为什么喜欢网上购物？

3. 网上购物有哪些优点？

4. 网上购物有哪些缺点？

最少要写到上述四点！

（二）怎样写

开头：Shopping online is a kind of fashionable thing today.

第一点：Shopping online has become ______________________.

第二点：Why do people like shopping online?（过渡句）Because __________ ______________________.

第三点：Shopping online has some advantages. ________________.（可以多写几个优点来拓展词数。）

第四点：But it has some disadvantages, too. ____________________.（可以多写几个缺点来拓展词数。）

结尾：So we should be careful to shop online.

Shopping Online

Today, people are busy with their work and study and have little time to go shopping. So shopping online has become an important part in their lives. It is convenient and we can save much time. Besides, with all the traffic problems in cities, going shopping is not an easy thing. Just sit at a computer, click and choose, you can find all kinds of different things online. You can also compare with the prices. So you can buy something you like but not expensive.

However, shopping online can bring you some trouble. Sometimes, you will find that the things you get are different from those you can see online. And, the quality of the things are not so good. Even, you will be cheated by others.

So we should be careful to shop online.

Topic 8 Sports and Entertainments

一、单元学习目标

(一)听力

(1)能听懂常见的关于运动的名称，如：球类、棋类、乐器等。

(2)能听懂生活中关于娱乐的词语，如音乐类、电影类、电视节目等。

(3)能听懂谈论运动、娱乐和表达对运动的喜好以及观点的对话。

(4)能听懂关于表达计划或是意愿的对话。

(二)口语

(1)能简单说出运动的词汇，如球类、棋类、乐器等。

(2)能简单谈论自己或他人的运动及娱乐观点。

(3)能表达自己的计划和意愿。

(三)阅读

(1)能看懂表达运动及娱乐的英语词汇，如打篮球、滑冰、听音乐等。

(2)能读懂关于表达计划和意愿的讨论和观点。

(3)能看懂介绍运动和娱乐的文章。

(四)写作

(1)能写出运动及娱乐类的单词或短语。

(2)能简单介绍喜欢的运动或娱乐。

(3)能写出关于计划或意愿建议的词句。

(4)能简单描述运动及娱乐在生活中的益处。

二、思维导图

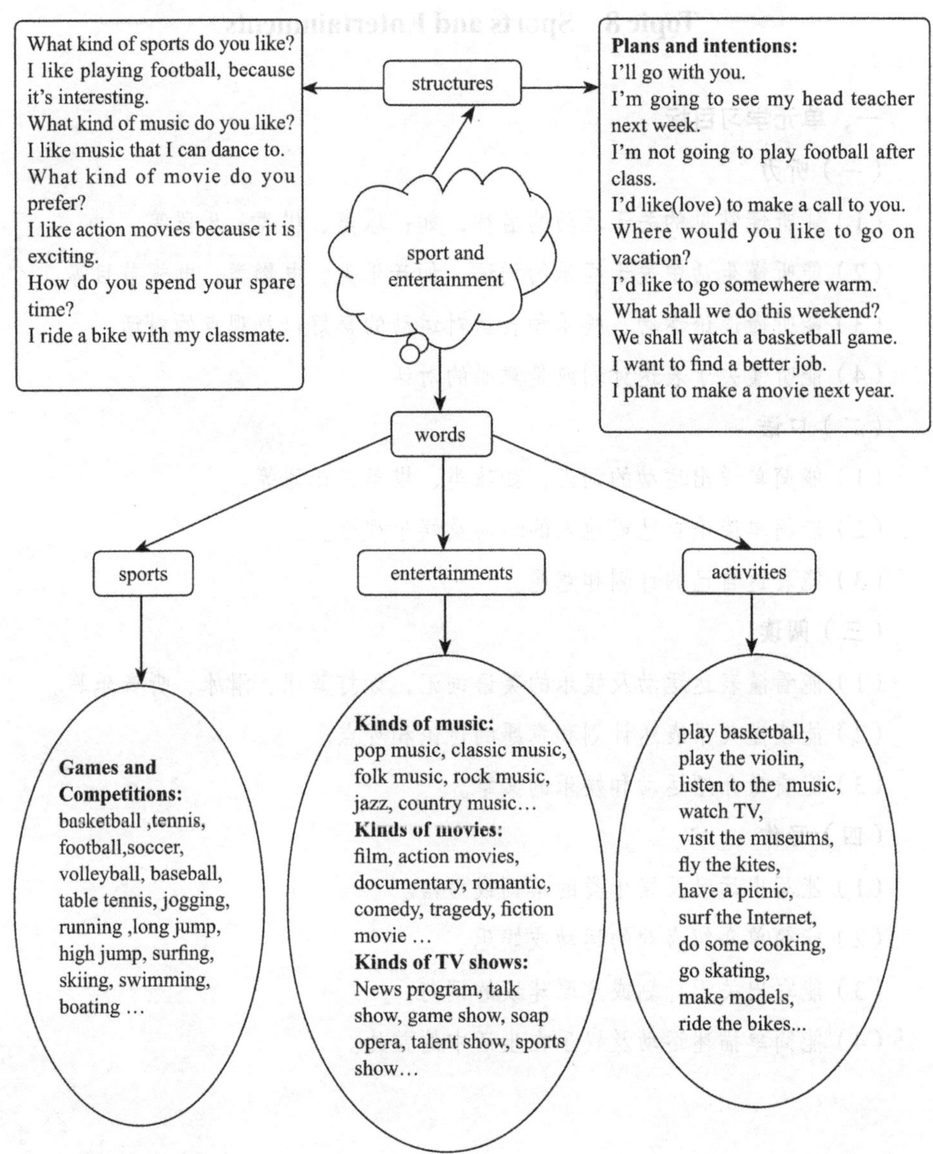

三、话题词语准备

(一) 话题单词

1. 与运动有关的词汇

tennis, volleyball, soccer, golf, baseball, basketball, running, jumping, surfing, swimming, badminton, champion, professional, P.E., record, etc.

2. 与娱乐有关的词汇

piano, violin, drum, classic music, gentle music, documentary, adventure movie, Jazz music, etc.

3. Answer the questions with "*my favorite sport is*..." according to the pictures.

What is your favorite sport?

（二）话题词组

词组复习的目的是帮助学生复习整理一些相关的词组，同时帮助学生复习相关建议句型。

1. 写出下列词组的英文或中文

弹钢琴 ________ 打网球 ________ 放风筝 ________

上网 ________ 帮助……做 ________ 游泳 ________

go hiking ________ walk through the jungles ________

go somewhere cool ________ visit museums ________ ride my bike ________

2. 根据情境进行语言知识的操练

Pair Work
T: What kind of sports do you like?
S: I like playing badminton.
T: What kind of music do you like?
S: I like classical music.
T: What kind of movie do you like?
S: I like action movies.

（1）同桌之间设计一个体育运动的对话。

（2）谈论家人周日的活动。

（3）假期将至，和你的同伴制订一个假期计划。

（4）根据不同的情境设计对话。

四、功能句和语法聚焦

（一）话题功能句和语法准备

话题功能句和语法准备的目的是帮助学生整理、归纳与本话题相关的重要句型。本章要求学生能熟练地运用“运动及娱乐的词汇”和“表达计划及意愿”的功能句进行真实对话。同时，在实际对话过程中熟悉不定式的用法。

1. 表达运动和娱乐爱好的常用句

What kind of sports do you like?

I like playing football, because it’s interesting.

What kind of music do you like?

I like music that I can dance to.

What kind of movie do you prefer?

I like action movies because it is exciting.

2. 表达计划和意愿的常用句

Where would you like to go on vacation?

I’d like to go somewhere warm.

What shall we do this weekend?

We shall watch a basketball game.

I want to find a better job.

I will plant to make a movie next year.

I'd like (love) to make a call to you.

（二）语法概念与比较

1. 中考聚焦：不定式的用法

（1）动词不定式是由“to + 动词原形”构成;其否定形式是“not to do”。

（2）不定式的用法。不定式在句中可以作主语、表语、宾语、宾语补足语、定语及状语。

2. 特别提醒

（1）动词不定式没有人称和数的变化，在句子中不能作谓语。

（2）在使役动词（let，make，have）和感官性动词（see，hear，watch，feel，notice）等动词后，用作宾语补足语的动词不定式省略“to”；但是变成被动句时，必须补上“to”。

（3）why not, had better, would rather等词组后接省略“to”的不定式。

（4）疑问代词（who, which, what）和疑问副词（how, where）与动词不定式连用。

（5）下面三个句型要注意掌握。

① be +形容词+动词不定式。

此外还有：be able to..., be afraid to..., be sorry to..., be sure to...等。

② be + too +形容词 + 动词不定式（太……而不能……）。

③ be +形容词 + enough + 动词不定式（够……可以……）。

（6）一些常用动词的用法。

① stop +动词不定式，表示“停下正在做的事去做另一件事”，表目的。

② stop +动词的-ing形式，表示“停止正在做的事”。

③ 有的动词或短语，如enjoy, finish, mind, practice, keep, spend, be busy, couldn't，help, be worth 等，其后只可用动词-ing形式（作宾语）。

五、话题语境运用

（1）目的：通过上节课的语句复习，本节课要求学生能将所复习的Topic words、phrases 和 sentences在语境中灵活运用。

（2）个人表述和小组讨论。

【口语训练】

Sample 1:

The students are talking about activities in Sentosa.

(A) Here are some of the things to do on Sentosa. In group of four, plan a day trip to the island. Decide together where you will go, how long you will stay at each place and what you will do there.

Museum	Siloso Beach Playing volleyball	Sky Tower	Tanjong Beach swimming
Water sports go surfing	shopping	Golf	Underwater World

Sample 2:

Here is Jennifer and Sonia's dialogue.

Sonia: Jennifer, where would you like to go in Sentosa?

Jennifer: I'd like to go to Water sport.

Sonia: What do you want to do?

Jennifer: I will go surfing.

Sonia: Well, how long will you stay there?

Jennifer: I 'll stay there for a day, then I'd like to visit Museum.

Sonia: Would you like to go shopping?

Jennifer: Sure, I'd like to buy some souvenirs for my parents. What about you?

Sonia: I'd like to go shopping too.

Jennifer: Ok. Let's go shopping first.

六、话题阅读

（一）篇章阅读

Some parents say their kids don't like sports. Why?

Some kids don't like sports because they don't know how to play sports. If the kids know how to play a new sport, maybe they will like it. Taking P.E. classes at school is a good way to learn new sports. Another way is to watch videos about sports.

Kids can also read some books about it.

Some kids don't like playing sports because they were once on a team and didn't have fun. For those kids, it's a good idea to talk with their teachers or parents. With their help, maybe the kids will like playing sports again.

There are many kinds of sports, so a kid should find the sports that suit him or her. If a kid doesn't like team sports, parents can ask him or her to try individual（个人的）sports, such as swimming and running.

Playing sports can help kids keep active and healthy.

Of course, many other activities can also keep kids fit, such as walking a dog, cleaning the room and watering the garden.

Read the passage and choose the right answer according to the Passage.（阅读文章内容，根据文章内容选择正确答案。）

1. The second paragraph tells us ________ ways to learn about new sports. (　　)

A. two　　B. three　　C. four　　D. five

2. Which is not the reason why some kids don't like sports? (　　)

A. They didn't have fun on the team.

B. They are not interested in sports at all.

C. They don't know how to play sports.

D. The sports don't suit them.

3. What does the underlined word "suit" mean in Chinese? (　　)

A. 爱好　　B. 相称　　C. 适合　　D. 衣服

4. Which activity is not mentioned in this passage? (　　)

A. Watering the gardens.　　B. Playing basketball.

C. Walking the dog.　　D. Cleaning the room.

5. Which of the following is true according to the passage? (　　)

A. Kids should only play team sports.

B. Playing sports can help kids keep active and healthy.

C. Most parents don't let their kids play team sports.

D. You can't be in good health if you don't playing sports.

(二)阅读策略指导

这是一篇关于sports的文章。文章以提问的方式开始，因此文章的中心主旨是很明确的。学生对这个话题也是熟悉的，因此可以充分提取学生以往经验，丰富关于话题的文化背景。

第一题：细节题，直接去原文找即可。先找出题目中的关键词“second 和 ways”，读懂了第二段后三句就可以找到答案B选项。

第二题：判断正误题。注意题目中的两个“not”，分析四个题干结合原文第二、三、四段的中两个“because”很容易排除A、C、D选项，所以答案B选项正确。

第三题：猜测词意题。这一类题最好是用翻译法加排除法，找到原文句子把选项的意思放进去，结合文章的意思来确定正确答案。本题的原句是“There are many kinds of sports, so a kid should find the sports that suit him or her. suit”后面接代词，是在谓语的位置，应该是动词，如此D选项可以排除；翻译此句为：有很多种类的运动，因此孩子应该可以找到一个_____他或她的运动，所以答案C选项正确。

第四题：判断正误题。关于mention 或是not mention之类的题目，最需要考生细致认真读完整篇文章，可以在看到与题目相关的内容时用笔钩出，以便做题时可以清晰准确地找到答案。本题的题干很简洁，在原文最后才找到原词“walking a dog, cleaning the room and watering the garden”，因此答案B选项正确。

第五题：判断正误题。关于True, Not true or False之类的题目，要求考生先要理解题目，分清要回答的问题是True还是False；接下来在读完文章的基础上把四个选项内容和原文进行逐个比对，找出选项错在哪里，对了又是在原文哪里，特别注意一些较“绝对化”的词，如all，only，everyone ...本题A、D选项就是很绝对的，C选项中的don’t let明显和原文不符，所以B选项是正确答案。

七、话题下综合运用

(一)话题句子

1. Open exercises like running, climbing are good for the young, while jogging and walking are more suitable for the old.

2. Reading is to the mind while exercise to the body.

3. Beijing will be the first city ever to host both the Summer and Winter Olympics.

4. I often practice playing the piano after school.

5. Sports and games make our life richer and more colorful.

（二）话题下读写综合运用

1. 信息归纳：阅读下面短文，完成信息卡

Everyone knows that exercise is important. It makes your heart and body strong. But you need to know the following things if you want to do sports scientifically（科学地）.

Get your body ready!

Before you do any exercise, make sure to warm up for about five minutes. This is really necessary and important, especially when you suddenly want to play after doing no exercise for a long time. During warming up you should stretch（伸展）all parts of your body.

Exercise enough, but not too much.

It is best to exercise twice each week. Thirty minutes each time is enough. Try all kinds of things until you find one, two or even three sports that feel right for you.

Exercise at fitness center.

There is a lot of equipment at fitness centers. The equipment will help exercise your arms, legs or other parts of your body to make you fit. Some people buy equipment for their homes. But the equipment is very expensive.

Stop playing when you are hurt!

If you get hurt when you are doing exercise, don't play again until you are well. Otherwise, it may become worse.

Don't get thirsty!

Drink a lot when you are playing sports because of easy thirst. If your body lacks（缺少）enough water, it will be harmful to you.

Information Card

The thing that makes your heart and body strong.	1.
Time that you need to warm up before doing exercise.	2.

续 表

The times that it is best for you to exercise.	3.
The place that there is much sports equipment.	4.
The reason why you need to drink a lot while playing sports.	5.

2. 书面表达

很多学校根据学生的爱好和兴趣开展了许多有益的课外活动，请你根据以下提示，写一篇不少于80词的短文。

内容包括：

（1）列举你们学校开展的三项课外活动。

（2）介绍你对哪些活动感兴趣，并说明原因，如这些活动给你带来的益处。

（3）为同学如何选择课外活动提两个建议。

（4）鼓励学生积极参加学校课外活动。

【写作策略】

（一）审题，找要点

1. 列举学校开展的三项课外活动。①

2. 介绍你对哪些活动感兴趣。②

3. 说明原因，如这些活动给你带来的益处。③

4. 为同学如何选择课外活动提出两个建议。④⑤

5. 鼓励学生积极参加学校课外活动。⑥

（二）怎样写

开头：（已给出）Nowadays, after-class activities are becoming more and more popular in schools.

第一点：We also have many kinds of after-class activities in our school, such as ________________.

第二、三点：I am interested in ____________, because ____________.

第四、五点：If you also want to take part in after-class activities, I have some suggestions. You had better ____________, you had better ____________.

第六点：Dear friends, please take part in after-class activities. I'm sure ____________.

结尾：Your school life will be colorful.

Nowadays, after-class activities are becoming more and more popular in schools. We also have many kinds of after-class activities in our school, such as English corner, playing basketball and swimming. I am interested in the English corner, because it can help me make some new friends there. If you also want to take part in after-class activities, I have some suggestions. You had better choose the activities which are good for you; you had better choose what you like.

Dear friends, please take part in after-class activities. I'm sure you will learn a lot and you will find it very interesting at the same time. Your school life will be colorful.

Topic 9　A Visit to Hong Kong

一、单元学习目标

（一）听力

（1）能听懂国内外的一些旅游胜地。

（2）能听懂旅游方式、活动、天气的简单介绍。

（3）能听懂旅游前的准备、定酒店等相关的简单对话。

（二）口语

（1）能简单介绍国内外的一些旅游胜地。

（2）能根据一次旅游进行情境对话。

（3）能简单描述过去的一次旅游或旅游计划和打算。

（三）阅读

（1）能读懂一些旅游胜地的介绍。

（2）能读懂对一次旅游的简单描述。

（3）能读懂对旅游目的地的要求和愿望的描述。

（四）写作

（1）能写出一些旅游胜地。

（2）能对旅游目的地的要求进行描述。

（3）能简单描述过去的一次旅游或旅游计划和打算。

二、思维导图

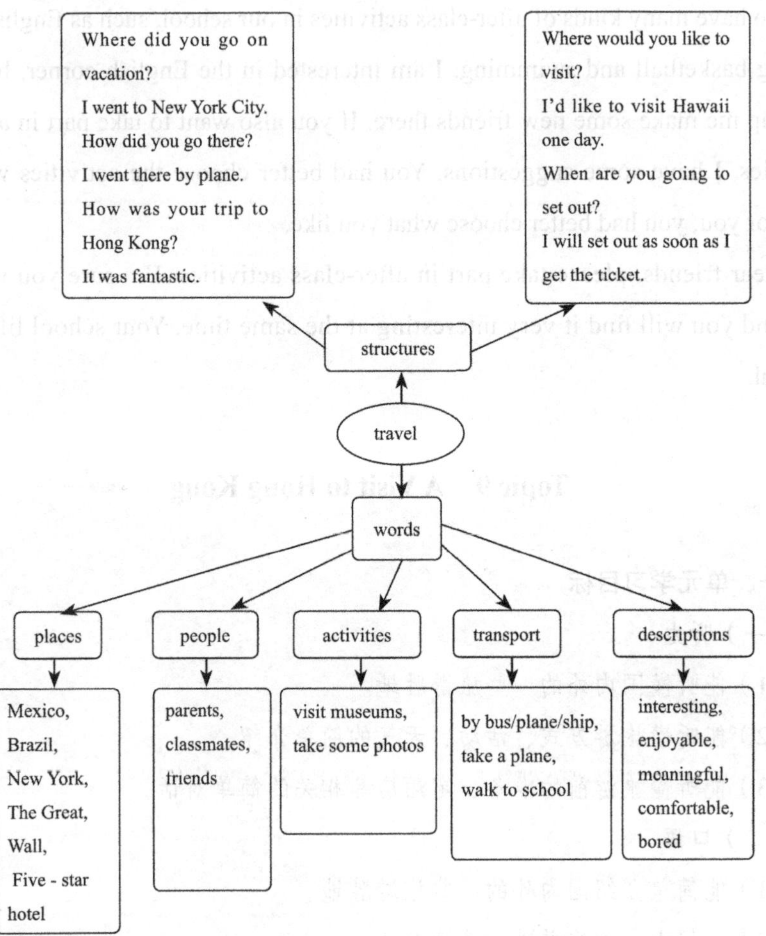

三、话题词语准备

（一）话题单词

1. 表示旅游地点的单词

Mexico, Hawaii, Brazil, France, Italy, New York, Sydney, California, places of interest, the Palace Museum, the Great Wall, the Eiffel Tower, the West Lake, the Bell Tower.

2.与旅游有关的形容词

interesting, exciting, fantastic, tiring, wonderful, enjoyable, terrible, comfortable, convenient, special, delicious, peaceful, educational, surprising, romantic, crowded, expensive, awful, meaningful, new, good, sunny, etc.

3. 与旅游有关的词汇

camera, map, swimming suit, umbrella, credit card, flight ticket, passport, airport, train, fantastic sights, hotel, etc.

（二）话题词组

1. 词组

be on vacation, go on a trip, take some photos, see sb. off, buy some gifts, take a walk, feed the animals, lie on the grass, play games, have a big meal, cook meals, do some shopping, enjoy oneself, etc.

2. 根据情境编写对话

（1）“五一黄金周”又要到了，请和你的同伴制订一个新颖、刺激的出游计划。你的朋友Jim暑假要来中国旅游，但他对中国不了解，希望你能推荐一下。请向他推荐我们的首都北京。

（2）你最希望去什么样的地方旅游？把你的要求和愿望告诉旅行社的Mr. Smith，请他帮你选一个理想之地。

四、功能句和语法聚焦

（一）话题功能句和语法准备

1. 语法聚焦的目的

语法聚焦的目的是帮助学生整理、归纳与本话题相关的重要句型，并让学生能熟练地就旅游的地点、方式、时间、感受进行真实对话。

（1）询问旅游目的地及应答的句型

Where did you go on vacation?

I went to New York City.

Where would you like to visit?

I'd like to visit Hawaii one day.

（2）询问交通方式的句型

How did you go there?

I went there by plane.

How long will it take us to go there by train?

About three hours.

（3）询问旅游时间的句型

When did you go there?

We went there last weekend.

When are you going to set out?

I will set out as soon as I get the ticket.

How long will you stay there?

For a week.

When will you come back?

I will be back in half a month.

（4）询问旅游感受的句型

How was your trip to Hong Kong?

It was fantastic.

How was the food there?

Everything tasted good.

Did everyone have a good time?

Yes, we did.

2. 语法概念与比较——动词和时态

（二）语法中考聚焦

1. 按照在句子中的功能，动词主要分为实义动词、助动词、系动词和情态动词四种。

2. 动词时态

动词时态在初中阶段共有八种：一般现在时、一般过去时、现在进行时、一般将来时、现在完成时、过去进行时、过去将来时和过去完成时。前面六种时态要求掌握，后面两种要求理解。

五、话题语境运用

（1）目的：通过上节课的语句复习，本节课要求学生能将所复习的Topic words、phrases 和 sentences在语境中灵活运用。

（2）小组讨论并完整地描述整件事。

【口语训练】

口语案例：

The students are talking about their vacation.

Pair Work

A: Where did you go on vacation?

B: I went to Shanghai.

A: When did you go there?

B: I went there last year.

A: How long will you stay there?

B: For half a month.

A: When will you come back?

B: I will be back in a week.

A: How was your trip to Shanghai?

B: It was amazing.

六、话题阅读

（一）篇章阅读

How do you go to school? Do you take the school bus to school? Every day, many students take the school bus to school and come back home. So the safety of the school bus is very important. Not only students, but also parents are concerned about the school bus safety.

To make sure that every student is safe on the school bus so that their parents aren't worried about their safety, China's Ministry of Public Security and Ministry of Education make a notice together. The notice asks schools across the country to carry out school bus safety rules strictly.

According to the notice, the registration system（登记系统）of school buses and drivers must be strictly carried out across the country. Every school bus and driver must register. Schools must register buses they own or rent as school buses with local education and public traffic management departments（管理部门）. Every bus must have a license. The driver must have a license, too. Schools can't rent private vehicles or use buses that are not safe.

The notice also says that all buses must take safety checks before every new semester. If schools don't take the check and use the buses, they will be punished. If school bus drivers don't have licenses, schools will be punished, too.

Read the passage and choose the right answer according to the passage.（阅读文章内容，根据文章内容选择正确答案。）

1. Why do China's Ministry of Public Security and Ministry of Education make a notice? (　　)

A. They want to punish some school.

B. Some school bus drivers do not have license.

C. School buses need to be checked.

D. They want to make sure that every student is safe on the school bus.

2. The underline phrase "concerned about" means ________. (　　)

A. thought about　B. talked about　C. worried about　D. discussed about

3. According to the notice, which is not true? (　　)

A. All school buses and drivers must register.

B. All buses must take safety checks before every new semester.

C. Schools can rent private vehicles.

D. Schools across the country must carry out school bus safety rules strictly.

4. What will happen if schools don't take the check and use the buses? (　　)

A. They will have to register again.

B. They will be punished.

C. They will not have the right to own a school bus.

D. They will have to carry out the notice.

5. What's the best title for the passage? (　　)

A. The safety of school buses.

B. The school buses.

C. The registration system（登记系统）of school buses.

D. The school bus is very important.

（二）阅读策略指导

这是一篇时事说明文。

第一题：细节题。在解答此类题目时，一定要抓住文中事件发生的时间、地点、人物、发展过程和结局等方面，答案一定要符合原文，切不可望文生义或主观臆造。在第二段可以找到与题目相同的句子，所以答案应该在第二段中找，A、B、C、D选项中，D选项是正确答案。

第二题：猜测词意题。猜词意是应用英语的重要能力，要准确无误地理解上下文，学会“顺藤摸瓜”，通过构词、语法、常识、上下文等确定词意。这里根据上下文，可以断定C选项是正确答案。

第三题：判断正误题。像这种判断正误，应该用排除法。通读全文后，逐个找出与文章不符合的句子，而且务必要符合原文，不能自以为是。从第三段的最后一句，可以得出正确答案是C选项。

第四题：细节题。从题目可以看出，答案应该在最后一段找。所以B选项正确。

第五题：就是所谓的标题，整篇文章都是讲校车的安全问题，所以选A选项。

七、话题下综合运用

（一）话题句子

1. There are many places of interest in Beijing such as the Summer Palace and so on.

2. Travel is a good way to open your eyes.

3. Don’t drink the wine if you drive a car. Don’t drive your car if you drink the wine.

4. We common people care most for clothing, food, shelter and transport.

5. You are always welcome to use my car at any time.

6. High iron make China travel is very convenient.

（二）话题下读写综合运用

1. 信息归纳：请阅读下面短文，完成表格

Sydney is on the eastern seaboard of Australia, near the Pacific Ocean. Sydney is the most crowed city in Australia. It is often known as the host of the year 2000 Olympic Games. Since Sydney beat Beijing in 1993 for the right to the host the Millennium（千年）Olympic, millions of dollars have been spent on the 110, 000-seat Olympic stadium known as the Stadium Australia. The three outstanding aspects of Sydney are its excellent sandy beaches, friendly and multicultural residents and clean atmosphere. The particular tourist attractions（旅游名胜）in Sydney are Sydney Opera House, Sydney Harbor Bridge and Bondi Beach. Sydney Opera House which is for both the poor and the rich looks like a ship sailing. Sydney Harbor Bridge which is known as "the coat hanger（衣架）" is the largest single arch（拱形） bridge in the world.

Information Card

The location（位置）of Sydney	1.
The money spent on the Stadium Australia	2.
The three aspects of Sydney	3.
The particular tourist attraction in Sydney	4.
The largest single arch bridge in the world	5.

2. 书面表达

现代人的生活压力都很大，所以人们喜欢通过旅游来缓解压力，请围绕下列内容写一篇不少于80词的短文。

（1）有的人喜欢独自旅行，有的人喜欢与别人结伴而行。

（2）两种旅行方式的好处。

（3）你更喜欢哪种旅行方式，为什么？

【写作策略】

（一）审题，找要点

1. 现代人的生活压力很大,所以人们喜欢通过旅游来缓解压力。

2. 有的人喜欢独自旅游，有的人喜欢与别人结伴而行。

3. 独自旅行的好处。

4. 与别人结伴旅行的好处。

5. 你更喜欢哪种旅行?

6.为什么?

最少要写出上述六点!

（二）怎样写

第一点：Now more and more people like ________. Because that can ________.

第二点：Different people have different opinions. Some ______, but some ______.

第三、四点：I think traveling alone ____________. And I think traveling with others ______________.

第五、六点：For me, I prefer to __________. Because __________.（写原因时可以拓展词数，可多写几个原因。）

结尾：If you would like to travel, wish you to have a great time.

Now more and more people like traveling around the world. Because which can make them relax. When it comes to traveling ways, different people will offer different opinions. Some like to travel alone, but some like to travel with their friends or parents. I think traveling alone is good for enjoying more freedom. And I think traveling with others who have the same interest can share something happy with others. As for me, I prefer to travel with friends rather than travel alone, because we can deal with the possible problems and difficulties in the journey. If you would like to travel, wish you to have a great trip!

Topic 10 Inventions

一、单元学习目标

（一）听力

（1）能听懂不同领域（如科技、交通、饮食、文学作品等）的重要发明的历史（如发明时间、发明人等）及用途的对话。

（2）能听懂评论各项发明的用处及特点的对话。

（3）能听懂文学作品等的介绍及评论。

（二）口语

（1）能简单介绍重要发明的历史及用途。

（2）能针对各项发明的用处及特点，发表自己的看法。

（3）能简单介绍文学作品的相关信息，并做简单的评论。

（三）阅读

（1）能读懂对各项发明及现代科技产品的介绍的文章。

（2）能读懂关于文学作品方面的简单介绍和简单评论。

（四）写作

（1）能写出各项发明及现代科技类产品的历史及用途。

（2）能针对各项发明的用处及特点，写简单的评论。

（3）能写出关于一些文学作品的文章，并写简单的评论。

二、思维导图

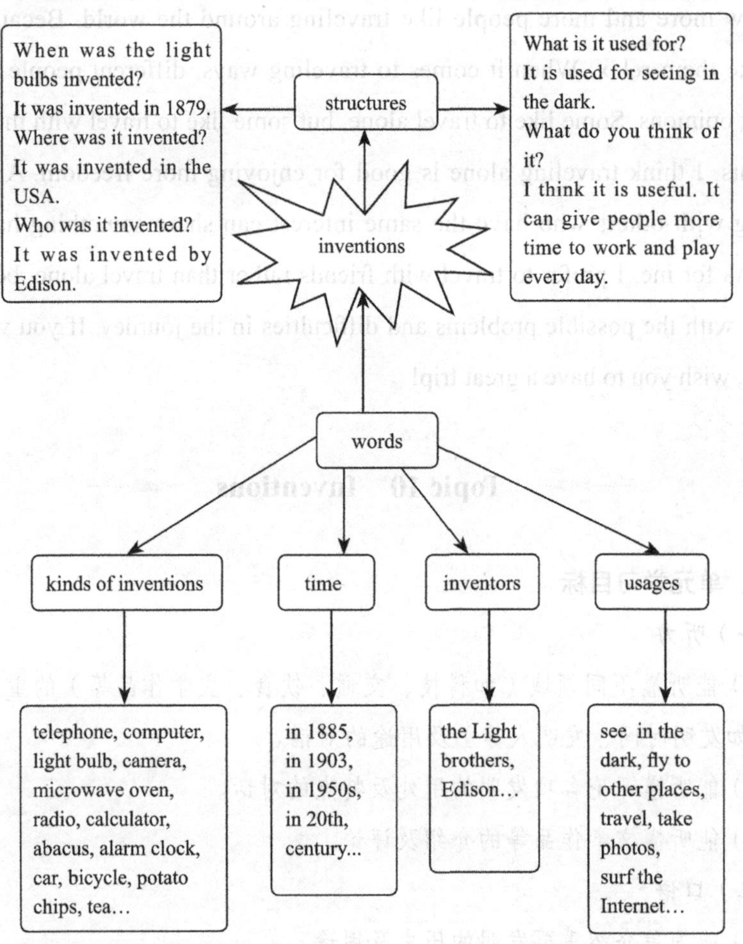

三、话题词语准备

（一）话题单词

1. 有关发明物的词汇

TV, computer, telephone, camera, microwave refrigerator, radio, abacus, alarm clock, car, bicycle, airplane, umbrella, potato chips, tea, etc.

2. 有关用途的词汇

see in the dark, cook food, change the style of the shoes, watch news, watch TV program, listen to music, surf the internet, send e-mail, send message, talk with people on line, etc.

3. 有关意见的词汇

useful, important, convenient, amazing, wonderful, creative, modern, popular, annoying, unimportant, terrible, etc.

（1）同学之间就一些发明设计对话。

（2）针对下列发明，和同伴之间讨论“what do you think is the most important invention in the world”，并且说明理由。

（二）话题词组

1. 词组

break off, come out, learn...by oneself, be made of, be made in, be invented, be used for, make tea, run out of, set up, etc.

2. 根据情境编写对话

____

____

A: When was the...invented?

B: It was invented in...

A: Where was it invented?

B: It was invented in...

A: What is it used for?

B: It is used for doing...

四、功能句和语法聚焦

（一）话题功能句和语法准备

1. 目的

话题功能句和语法准备的目的是帮助学生整理、归纳与本话题相关的重要句型，并让学生能熟练地运用所学的功能句对发明进行真实对话。同时，在实际对话过程中熟练运用被动语态。

2. 关于发明的常用句

When was/were …invented?

It was/ They were invented in …

Where was/ were …invented?

It was/They were invented …

Who was/were …invented by?

It was/ They were invented by …

What is it/ are they used for?

It is / They are used for …

What do you think of it/them?

How do you like it/ them?

I think it is / they are …

What do you think is the most useful/important/ annoying invention?

(二)语法中考聚焦

语态是动词的一种形式，用来说明主语和谓语动词之间的关系。

英语语态有两种，即主动语态与被动语态。主动语态是动作的执行者，被动语态是主语动作的承受者。

一般情况使用如下形式：

(1)一般现在时：am/is are +过去分词。

(2)一般过去时: was/were +过去分词。

(3)情态动词：can/may/must/should + be+过去分词。

(4)一般将来时：will + be + 过去分词。

(5)行为主体不明确，不必说出或者无法说出动作的执行者时用被动语态。

(6)不易找到或根本就找不到动作的执行者时用被动语态。

(7)英语中表达“据说”“据报道”“据了解”等含义时用被动语态。

特别注意：

(1)在主动句中，有些动词如：see, watch, hear, feel, make, let等，它们后面的作宾语补足语的动词不定式是不带to的，而在被动句中则仍应加上to。

（2）某些动词形式上是主动语态，但含有被动的意思。如：

This dictionary sells well. 这本字典很畅销。

A new bookshop is building. 一间新书店在建造中。

This flower smells very sweet. 这花闻起来很香。

五、话题语境运用

（1）目的：通过上节课的语句复习，要求学生能将所复习的Topic words、phrases和sentences在语境中灵活运用。

（2）小组讨论并设计对话。

【口语训练】

口语案例：

Mobile phone is a popular invention. Most students have mobile phones. Some use it to make calls, some use it to surf the Internet, some use it to play games. What about you? Talk about your opinions on mobile phones with your partner.

Useful expressions:

What do you think of …

How do you like …

It's good/convenient/ wonderful/useful/ important…

It's bad/ annoying/ terrible…

It's good/bad for…

It makes…

It helps …

Sample:

A: Wow, what a cool mobile phone! You bought a new mobile phone?

B: No, my mother bought for me as my birthday present. I love it so much. It's very cool. I can listen to music and surf the Internet by moving my fingers.

A: Now more and more students have mobile phones, what do you think of them?

B: In my opinion, mobile phones are kind of necessary. It keeps me in contact with others. Besides I can have lots of entertainment such as listening to music, watching movies as well as taking photos.

A: Yeah, mobile phones make our life more convenient. But it causes some troubles too. People spend less time hanging out with families and friends.

B: It's true. And they also disturb us when we are trying to work or study.

A: And people spend lots of money buying the latest ones. It's a waste of money.

B: I agree with you. Though we created mobile phones, we should choose to use it more carefully.

A: Yes, especially our students, we'd better concentrate more on our study.

六、话题阅读

(一)篇章阅读

Science and new technology have made such rapid progress in agriculture that modern machines can do almost all farm work. More and more vegetables and fruits are in greater need. But can orchard(果园)workers harvest fruits with machines as farmers to crops? Yes, they can. Scientists have already invented many different fruit-harvesting machines. Now, let's take cherry-picking machine for example.

The cherry-picking machine first shakes a cherry tree, and then catches cherries in heavy sheets and pushes the fruit along belts. The cherries are then dropped into huge containers of water, in which they are washed and cleaned, and look fresh and pretty when they are placed into plastic boxes which come along the belt one after another. All this work is finished within three minutes. In this way two orchard workers are able to finish the harvesting work of a cherry orchard within two days which was done by over one hundred workers for two weeks. New machines that are now being tested will pick apples, peaches, pears and strawberries.

It is also believed that with the development of science and new technology, farm working conditions will be greatly improved. More and more work will be done by machines instead of men so that people's living standard will be greatly improved in the future.

Read the passage and choose the right answer according to the passage.(阅读文章内容,根据文章内容选择正确答案。)

1. The underlined word “agriculture” in the first paragraph means ________ in Chinese. (　　)

A. 工业　　B. 农业

C. 旅游业　　D. 航空业

2. ________ are in greater need. (　　)

A. More and more fruits

B. More and more orchard workers

C. More and more vegetables

D. More and more vegetables and fruits

3. Which of the following is the correct order of how cherry-picking machine works? (　　)

① drop cherries into huge containers of water

② push cherries along belts

③ wash and clean cherries

④ catch cherries

⑤ shake a cherries tree in heavy sheets

⑥ place cherries into plastic boxes

A. ④⑤①②⑥③　　B. ⑤④①②③⑥

C. ⑤④②①③⑥　　D. ④⑤②①⑥③

4. Which of the following is not right? (　　)

A. Orchard workers with machines spend less time harvesting fruits.

B. Scientists have invented few fruit-harvesting machines.

C. Apples, peaches, pears and strawberries will be picked by new machines.

D. Thanks to cherry-picking machine, it takes two orchard workers two days to finish the harvesting work of a cherry orchard.

5. With the development of science and new technology, what will happen in the future except ________. (　　)

A. farm working conditions will be much better

B. machines will do more and more work

C. people's living standard will be greatly improved

D. more and more people will lose jobs

（二）阅读策略指导

我们可以看出这是一篇总分总的现代科技文章。第一段讲了现代科技的发展给农业带来的进步。第二段以“cherry-picking machine”为例，讲述了摘樱桃机器是如何工作的。第三段总结现代科技的发展使人们的生活水平提高了。

第一题：猜测词意题。从第一段第一句的“farm work”，可以推测出“agriculture”指的是农业，所以选B选项。

第二题：细节题，直接去原文找即可。从第一段的第二句“More and more vegetables and fruits are in greater need”可以找出答案。所以D选项正确。

第三题：排序题。题目中主要问摘樱桃机器的工作程序，由文中的第二段的第一、二句可以判断出C选项是正确的。

第四题：判断正误题。像判断正误、mention or not mention和选标题几类种题，为了保证考试时间一定要放在最后做。由于你做完所有的细节题对全文有掌握了，更好做题。而且对于这种题，出现在篇幅较长的文章中，要从选项中找。A选项提到有了机器，果园工作者会花费更少时间收获水果。从文中的第二段“In this way two orchard workers are able to finish the harvesting work of a cherry orchard within two days which was done by over one hundred workers for two week”可以推测出A选项是正确的。B选项说的是科学家几乎没有收获水果的机器。从文中的第一段“Scientists have already invented many different fruit-harvesting machines.”可以看出B选项是错误的。选项错在few，几乎没有，表否定。C选项说苹果，桃子，梨子和草莓将会被新机器采摘。由文中的第二段的最后一句“New machines that are now being tested will pick apples, peaches, pears and strawberries.”可以推测出C选项是正确的。D选项说多亏有了摘樱桃机器，两名果园工作者可以在两天内完成整个果园的采摘工作。从文中的第二段“In this way two orchard workers are able to finish the harvesting work of a cherry orchard within two days which was done by over one hundred workers for two weeks.”可以判断出D选项是正确的。所以答案为B选项。

第五题：细节题。题目中说随着科技的发展，给生活带来了什么样的改变。从第三段可以判断出A、B、C选项是正确的。D选项文中没提及，所以选D选项。

七、话题下综合运用

（一）话题句子

1. China's Tu Youyou has become the first scientist on the mainland to win Nobel Prize for achievements in Medicine.

2. Books are very important to us. Sometimes, a good book can change one's life .

3. With the help of computers, it will be possible for people to see a doctor at home.

4. In a way, the popularity of the Internet, PC and 4G make a great difference to our life.

5. One of the biggest reasons for this is broadband and wifi.

6. Now satellites are helping to forecast the weather.

（二）话题下读写综合运用

1. 信息归纳：阅读下面短文，然后按照信息卡中项目要求填入相关信息

Henry Ford was the eldest son of a farmer. He grew up on a farm in Michigan. Like most farmers at that time, his father William hoped his eldest son would help him on the farm, but Henry was not interested in farm work at all. He did everything he could do to avoid（逃避）it. Once he wrote, "What a waste it is for a man to spend hours behind a slowly moving horse."

However, Henry was not a lazy boy. He liked to do mechanical（机械的）work very much. When he was twelve, he became quite interested in clocks and watches. He mended clocks and watches for his friends in his bedroom. He loved this and learned much from it.

Later he took a job as a mechanic（技工）in Detroit. He began to show great interest in steam engines（蒸汽发动机）at this time, then he built his first car. In 1908, he built a famous "Model T". This car was so popular at that time that it was unchanged for twenty years. Five years after that he started the Ford Motor Company which is one of the most famous companies in the world. We can see many kinds of cars produced in the company everywhere.

Information Card

Ford's Nationality.	1.
His father's job.	2.
The thing he wasn't interested in.	3.
The place he worked as a mechanic.	4.
The time Ford started the Ford Motor Company.	5.

2.书面表达

历史上有很多发明，起着重要的作用，其中一些改变了世界。依你之见，什么是最重要的发明，并说明原因，比如它起的作用（不少于三点），80词左右。

【写作策略】

（一）审题，找要点

1. 什么是最重要的发明？

2. 重要的原因（三点）。

最少要写出上述四点！

（二）怎样写

开头：There are a lot of inventions in the history. Some of them play an important role in people's life and some have greatly changed the world.

第一点：In my opinion, I think ________________.

第二点：First, ______________________________

第三点：Second, ____________________________.

第四点：Third, ______________.（还可以多写几个原因来拓展词数。）

结尾：In a word, I do agree that ___________ are the most important invention.

The Most Helpful Invention

There are a lot of inventions in the history. Some of them play an important role in people's life and some have greatly changed the world. In my opinion, I think the most important invention is the car. First, people used to travel by train or by plane.

But now, they can go any place by car. Second, when holiday comes, they can visit their family and friends by car. Third, they can also go to many places of interest to enjoy themselves.

In a word, I do agree that cars are the most important invention.

Topic 11 Holidays and Celebrations

一、单元学习目标

（一）听力

（1）能听懂中西方节日和庆典的名称，如名称、时间、由来、习俗等。

（2）能听懂对中西方传统节日的描述，如食物、服装、传统活动等。

（3）能听懂不同节日里人们所说的祝福语。

（二）口语

（1）能简单介绍中西方传统节日和庆典。

（2）能简单描述人们庆祝不同节日的方式和习俗。

（3）能说出各种节日的传统食物和祝福语。

（三）阅读

（1）能读懂中西方传统节日和庆典。

（2）能读懂关于中西方传统节日和庆典的介绍。

（3）能读懂对对中西方传统节日的比较。

（四）写作

（1）能写出中西方传统节日和庆典的名称。

（2）能简单描述人们庆祝不同节日的方式和习俗。

（3）能简单地比较中西方传统节日的不同。

二、思维导图

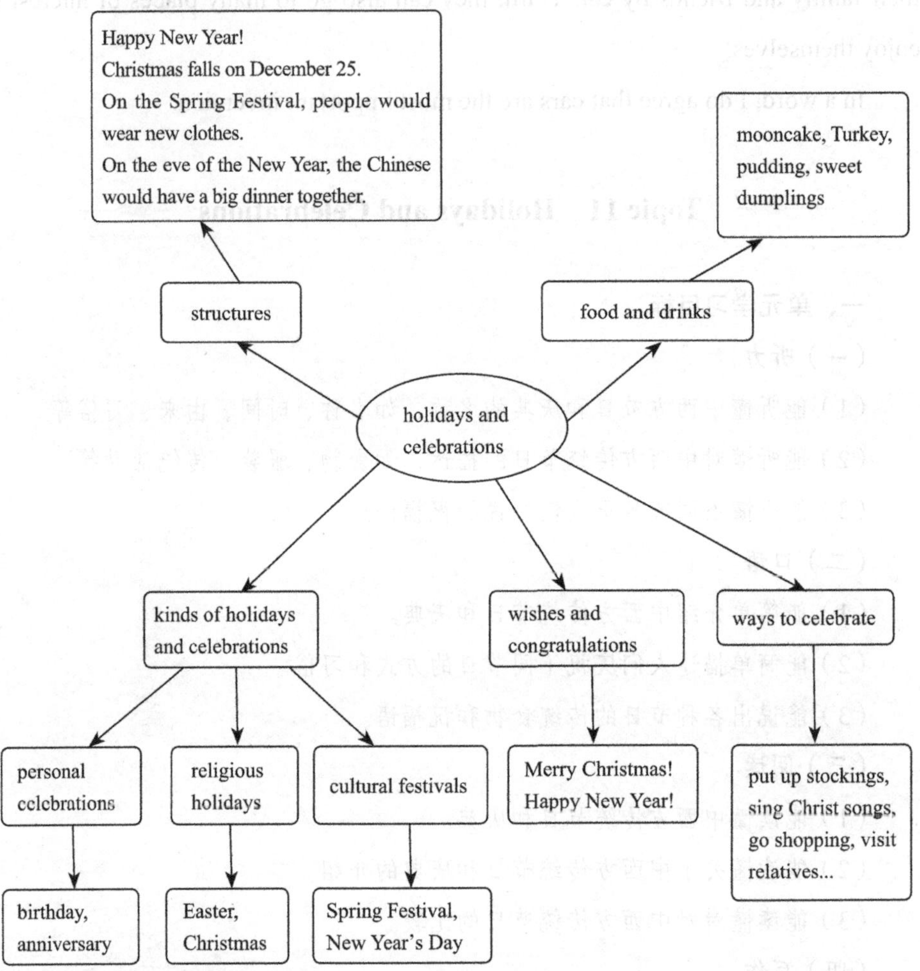

三、话题词语准备

1.节日、庆典的名称

the Spring Festival, the Dragon Boat Festival, the Mid-autumn Festival, Lantern Festival, Double Ninth Festival, New Year's Eve, Christmas Day, Halloween, Easter Day, Thanksgiving Day, National Day, Mother's Day, April Fool's Day, Women's Day, Wedding anniversary, etc.

2.与节日有关的词汇

card, flower, gift, party, picnic, firework, lucky money, new clothes, santa hats, mooncake, Turkey, give thanks for, go to church, put up stockings, sing Christ songs, get together, go shopping, visit relatives and friends, decorate Christmas tree, clean the house, set off firework, perform lion and dragon dances, eat sweet dumplings, etc.

四、功能句和语法聚焦

（一）话题功能句和语法准备

1. 话题功能句和语法准备的目的是帮助学生整理、归纳与本话题相关的重要句型。

2.谈论节日、庆典的常用句型。

National Day is coming.

Christmas falls on December 25.

The Spring Festival usually falls in January or February.

They are celebrating National Day.

On the eve of the new year, the Chinese would have a big dinner together.

On the Spring Festival, people would wear new clothes.

The Spring Festival is always the most important and happiest time for the Chinese.

Mid-autumn Day is a traditional festival for the Chinese.

On that day, people would eat mooncake while appreciating the moon.

Happy New Year!

Merry Christmas!

（二）语法中考聚焦

英语句子根据用途可以分为：陈述句、疑问句、祈使句、感叹句。

1. 陈述句

陈述句用来叙述一件事或一种看法。

2. 疑问句

疑问句分为一般疑问句、特殊疑问句、选择疑问句和反意疑问句。

（1）一般疑问句：用yes或no回答的疑问句。

（2）特殊疑问句：以特殊疑问词wh-/how开头的疑问句。特殊疑问词wh-/how + 一般疑问句。

（3）选择疑问句：

选择疑问句的结构有下面两种：

① 一般疑问句 + or + 一般疑问句。

② 疑问句+选择部分 + or + 选择部分。

（4）反意疑问句：提问者有一定主见，但没有把握，希望对方来证实的问题。

3. 祈使句

祈使句表示请求、建议、命令或劝告等。有肯定和否定形式，多省略主语。中考仅理解。

4. 感叹句

感叹句用来表示强烈感情，由感叹词what或how引导。

注意：把肯定句变成否定句或是一般疑问句时，一般把含有some/something/somebody 等不定代词变为相应的any/anything/anybody。也可以用no/nothing/nobody 来替换all/everything/everybody，而不必加助动词和not就能变成否定句。

五、话题语境运用

（1）目的：通过上节课的语句复习，本节课要求学生能将所复习的Topic words、phrases 和 sentences在语境中灵活运用。

（2）小组讨论并设计对话。

【口语训练】

These are Chinese traditional festivals. When are they and what people usually do on these special days? In pair, discuss and make your conversation.

the Mid-autumn Festival	the Spring Festival

Sample:

A: What is the most important Chinese traditional festival?

B: I think the Spring Festival is the most important.

A: When is the Spring Festival?

B: It usually falls on January or February.

A: What do people usually do on that day?

B: People usually wear new clothes, have a big meal and set off firework.

A: Is the Mid-autumn Festival Chinese traditional festival?

B: Yes, it is.

六、话题阅读

(一)篇章阅读

Festivals and Holidays

People everywhere celebrate special and important days known as festivals or holidays. Although each festival or holiday has a different purpose, they seem to have something in common. Many are related(有联系的)to traditions. For example, people in western countries like decorating a tree at Christmas.

Festivals and holidays also bring people together in plenty of ways. On some holidays, people come back home and join together to celebrate the coming of a new year — such as the Spring Festival in China. Other holidays, such as Halloween, are for exciting celebrations.

The word "festival" comes from the word "feast (a big meal)". Many festivals were originally connected with the planting or harvesting(收获)of crops. Food still plays an important <u>role</u> in many festivals and holidays today. The turkey eaten on Thanksgiving Day and mooncake eaten on Mid-autumn Day are examples of traditional food of holidays. The word "holiday" originally meant "holy(神圣的)day". Many holidays are still religious(宗教的).

Read the passage and choose the right answer according to the passage.(阅读文章内容，根据文章内容选择正确答案。)

1. When do people in western countries usually decorate a tree? (　　)

A. During the Spring Festival. B. At Christmas.

C. On weekends. D. On Halloween.

2. What's the purpose of the Spring Festival? (　　)

A. To celebrate the coming of a new year.

B. To celebrate the harvest.

C. To enjoy the beautiful moon.

D. To show respect to a great person.

3. What does the underlined "role" mean? (　　)

A. game.　　B. part.　　C. time.　　D. person.

4. What traditional food of holidays is mentioned in the text? (　　)

A. Mooncake.　　B. Turkey.

C. The Christmas tree.　　D. A and B.

5. Why does the author write the third paragraph? (　　)

A. To introduce more holidays.

B. To show the difference between holidays and festivals.

C. To explain the original meanings of "holiday" and "festival".

D. To introduce religious holidays.

（二）阅读策略指导

这是一篇说明性文章。

第一题：细节题。在解答此类题目时，答案一定要在原文中找，切不可望文生义或主观臆造。在第一段可以找到与题目相同的句子，所以答案应该在第一段找，A、B、C、D选项中，B选项是正确答案。

第二题：理解题。文章中没有出现与题干一样的句子。但是提及"the Spring Festival"只在第二段，所以答案可以在第二段中找，而恰好选项中有符合的。这里根据上下文，可以断定A选项是正确答案。

第三题：猜测词意题。像这种题要求学生平时要有较大的阅读量，掌握或认识较多的课外词汇。实在猜不到，应该选用排除法，把单词放到文章中，逐个推敲，根据上下文，这题答案应是B选项。

第四题：细节题。从题目可以看出，答案应该在最后一段中找。所以D选项正确。

第五题：主旨题，主要考查学生对文章的理解程度，考查内容包括作者的写作目的、文章的中心思想等。只有读懂全文，才能正确答题。整段看来，C选项是正确答案。

七、话题下综合运用

（一）话题句子

1. On New Year's Eve, Chinese people often have a big dinner.

2. On Christmas afternoon, people usually stay at home and open the gifts that\which were gathered around the Christmas tree.

3. Many countries set off fireworks to celebrate their national days .

4. We look forward to sharing China's story with players to the 2016 Rio de Janeiro Olympic Games.

5. In order to celebrate Dragon Boat Festival, the Chinese people have three days off.

6. The first of April is April Fool's Day, and it is common to play a trick on a friend on this day.

（二）话题下读写综合运用

1. 信息归纳：请阅读下面短文，并按照信息表中项目要求，填写信息卡

The Internet has become part of teenage life. There's a report on 3,375 students aged from 10 to 18 in seven Chinese cities. It says that 38% of them believe they use the Internet often. While most of them get useful information and use the Internet to help in their studies, some are not using it in a good way. Many are playing online games too much. A few even visit websites they should not look at. Bad things can happen if young people spend too much time on the Internet. In order to help young people use the Internet in a good way, a textbook on good Internet behavior has started to be used in some Shanghai middle schools this term. It uses real examples to teach students all about good ways of using the Internet. It gives useful advice such as it's good to read news or find helpful information to study. Some students also make online friends. But if you are meeting a friend offline, let your parents know. Teachers and parents all think the book is a very good idea. It will teach students how to be a good person in the online world. It will be a guide for teens using the Internet and keep students away from bad sites.

Information Card

__________ has become part of teenage life.	1.
The number of students on the report is __________.	2.
Most students do __________ on the Internet.	3.
__________ has started to be used in some Shanghai middle schools this term.	4.
The reason parents and teachers think the book is a very good idea .	5.

2. 书面表达

现在很多学生喜欢上网，作为一名中学生，从正反两个方面谈论一下在业余时间该不该上网，并说明原因。写一篇不少于80词的短文。

【写作策略】

1. 审题，找要点

（1）上网的优点。

（2）上网不足的方面。

（3）作为一名学生如何平衡上网时间？

2. 怎样写

第一点：But we also know it has advantages and disadvantages. On the Internet, we can get____________________.

第二点：disadvantages about Internet...

第三点：Call on students to use the Internet correctly.

Should students surf on the internet? We divide the opinions into two parts.

We know the Internet is becoming more and more popular in our daily life. But we also know it has advantages and disadvantages. On the Internet, we can get information as much as we can. We can send emails to our friends and talk to them as well. Besides, on the Internet we can read books, enjoy music and watch ball games. We can also do shopping without leaving our homes. It's good for us to use the Internet.

But now as students, we spend too much time playing computer games. It is bad for our eyes and our study, we should put our hearts into our study. Besides, some students often chat with strangers on the Internet, it's easy to be cheated. Seriously, sometimes some students can leave home to look for their strange friends.

So we should use the Internet correctly.

Topic 12 Weather

一、单元学习目标

（一）听力

（1）能听懂描述天气状况的形容词，如晴天、阴天、雨天、多雾天气、刮风天气、热、冷等。

（2）能听懂世界各大城市的天气状况，并能够简单地描述所听到城市的天气状况。

（3）能听懂简单的谈论天气及人们正在从事的活动的对话以及简单的城市天气预报。

（二）口语

（1）能用所学语言谈论天气，并能够谈论天气预报。

（2）能描述一下天气状况，如阴天、晴天、雨天、多雾天气、雪天、冷、热等。

（3）能够简单地描述人们在不同的天气情况下从事的不同活动，如看电视、打篮球、登山、滑雪、放风筝等。

（4）能够表述简单的天气预报及穿着，如雨衣、外套、裙子、衬衫、毛衣等。

（三）阅读

（1）能读懂描述天气状况的形容词，如晴天、阴天、雨天、多雾天气、刮风天气、热、冷等。

（2）能读懂天气状况，如阴天、晴天、雨天、多雾天气、雪天、冷、热等。

（3）能读懂描述人们在不同的天气情况下从事的不同活动，如看电视、打篮球、登山、滑雪、放风筝等。

（4）能够读懂简单的天气预报及穿着，如雨衣、外套、裙子、衬衫、毛衣等。

（四）写作

（1）能写出描述天气状况的形容词，如晴天、阴天、雨天、多雾天气、刮风天气、热、冷等。

（2）能写出天气状况，如阴天、晴天、雨天、多雾天气、雪天、冷、热等。

（3）能写出描述人们在不同的天气情况下从事的不同活动，如看电视、打篮球、登山、滑雪、放风筝等。

（4）能够写出简单的天气预报及穿着，如雨衣、外套、裙子、衬衫、毛衣等。

二、思维导图

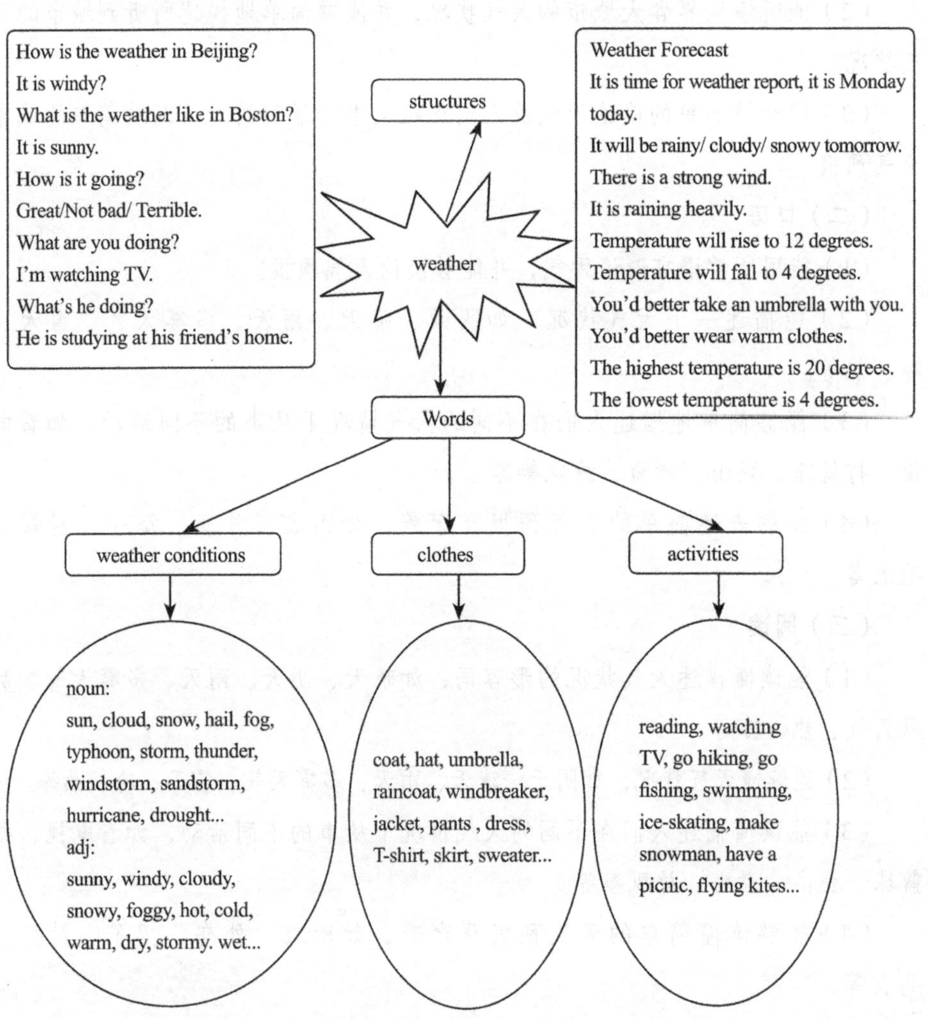

三、话题词语准备

（一）话题单词

1. 天气类以及主要城市的名词

weather, rain, snow, cloud, wind, rainy, snowy, cloudy, windy, sunny, dry, hot, cold, warm, wet, foggy, humid, muggy, close, freezing, flood, heatwave, etc.

2. 衣服类的名词

coat, sweater, raincoat, hat, T-shirt, dress, glove, windbreaker, scarf, etc.

3. Functional language: Answer the questions with "It is…", according to the words about the weather.

Different weather and different activities What's the weather like?/ What are they doing? Sunny—swimming　　snowy—making a snowman—rainy—watching TV

（二）话题词组

1. 词组

strong wind, heavy rain, the highest temperature, the lowest temperature, weather forecast, visit friends, make a snowman, sit by the pool, wear a hat, take an umbrella, pretty good, not bad, etc.

2. 根据情境编写对话

（1）同桌之间设计不同的天气情况下开展不同的活动的对话。

（2）根据话题词语提示进行对话。

（3）在话题词语训练熟练的基础上，自己设计情境，在不同的天气情况下进行的不同的活动的对话。

四、功能句和语法聚焦

（一）话题功能句和语法准备

话题功能句和语法准备的目的是帮助学生整理、归纳与本话题相关的重要句型，并让学生能熟练地运用以“天气”为中心的功能句进行真实对话。同时，在实际对话过程中掌握主谓一致的用法。

1. 询问天气及应答的常用句型

How is the weather in Beijing?

It is windy?

What is the weather like in Boston?

It is sunny.

How is it going?

Great/Not bad/ Terrible.

What are you doing?

I'm watching TV.

What's he doing?

He is studying at his friend's home.

2. 与天气预报相关的常用句型

It is time for weather report, it is Monday today.

It will be rainy/ cloudy/ snowy tomorrow.

There is a strong wind.

It is raining heavily.

Temperature will rise to 12 degrees.

Temperature will fall to 4 degrees.

You'd better take an umbrella with you.

You'd better wear warm clothes.

The highest temperature is 20 degrees.

The lowest temperature is 4 degree.

(二) 语法中考聚焦

主谓一致是指主语和谓语动词在人称和数上保持一致，主要包括语法一致原则、意义一致原则和就近原则，具体内容如表7–7所示。

表7–7 中考语法

主谓一致原则	1. and 或both...and连接两个名词时，谓语用复数； 2. each 与every作主语时，谓语用单数； 3. 不定代词either，neither，each one，the other，another及复合不定代词somebody，nothing 作主语，谓语用单数	1. a number of +复名，谓语用复数；the number of +复名，谓语用单数； 2. 主语后接with，along with，together with，as well as，including，besides，except，but, like 等词，谓语动词的数由主语决定； 3. 不定式或动名词作主语，谓语用单数； 4. the+姓氏复数名词，谓语用复数名词； 5. a lot of /lots of +名词以及"分数或百分数+名词"作主语，谓语动词的单复数取决于名词
意义一致原则	1. family，team，class，group，government等，强调"整体"时谓语用单数，强调"集体中的成员"时用复数； 2. people，cattle，police 谓语用复数	表示价格、时间、度量、长度的复数名词或短语作主语，谓语用单数
就近原则	either...or, neither...nor..., not only...but also..., not...but..., 或or谓语动词的单复数形式要和离得最近的主语保持一致	there be 句型也要遵循就近原则

五、话题语境运用

1. 目的：通过上节课的语句复习，本节课要求学生能将所复习的Topic words、phrases 和 sentences在语境中灵活运用。

2. 小组讨论并设计对话。

【口语训练】

Three people are on holiday, they have been asked what the weather is like, and how they feel and why. Choose one of them to discuss the weather, their feelings of the holiday.

Relevant information

Name	Bob	Sue	Amy
Weather	Rainy	Snowy	Hot
Feeling Reason	Sad Couldn't go hiking	Excited Make a snowman First time she has seen it	Uncomfortable Isn't used to this kind of weather

Useful expressions:

What was the weather like?

What were you going to do before?

What did you do instead?

Come back from...

A bit too hot and too sunny

You should put on...

Sample：

A: Hi! Amy. You have just come back from holiday, haven't you?

B: Hi! Wang Bo. Yes, I have.

A: Where was it you went again? The USA?

B: No, we went to Perth. Me, my mom and my dad.

A: In Scotland?

B: No, silly! In Australia.

A: Oh, right. I've never been there. What was it like?

B: Well, the weather was absolutely fantastic. It didn't rain once!

A: That's great. So what did you do?

B: First, we visited a farm. I got to see kangaroos and sheep, and learned all about them. Then we took a plane and went to the Gold Coast. That was really fun, there were amusements and the beach is great. There were many things to do that we couldn't fit them in.

A: Was the weather good there too?

B: Yes, it was the same. Actually it was a bit too hot and too sunny. I got sunburnt one day. It was really painful.

A: You should have worn clothes that covered you and you should have put on some sun cream.

B: I know that now.

六、话题阅读

（一）篇章阅读

Do you think it'll rain tomorrow? Will it be cold or sunny? In many places, people often listen to the weather reports because they want to wear right clothes for the weather. But the weather can mean more than changes in clothing. Studies show that the weather affects people's moods —— it changes the way people feel. Rainy or cloudy weather can have a bad effect on people. In Poland, scientists studied the effects of weather on the building industry. They found that the number of accidents on building sites went up when the weather was bad. Years ago in England, when the London fog came up and it was dark outside the whole day, the Bank of England put away its most important papers. The bank found that bank employees made a lot of mistakes because of the bad weather. In recent years, scientists find out a new illness. They call it seasonal affective disorder（季节性情绪失调）. People with this illness get very sad during the long dark days of winter when there is little sunlight. But when people with the illness sit under a sunlamp for some time every day, they will usually feel better. So next time when you are sad or feel strange, maybe you can blame it on the weather.

Read the passage and choose the right answer according to the passage.（阅读文章内容，根据文章内容选择正确答案。）

1. If you want to wear right clothes, you can ________. (　　)

A. listen to the weather reports　　B. ask some people for help

C. go to the shop　　D. have a family meeting

2. In Poland, scientists found out that ________. (　　)

A. the weather could mean changes in clothing

B. the weather affected people's moods

C. the accidents on building sites went up because of bad weather

D. the bank employees made many mistakes because of bad weather

3. Scientists found out a new illness called ________. (　　)

A. people's moods　　B. clothing changes

C. building sites　　　　D. seasonal affective disorder

4. The word "blame" in the last paragraph means ________.(　　)

A. 批评　　B. 表扬　　C. 责怪　　D. 咒骂

5. The passage is mainly talking about ________. (　　)

A. effects of the weather on the building industry

B. effects of the weather on people's mood

C. the weather

D. people's illness

（二）阅读策略指导

本文主要是围绕"weather"这个话题进行的，主要阐述了天气和人们心情之间的关系。

第一题：细节题，直接去文中找答案即可。在第二句中即可找到答案，注意"because"这个关键词。所以选择A选项。

第二题：细节题，直接去文中找答案即可。关键词是"In Poland"，所以C选项正确。

第三题：细节题，直接去文中找答案即可。关键词是"a new illness"，因此D选项正确。

第四题：猜测词意题，根据上下文可以推断出blame的意思。因此C选项正确。

第五题：文章主旨题。通读并理解全文即可把握文章的主旨，所以B选项正确。

七、话题下综合运用

（一）话题句子

1. It will probably rain tomorrow, so I will stay at home and read a book.

2. Do you think weather can influence you a lot in your daily life?

3. Is it very useful for us to listen to weather report every day?

4. Why do British people often take umbrellas with them while going out?

5. If it is fine this afternoon, we will have a picnic in the open air.

6. The weather is expected to be terrible through the weekend.

7. There is a cold from the north moving down through Guangdong.

（二）话题下读写综合运用

1. 信息归纳：请阅读下面短文，完成表格

Your junior school years are coming to an end. After this term, you will study in a senior school. What are you expecting from senior school? Let's hear what some teen readers think the future will be.

Chen Gang, 14, from Dongguan, Guangdong I hear that although Senior 3 is a hard year, Senior 1 and Senior 2 are less stressful. I hope there' ll be time then to enjoy sports.
Zhao Jie, 16, from Harbin, Heilongjiang I really enjoy science. I am also interested in UFOs. I'm crazy about making model planes, although I'm not very good because I don't really have the science knowledge. I'll learn more science in senior school. Anyway, sometime in the future I'm going to build an amazing model plane!
Wang Lin, 15, from Xiamen, Fujian I hope I can be taller in senior school. I am only 155 cm. Many children grow faster in senior school and I hope so. I want to be 162 cm. But I am not sure, since most girls in my family don't grow any taller than 160 cm. I hope I am different.
Zhang Chen, 14, Puyang, Henan I expect that I'll make more friends in senior school. I study in a middle school affiliated to（附属）a factory. Most of my classmates live nearby. In senior school, I'll meet people from different areas. I can learn new things from them.

Information Card

the age of is Chen Gang	1.
the place Wang Lin comes from	2.
the things Zhao Jie like to do	3.
the name of the oldest kid	4.
the things Zhang Chen hope to do	5.

2.书面表达

最近，班里召开了以“我的中国梦”为主题的班会活动，每名学生都畅谈了个人对中国梦的理解。请你写一篇日记，描述班会情况及个人感受。

内容要点：

（1）谈谈个人梦想。

（2）为什么有这个梦想？

（3）如何实现个人梦想？

【写作策略】

（一）审题，找要点

1. 对中国梦的理解。

2. 个人梦想是什么？

3. 为什么有这个梦想？

4. 如何实现个人梦想？

最少要写出上述四点！

（二）怎样写

第一点：Everyone talked about his understanding of the Chinese Dream. We all believe that this dream will come true in the future.

第二点：I also talked about my own dream.（过渡句）My dream is to be ____________________________________.

第三点：Let me tell you why I have this dream?（过渡句）________________.（可以多写几个原因来拓展词数，可以写一两件事情来说明原因。）

第四点：How will I make my dream come true?（过渡句）I will ____________________________________.（可以多写几条来拓展词数。）

结尾：I believe I'll be a good…in the future.

Everyone talked about his understanding of the Chinese Dream. We all believe that this dream will come true in the future. I also talked about my own dream. My dream is to be a doctor. Let me tell you why I have this dream. When I was in Grade Seven, I was sick and often went to see doctors. The doctors were very friendly to me and they often cheered me up. With the help of them, I was getting better. Now I'm very healthy. Since then I have hoped to become a doctor.

How will I make my dream come true? I will study hard to get good grades. I'll read more books about medicine. I believe I'll be a good doctor in the future.

第三部分　初中英语教材话题下单元整合介绍

（一）单元整合需要把握的教学理念

1. 把握语言学习的过程性，加强对教学过程的指导与帮助

鼓励学生在教师的指导下，通过体验、实践、参与、探究和合作等方式，发现语言规律，逐步掌握语言知识和技能，不断调整情感态度，形成有效的学习策略，发展自主学习能力，体现学习的过程性。

（1）如何体现学习的过程性？

以学生为主体，以学习为中心，努力改变“有记忆，无认知”的教学；设计尽可能真实的教学情境，引导学生参与教学过程，不仅是行为参与，更需要思维参与；帮助学生实现在学习过程中的角色转换。教师在教学中呈现出来的教学应该不是体力活，而是科学、艺术和智慧。

（2）话题下单元整合的过程性如何体现？

PWP model 体现的是Pre-learning，While-learning，Post-learning，教师围绕本节课的话题主线，要求学生在活动中，获取、阐释和评判所学话语的意义，表达个人观点、意图和情感态度，分析中外文化异同，发展多元思维和批判性思维，从而提高学生英语学习和实际运用语言的能力。

Task-chain 体现的是任务链教学思想，即根据任务型教学思想，将一个大任务分解成若干个小任务，每一个小任务都是大任务链条上的一环，各个小任务之间拥有一定的教学逻辑，环环相扣，互为支架，螺旋上升，形成一个从语言输入，到语言内化，最后到语言输出的完整过程。

Discovery method 教师通过图片或教师语言搭建支架，让学生在操练中习得，最终发现语言结构规则。

2. 把握任务型教学思想，发展学生的语言运用能力，使其学会用语言做事情

什么是任务（task）？

任务就是人们在日常生活中所做的任何有目的的活动，如打电话、填写表格、点菜等。

任务的特点：具有明确的目的，具有真实意义，与现实生活相近，涉及语言信息的接收、处理和传递，涉及不同语言技能的运用。它是一个完整的交际过程，有一个语言的或非语言的结果。

3. 重视学习策略培养，发展学生的自主学习能力

学习策略指学生为了有效地学习和使用英语而采取的各种行动和步骤以及指导这些行动和步骤的信念。英语学习策略包括认知策略、调控策略、交际策略和资源策略等。

4. 重视词块（Lexical chunks）教学，提高词汇学习效率

（1）词块 Lexical chunks指固定短语、常见搭配、习语和俚语、句型框架。

（2）词块教学的意义：整体输入，整体输出；提高学生记忆和表达的效率和准确性。

5. 把握多元化教学思想，培养学生的跨文化交际意识和能力

2011版课程标准指出语言有丰富的文化内涵。在外语教学中，文化是指所学语言国家的历史地理、风土人情、传统习俗、生活方式、行为规范、文学艺术、价值观念等。教材中的文化是英语国家文化、非英语国家文化、中国文化。

文化对学生的发展功能：

（1）外国文化：理解、包容、国际视野。

（2）祖国文化：祖国意识、爱国精神、家国情怀。

（3）向世界：讲好中国故事，传播好中国声音。

（二）话题下单元整合的思路和整体教学的做法

1. 综合模式

话题+功能+结构+任务，即Topic + Function + Structure + Task。

2. 分层设计

（1）Section A 语言的呈现与训练：以听说为主。

（2）Section B 语言的运用与拓展：以读写为主。

3. 板块设计

听说板块、语法板块、阅读板块、写作板块 、检测板块。

4. 听说领先，读写跟上

听说领先、读写跟上是整合教材编写的一个特点，较符合先声音后文字的语言学习规律，较符合先输入后输出的语言教学原则。

5. 单元整体教学整合原则

以话题带动词汇的学习，以功能带动结构的学习，以任务带动语言的运用。围绕一条主线：话题；两个层次：Section A 语言的呈现与训练，Section B 语言的拓展与运用；三个支柱：知识、技能、运用；四个维度：话题、功能、结构、任务；五个板块：听说、语法、阅读、写作、检测。

（三）整合后面临的问题

增加阅读是为了增加可理解性输入。人教版教材GFI，七年级上册、七年级下册、八年级上册与八年级下册和九年级在阅读量和阅读难度上不够平衡，缺乏合理梯度。

2011版课程标准指出英语课程具有双重属性，即工具性和人文性。

人文性：情感态度、价值观念、思维方式、思想品格、审美情趣、文化素养、国际视野及跨文化意识。

话题下单元整合涉及显性变化和隐性变化。

显性变化：增加了话题下的篇章阅读量和阅读难度，便于教学中有梯度衔接，适当地减小了部分单元阅读的长度和难度，形成一个单元在话题下阅读教学格局。

隐性变化：在整合的篇章中增强了社会主义核心价值观教育。

1. 怎么办

教学难度主要来自于话题下语篇以读促写和话题下篇章作文。

话题下语篇以读促写和话题下篇章作文的目的是增加学生的可理解性输入，培养其语感；培养学生的阅读策略和阅读技能；拓展学生的文化知识；强化语言知识在真实语境中的运用；增强学生的语篇意识。话题下语篇教学有利于学生综合语言运用能力的培养。

2. 教材中词汇怎么教

在整合教材中我们关注了第一层次：课标要求的词；第二层次：话题拓展词；第三层次：行文需要的词。

在课堂教学中注意以下几点：

（1）不宜平均使用力量。把握重点，分清层次，切忌眉毛胡子一把抓。只要重点关注课文中课标要求的词汇和本单元的目标、语法即可。

（2）不宜提前教学。对于一些提前出现的词汇或语法现象，只要让学生根据语境能够理解、翻译即可，不宜拓展教学。

（3）不宜过度教学。对于课文中的语言知识应有选择性地教学，不宜做“开花式”教学。

（4）不要求一步到位。不要见到什么就讲什么，不要一讲就讲个彻底。

（5）应把课文当作语篇来教学。不要把所有精力都放在对课文语言点的解读上。在整合时，我们考虑：教课文，还是用课文来教？因此，我们充分考虑了如何处理好教材与教学的关系。以前，教材是学生的世界。现在，世界是学生的教材。

第四部分 教材中的三个案例展示

案例1：GFI Unit 8 How was your school trip? B3

Topic: school trips

一、单元整合整体规划

（一）教材分析

UNIT 8 How was your school trip？以“school trips”为话题，让学生学会谈论过去所发生的事情，包括去了哪里、怎么去、做了什么、看了什么、心情怎样等。在实际生活中，学生要学会根据个人的实际的情况，向他人进行描述，从而进行交流沟通，达到交际的目的。

在教材中，本单元紧紧围绕“events in the past”，共设计Section A，Section B 和Self Check三个部分的内容。下面就这三个部分对教材进行具体的分析：

Section A 共有两个模块：

第一个模块在1A部分围绕“last school trip”的活动介绍了本单元的第一个目标语言，介绍了在school trip里所做的事情，也就是activities。然后展开思维，让学生产生头脑风暴（Brain Storm），输入各种各样的动词过去式的动词短语的。紧跟着的听力训练1B给学生提供了在口语交际中理解和掌握目标语言的训练，更深化了动词短语的应用。接下来的1C让学生模仿对话，代入所学的动词短语进行机械操练，使学生在口语交际中学会使用目标语言。接下来的2A和2B部分以听力做切入点，继续深化学生对School trip中活动的运用，并且在1C中用听力情境进行语言操练，达到对目标语言的掌握。在此模块中，从语言风暴的输入到听力，到理解、机械操练，到具体语境的训练，由浅入深，反反复复，但又形式多样不显枯燥，符合学生的认知规律，从而达到掌握目标语言的目的。

第二个模块在School trip活动的基础上，完整地展示了什么是School trip，以School trip 为载体，向学生展示了应该怎样讲述过去的事，就像语文中的记叙文一样，包括了人物、时间、地点、活动、经过、结果等几个基本要素。通过阅读小短文，让学生学会怎样讲述过去的事，并配有相关的阅读训练，更深化学生对人物、时间、地点、活动、经过、结果这六个要素的学习。接下来的故事接龙，从口语方面考查学生对讲述过去事情的基本结构的操练，即包括哪几个方面的练习。在这个模块中，我们加入了写作，也就是写自己曾经旅游的经历，要求按照范文进行模仿写作，把书本上的东西变成学生自己的东西。

总之，Section A部分从听、说、读、写四个方面，以输入目标语言和使用目标语言为中心让学生真正学到东西。

Section B 共有两个模块：

第一个模块在1A中输入了新的目标语言，如sleep late, go for a drive等，让学生认知到不只是School trip才精彩，生活到处都有风景。1B使用目标语言进行简单的口语训练，但是加入了个人评价和看法，引入了新的目标语言，进而让学生巩固学习Boring，Interesting等表观点的形容词。而在2A和2B中，通过使用听力材料的真实情景，让学生进一步理解目标语言。2C部分让学生在口语训练中学会使用目标语言，并融入个人的主观思想，对学生进行思想教育，让学生学会区分怎样过才有意义。这一模块拓展了学生的学习，陶冶了学生的思想情操，也让学生在实际生活中能够解决问题。

第二个模块以读、写为主，设计了3A、3B、3C以及PART 4四个部分，让学生在读、写训练方面提高对目标语言的综合运用能力，让学生从输入变为输出，完成了对本单元目标语言的掌握和熟练运用。

Self Check 共有两个模块：

第一个模块以选词填空的形式对本单元所学的词汇进行训练，检查学生有没有掌握。第二个模块创设情境，对本单元所学目标语言进行口语交际和写作方面的训练，进一步检测学生的语言运用能力。

因此，根据对教材的分析，我们进一步整合教材，分四个课时对本单元进行教学。

在第一课时中，主要是让学生了解本单元基本的语言目标，包括地点名词、动词的一般过去式、基本句型的一般疑问句形式及其简单回答。根据要达到的语言目标，我们把第一课时定位为说写课。通过反反复复地说，进行由浅入深地操练，从而落实到笔头上。因为本单元的功能语言是让学生学会谈论自己过去的事情，所以，我们初步引出好像语文记叙文教学的五要素，包括时间、地点、人物、事件经过、感想等，让学生遵循一个特定模式，达到人人都能动口、动笔，从而真正掌握目标语言。

在第一课时对本单元目标语言大概掌握的基础上，我们把第二课时的课型定位为读说课。通过对第一课时中动词一般过去式及其句型的复习，温故而知新，进入到阅读，为学生理解文本内容做好充分的铺垫。在第一课时的基础上步步为营，加深加难，通过阅读和小组活动让学生学会使用英语。课堂练习作为辅助，让所学知识和中考挂钩，在口语练习的基础上加大笔头练习，让学生牢固掌握本单元所学知识。

第三课时，继续围绕本单元的目标语言设计课堂活动，把它定位为读写课。从第二课时对动词一般过去式的机械复习，在本课时中通过游戏更加深入对这一时态的理解和运用，体现了学生的认知规律，由浅入深，层层递进。这一课时的读我们加入了阅读策略的训练，即引导学生掌握时态发展的联系词，为后一阶段的写埋下伏笔，做好铺垫。第一课时中的写只是机械的模仿，那么在这一课时中我们深化了学生写的能力，把它变成了一个活生生的故事，更加有吸引力。

第四课时继续第三课时拔高的话题，由听力入手，了解别人在休息日的活动，定位为听写课。主要进行听力技能技巧的训练，引导学生在听力题目中怎样获取信息，培养学生猜的能力，进而提高听力水平，使学生充分灵活利用听力材料，进行人称的转换，能站在别人的立场来讲述别人过去的经历，从而更加明确动词一般过去式的用法——它不随人称的变化而变化。

总之，四个课时的编排全部围绕本单元的目标语言而进行，从最基本的字、词、句的输入到文段的模仿，最后到个人创作，到讲述他人的故事，层层递进，符合学生的认知规律，也让学生由简单到复杂，逐渐掌握本单元的语言目标，从而达到任务型教学的目的。所有课型的设计，都全方位地训练学生的听、说、读、写技巧，从而切实地提高学生学习英语的能力。特别是说英语的能力和写英语能力的大量训练，让学生切实落实到口头上、笔头上，为以后中考的口语考试和笔试打下坚实的基础。

（二）学情分析

中山市小榄镇华侨中学是一所全日制农村中学，学生本着片区招生的原则入学，所以学生的基础相对薄弱，但是可塑性很强。因为大部分学生来自农村，所以他们对语言的敏感度不是很强，也不是很自信，这给英语课堂教学带来了不便。加上本年级一共有十个教学班级，每个班人数都在五十人以上，属于大班授课，在客观上加大了课堂教学的难度。此外，学生来自不同的小学，英语水平参差不齐，如果没有一定的吸引力，根本引不起学生学习英语的兴趣。但是学生比较单纯，很容易接受新的事物，所以教师要抓住学生的这一特点，整合英语教材，从各个方面激发学生学习英语的兴趣，想办法、出点子，用精品，上精品课来最大限度地提高学生学习英语的积极性，达到一定的效果。而本单元的话题容易激发学生的兴趣，主要体现为两方面：一方面，学生刚好在上本单元之前的两个星期去了番禺的长隆游乐园，所以对所学内容非常熟悉，是学生亲身体验过的，所以有话说；另一方面，大部分内容是学生在以往就学过的，只不过换了一个方式呈现在他们面前。本单元就是在温故而知新的基础上，结合生活体验，联系跨学科语文对记叙文的铺垫，从而达到对语言目标的掌握。

（三）总体教学目标（见表7-8）

表7-8　总体教学目标

语言功能	语言目标
描述过去发生的事情	1. What did you do on your school trip? 2. Did you go to the zoo? No, I didn't. I went to the aquarium. 3. Were there any sharks? No, there weren't any sharks, but there were some really smart dolphins.
语言结构	**重点词汇**
1. 规则动词和不规则动词的一般过去式； 2. 一般过去式的肯定句与否定句； 3. Did引导的一般疑问句； 4. Were there...以及简单回答	1. aquarium,science,center,gift shop； 2. seal,shark,octopus； 3. autograph,win； 4. ate,took,hung out, got； 5. go for a drive,sleep late, yard sale,day off
技能目标	**情感目标**
1. Listening skill； 2. Speaking skill； 3. Reading skill； 4. Writing skill	1. 爱祖国，爱家乡； 2. 在活动中增进感情； 3. 设身处地为他人着想； 4. 反省过去，添彩未来； 5. 跨文化意识
学习策略与思维技巧	**多元智能**
1. 个性化的学习； 2. 合作学习； 3. 反思与实践	1. 人际交往； 2. 逻辑表达； 3. 内省智能

（四）重点

1. 对基本句型的掌握

（1）What did you do on your school trip?

I watched a dolphin show.

（2）Did you go to the zoo?

No, I didn't. I went to an aquarium.

（3）Were there any sharks?

Yes, there were.

2. 对目标语言的综合运用

从听、说、读、写四个方面整体提高学生对英语语言的运用能力，特别是对阅读技巧和写作技能的训练，最大限度地培养学生的语言综合运用能力。通过对个人精彩一天或假期的描述，逐渐培养学生写日记的学习英语的良好习惯。

3. 情感目标的实现

通过各种形式的课堂活动，学生能了解身边的人周末或者节假日的安排，并且通过对照，能自己内省，学会从过去吸取经验教训，学会合理安排自己的时间，珍惜每一天，珍惜生命，珍惜身边所有的人与事物。

（五）难点

（1）在口语交际中，由于所有语言材料来源于生活体验，学生参与积极性比较高，课堂会比较活跃，但如何让学生说英语而不是中文，怎样控制课堂是考验教师的一大难点。

（2）在目标语言运用上，一是能否熟练运用所学句型进行交际；二是能否正确使用动词的过去式，包括不规则变化的动词；三是对难句There be 句型过去式的运用以及它的一般疑问句形式：Were there any sharks？的掌握。

（3）在目标语言的读写运用中，能否用所学目标语言进行实际生活中的口语交际和通过写作表达自己的生活经历。

（4）能否引起共鸣，真正让学生通过这一单元的学习，能够合理安排自己的课余时间，过得精彩而有意义。

（六）教学策略和教学方法

（1）个性化的学习。

（2）合作学习。

（3）推测词义。

（4）“三P”教学法。

（5）交际法。

（6）任务型教学方法。

（七）课时安排

全单元安排四个课时：

第一课时——主要是让学生了解本单元基本的语言目标，本单元核心词汇，了解基本语言结构，以听促说。

第二课时——在第一课时对本单元目标语言大概掌握的基础上，拓展本单元话题下的词汇及结构语言的运用，以读促说。

第三课时——围绕本单元的话题，整合教材，补充相关话题阅读，以读促写。

第四课时——引导学生思考并实践在单元话题下进行篇章写作。

二、教学设计

（一）The first period

Analysis of teaching target

Teaching aims	Language goals	1. Talk about events in the past; 2. Simple past of regular and irregular verbs; 3. Affirmative and negative statements in the past tense
	Ability goals	Developing students' abilities of speaking and reading
	Teaching strategy	Task based teaching, cooperative learning
	Emotional goals	Enable the students to enjoy different kinds of activities
Important points	Did you, were there ..., affirmative and negative statements	
Difficult points	Reading comprehension	

Teaching process

Activities	Content	Intention
Activity 1 leading-in Activity 2 in put Activity 3 pair work Activity 4 survey	Have a competition about activities Lean new words and present sentences A: Were there any seals in the aquarium? B: Yes,there were./No, there weren't. A: Did you go to the beach? B: Yes, I did./No, I didn't.	1. Attract students' attention; 2. Arouse interest; 3. Put in new language points

续 表

Activities	Content	Intention
Activity 5 reading Activity 6 summary Activity 7 exercises Activity 8 homework	Make a conversation according to pictures(three or four pairs) Ask students to make a survey and make a report Ask students to read the passage and answer the questions Did you, were there questions Ask students to finish exercises Write a passage about how your school trip was	Practice news language Improve ability of commanding new language Improve ability of reading Consolidate new knowledge

Teaching producers

Steps	Students' activities	Teacher's help	Purposes
Leading in	1. Greetings; 2. Going over the words	Ask some questions about trip	1. Bring out the topic; 2. Revise simple past of regular and irregular verbs
Warming-up	Read out the words about activities	competition	Make students master the important words and sentences
Task 1 Pair-work	Sentence structure	Show students sentence structures	Practice speaking skill
Task 2 Interview	Ask and answer	As a guide	Encourage student to improve oral English
Task 3 Reading	Ask students to reading 3a	As a guide	Improve students reading skills
Summary	Conclusion the sentences structures	Helper	Feedback
Homework	Write a passage about your school trip	As a helper	Consolidation

Handwriting on the blackboard

Activities:

went to the beach, had some ice-cream, saw some seals, went shopping,

went to the aquarium, took photos, hung out with friends.

Animals:

seals, sharks, tiger, money, goldfish, octopus, dolphins, sea horses.

Sentences:

Were there any … in the aquarium?

Yes, there were / No, there weren't.

Did you …

Yes, I did. / No, I didn't. I…

(二) The second period

Analysis of teaching target

Teaching aims	Language goals	1. Talk about events in the past; 2. Simple past of regular and irregular verbs; 3. Affirmative and negative statements in the past tense
	Ability goals	Developing students' abilities of commanding English
	Teaching strategy	Task based teaching, cooperative learning
	Emotional goals	Comparing differences culture
Important points	Did you, were there questions ,affirmative and negative statements	
Difficult points	How to express	

Teaching process

Activities	Content	Intention
Activity 1 warming up	Show some pictures about activities	
Activity 2 leading-in	To be familiar with the target language and the key word	
Activity 3 in put	Read and practice the target language	
Activity 4 pair work	Make a conversation according to pictures (three or four pairs)	
Activity 5 group work	Let's read	
Activity 6 exercises	Make a survey then make a report	
Activity 7 summary	Did you, were you questions	
Activity 8 homework	Finish the report	

Teaching procedures

Aim	Teacher's Activity	Student's Activity	Preparation
Warming-up	What did you do on your last school trip?	Pair work to talk about their past activities Listen and read	
To be familiar with the target language and the key words	1. Ask some students to read the conversation 2. Ask some students to answer the questions 3. Show the target language: Did you go to the zoo? No, I didn't.I went to the aquarium. 4. Show the target language About 10 kilometers. Were there any sharks? No, there weren't any sharks 5. Ask the students to sum up the language points	Try to answer the questions Use the target language, and talk to others Use the target language, and talk to others Sum up the language points Look and read 3a	Textbook Group work Pair work
Reading practice using the target language	① Look at the picture and read the article ② Read and correct the statements ③ Ask and answer questions to the article	Correct the statements Listen One asks and the other two fill in the blanks	Recorder Group work
Use the target language to make their own conversation	6. Sum up the language points ① Ask the students to work with two other students ② Ask the students to do exercise ③ Move around the room and give support as need	Talk to each other	Group work Pair work
Homework			Group work Group work

Handwriting on the blackboard:

What did you do on your last school trip?

I went to the aquarium.

Did you see any seals?

Yes, I did. I saw some seals.

Were there any sharks?

Yes, there were some sharks.

（三）The Third Period

Analysis of teaching target

Teaching aims	Language goals	master how to talk about events in the past
	Ability goals	Enable the students to write a story and improve students' reading and speaking abilities
	Teaching strategy	Task-based teaching, cooperative learning
	Emotional goals	Enable the students to form positive attitudes towards life through past events
Important points	Past events	
Difficult points	The structure "She did some washing yesterday."	

Teaching process

Activities	Content	Intention
Activity 1 warming up	Listen to an English song	Attract students' attention
Activity 2 leading-in	Guessing game about what people did in the pictures showing on the screen	Arouse interest
Activity 3 in put reading time	1. Predict what Nick did on his day off according to the picture; 2. Scan and skim the letter to get information. Share their own information with the whole class	Read and get information
Activity 4 further reading	Consolidate the knowledge about how to describe past events	Get students to express their ideas
Activity 5 writing a letter	Write a passage Have Ss learn to make a story in group	Consolidate
Activity 6 telling a story and have a PK	Give a conclusion	Improve ability of speaking, predicting and cooperating
Activity 7 summary	Write to foreign English teacher, Lake, about your last Mid-autumn Day or National Day	Consolidate new knowledge
Activity 8 homework		Consolidate new knowledge

Teaching Procedures

Steps	Students' activities	Teacher's help	Purposes
Leading in	1. Greetings; 2. Watch some photos and guess	1. Show some photos; 2. Ask some questions about the photos	1. Bring out the topic; 2. Stimulate the students; 3. Revise simple past of regular and irregular verbs
Task 1 Information collecting	1. Predict what Nick did on his day off according to the picture; 2. Scan and skim the letter to get information	1. Show the students picture; 2. Give proper instructions	Make students get some information form the letter
Task 2 Feedback	Share their own information with the whole class	A guide	Encourage student to express their opinions
Task 3 Telling a story	Tell a story about Nick's evening	Show students 5W of the story	1. Talk about events in the past; 2. Practice spoken English
Task4 Writing a story	Write a story about what happened to Tom	As a guide	1.Talk about events in the past.; 2.Practice writing
Summary	Conclusion	Helper	Feedback
Homework	Write to our foreign English teacher, Lake, about your last Mid-autumn Day or National Day	As a helper	Consolidation

Handwriting on the blackboard:

(1) Time: yesterday, on your last school trip, on you day off .

(2) Where/ What/ When/ Who/ How

(3) PK: Story telling

Group A // Group B

（四）The fourth period

Analysis of teaching target

Teaching aims	Language goals	1. Talk about events in the past; 2. Simple past of regular and irregular verbs; 3. Affirmative and negative statements in the past tense
	Ability goals	Developing students' abilities of listening and writing
	Teaching strategy	Task-based teaching, cooperative learning.
	Emotional goals	Enable the students to enjoy different kinds of activities.
Important points	Did you, were there ..., affirmative and negative statements	
Difficult points	Listing comprehension	

Teaching procedures

Steps	Students' activities	Teacher's help	Purposes
Leading in	1. Greetings; 2. Going over the words	Ask some questions about trip	1. Bring out the topic; 2. Revise simple past of regular and irregular verbs
Warming-up	Read out the words about activities	Give proper instructions	Make students master the important words and sentences
Task 1 Listening practice1	Listen materials	Show students listening strategy	Practice listening skill
Feedback	Share their own answer with the whole class	As a guide	Encourage students to find the best way to improve listening skill
Task2 Listening practice 2	Listen material	As a guide	Encourage students to find the best way to improve listening skill
Summary	Conclusion	Helper	Feedback
Homework	Write your day off	As a helper	Consolidation

三、教学实录

（一）The First Period

T: Good morning, boys and girls!

Ss: Good morning, Ms. Li.

T: Sit down, please. Just now we listened to a wonderful English song. Do you like it?

Ss: Yes. (Ok/ So-so)

T: Today we come to Unit 8. What's the topic of Unit 8?

Ss: How was your school trip.

T: Yes. Before we start this class, let's listen to the duty report from Anna Hong, welcome!

(Applause!)

T: Thank you, Anna! Ok, boys and girls, what did Anna talk about in her report?

Ss: Her last school trip.

T: Good! Today we are going to talk about our school trip. First, we are going to learn to talk about events in the past; We also hope to improve our speaking and writing skills through collaborating and Task-based learning. After this class, I hope you can love their lives and enjoy different kinds of activities.

Ok, everyone likes going out for a trip. Here I prepare some beautiful places. Let's see where they are. Where's here?

Ss: An amusement park.

T: And here?

Ss: An aquarium.

T: What about here?

Ss: A space museum.

T: And here?

Ss: A zoo.

T: And this one?

Ss: A beach.

T: Yes! What a beautiful beach! Where's here?

Ss: A water park.

T: And here?

Ss: Disneyland! (Students shout it out!)

T: Good! When we go out, we often do many activities. Here are some. Let's read them.

Ss: Go to the beach, go fishing… (Students read them twice a word.)

T: Now I'd like you to read all the words about places and activities together.

(Students read them together.)

T: Then, how do we talk about a trip? Let's do it like this.

(Students read the dialogue sentence by sentence.)

Ss:

A: Did you go to the zoo on your last trip?

B: Yes, I did. I went to the zoo.

A: Were there any pandas there?

B: Yes, there were.

A: Did you take any photos?

B: Yes, I did. I took lots of photos.

(Do another example and Ss practice the dialogue.)

Ss:

A: Did you take any photos?

B: No, I didn't. I went to the space museum.

A: Were there many people?

B: No,there weren't.

A: What did you do?

B: I bought some souvenirs.

T: (Show another dialogue struture.)

Now I'd like someone to fill in the dialogue orally. Any volunteer? Blair, please.

S1: (Fill in the blanks and read the dialogue.)

T: (Show another dialogue structure with some sentences unfinished. Students read the dialogue together.)

T: Now who'd like to finish the dialogue? Ok, Martin, please. (Ss read the dialogue together.)

S2: (Fill in the blanks and read the dialogue.Students read the dialogue together.)

T: All the students did a good job! Now, class, please work in pairs and practice the dialogue with the following sentence structures.

(Students practice it in pairs.)

(Three minutes later.)

T: Be quiet, please. Betty and Tom, please share your dialogue with us.

(The two students did a good job.)

T: Thank you! You did a good job! If you could speak a little louder, that would be better.

(Ask two more pairs to show their dialogues.)

T: As we know now, when we talk about trip, we usually talk about these aspects: where, when, who, what and how. (Students say them with the teacher together)

Now I'll show you another great trip. Look at this picture, can you guess where it is?

S3: Shanghai.

T: Great! It's Shanghai. Do you know what's happening in Shanghai now?

S4: Shanghai Expo!

T: Yes! It is holding the 2010 Expo and it's topic is "Better city, better life". My cousin went to Shanghai to see the Expo recently. Let's imagine, if you were Amy, please talk about with your partner about the trip.

First, you can discuss it in groups, then 5 minutes later, you'll write them down in a passage on your paper. Go!

(The teacher gives some advice on some guidance to the students.)

(Five minutes later, students begin to write articles.)

T: Now, who'd like to share your trip to Shanghai with us? Hands up, please!

Jane, please. (The student comes to the front and reads her passage.)

T: Good job!

(Ask two more students to read their articles and give some comments.)

Everyone may has his or her own unforgetable trip. But which is the best one?

Lucy talks about her mother's trip to Hainan Island and she thinks it's a great trip. I'd like you to tell your or your family members' great trip and then discuss in groups to see whose trip is the best one. Do it after class as our homework.

Ss: Ok!

T: Good. Today, we mainly talk about the past events with where, what, when, how, who. And we practice our speaking and writing abilities fully. Don't forget our home work on the screen.

See you. Good-bye， boys and girls!

Ss: Good-bye, teacher!

（二）**The Third Period**

T: Good morning, boys and girls!

Ss: Good morning, Ms. Chen.

T: It's a sunny day, isn't it?

Ss: Yes, it is.

T: What do you like to do on sunny days?

S1: Go swimming or play basketball.

T: Good idea! Girl, what about you?

S2: I like going shopping with my friends.

T: That's good. Then what did you do yesterday, Ken?

S3: I stay at home and do my homework, oh, no, I stayed at home and did my homework.

T: Good job! So, class, (to the whole class) what did Ken do yesterday?

Ss: He stayed at home and did homework yesterday.

T: Now please look at the picture. What did she do, can you guess? Boy, please!

S4: She washed her clothes.

T: Good, she did some washing yesterday. Read together, please.

Ss: She did some washing yesterday.

T: Guess, what did Yao do last night?

S5: He read a book.

T: What about this picture, what did they do on the school trip?

(Together)

Ss: They watched a seal show on the school trip.

T: And what did she do on her day off ?

Ss: She played the guitar on her day off.

T: Then, which of these activities do you want to do most on your day off ? Why?

S6: I want to play the guitar because I think it's really relaxing.

T: Good. Thank you. Sit down, please. And you, boy?

S7: I want to watch a seal show because it's funny.

T: Great! In fact, you can choose to do a lot of things on your day off. Then, what about people in this picture, what did they may do on their day off? First, let's see who they are? They are …

Ss: They are Nick, Uncle Martin and Nick's cousin.

T: Yes, and what did they do?

Ss: They had a yard sale.

T: That's right. But what's a yard sale? Let's see, yard sale means selling second-hand things in your yard. Through yard sale, you can both deal with some old things and get some money. Have you ever had a yard sale?

S8: No, never.

T: Oh, it's a pity! But it doesn't matter, you can have a try next time. Now let's know more about the people's day off. Please read the passage quickly, find the answers and fill in the blank quickly, please.

(About one minute later.)

Now, please show me your answers. First, who is this letter from?

S8: It's from Nick.

T: Good job! Then whom is this letter to?

S9: It's to Tom.

T: Very good. Then, what's the weather like that day?

S9: Oh, it rained all day.

T: How did Nick feel?

S10: He felt sad, or maybe unhappy.

T: Yes, he did. Now I want to know besides having a yard sale, what else did Nick do on his day off ? Please read it again and find the answer as quickly as possible.

Ss: He watched DVDs, played computer games and read.

T: Well done! Nick did lots of things on his day off. Who'd like to give a report according to it? Frank, please.

S11: Nick stayed at home on his day off. He watched DVDs, played computer games and read some books. Then he visited Uncle Martin and had a yard sale. But unluckily, it rained and no one came to the sale.

T: Quite good. Thank you very much. What do you think of Nick's day off ?

S12: In my opinion, I think it's a little boring.

T: Good! Here I'd like to share the strategics with you. When we want to find some information, we usually try to find it directly according to what we need, then we would not read it any more. We call it Scanning or Skimming.

For example, in this passage, we could mainly focus on the information about "Where" "What" and "How".

Now, please read another passage and try to find the three "Ws".

(Students read the passage and underline the answers.)

T: Ok! Time's up. Now, show me your answer as loudly, quickly as you can. First, where did the writer go on vacation?

Ss: Guilin.

T: Good! What did he do?

Ss: He showed me around the city. I also went to his school. His students like him very much. I bought a special bag for you and a silk tablecloth for Mom.

T: Wonderful! What did he think of his vacation?

Ss: He thinks that it's a beautiful place and the people are kind there and he has some new friends.

T: If you are Amy, since you had such a nice day, please write a letter to your friend Maria and tell her about your vacation. Do it now.

(Time for writing! Then have a student read out his or her letter.)

T: You did a good job. I like your writing very much. If you could read it a little loudly, it would be better.

(Look at the screen.)

And pay attention please, when we are writing a letter back to someone, we should give direct answers to the questions mentioned in the letter. Also, we have to use the right forms of all the verbs. When we can also use then, after that, next, finally and other words to talk about orders.

Do you understand?

Ss: Yes.

T: Now let's see what happened to Tom according to Picture 2. Then guess what happened, how to solve the problem and what the ending is. Discuss in group within 3 minutes, please.

(Students talk in groups, and the teacher gives some guidance.) Pay attention to the tense of the verbs.

T: Now, class, let me share your stories together.

(Pick up one student.)

S13: Xiaoming didn't bring his homework today, so he copied other's homework. Then the teacher discovered that and the teacher told him not to do that again because it would start a bad habit. XiaoMing said sorry to the teacher and decided that he would not do that anymore.

T: Good job and good imagination. Now please write your stories down.

T: Ok, today, we've learned how to use the simple past tense, how to collect information from the article. And we've worked to make the reading and writing connection.

T: Look at the homework on the screen: write to our foreign English teacher, Lake, about your last Mid-autumn Day or National Day and give your opinion. What did you do on that day? What was your feeling?

Ok, that's all for the class. Thank you.

Good-bye, boys and girls.

Ss: Good-bye, teacher.

四、教学经验

（一）教学反思

1. 第一课时

（1）面向全体学生，为学生全面发展和终身发展奠定基础。①创设各种情境，鼓励学生大胆地使用英语，对他们在学习过程中的失误和错误采取宽容的态度；②为学生提供自主学习和直接交流的机会以及充分表现和自我发展的空间；③鼓励学生通过体验、实践、合作、探索等方式，发展听、说、读、写的综合能力；④创造条件让学生能够探究他们自己的一些问题，并自主解决问题。

（2）关注学生情感，创造民主、和谐的教学气氛。①尊重每个学生，积极鼓励他们在学习中尝试，保护他们的自尊心和积极性；②把英语教学与情态有机地结合起来，创造各种合作学习的活动，促进学生互相学习，互相帮助，体验成就感，发展合作精神；③关注学习有困难的或性格内向的学生，尽可能地为他们创造使用语言的机会；④建立融洽、民主的师生交流渠道，经常和学生一起反思学习过程和学习效果，互相鼓励和帮助，做到教学相长。

2. 第二课时

（1）巧妙导入。常言说："良好的开端，成功的一半。"增强趣味性，最大限度地吸引学生，激发学生的学习兴趣，把注意力放到课堂上来，要靠教师巧妙构思，设计合情合理的导入方式。这节课从教师询问学生"last school trip"开始，极大地刺激了学生的兴奋神经，一下子把学生吸引住了，连后进生也跃跃欲试，积极配合。

（2）教与学有机结合在一起。在教学过程中，既有教师灵活的教，也应有学生积极主动的参与，才是真正意义上的教学。课堂中避免了以往教师"满堂灌"，学生被动学习这一模式，使学生由被动变为主动，既增强了学习趣味性，引发学生思考、记忆，又体现了学生的主体性，教师的指导性；既完成了教学任务，学生在学到知识的同时也学得开心、有趣。

（3）创造性教学。学习，不但要学习前人的丰富经验，牢记、掌握固有知识，还要学会灵活应用，才是学习的根本目的。

（4）学习过程同时也是发现归纳的过程。学生是学习的主体，不但要跟随教师学习，也应在学习过程中善于归纳总结，得出自己的结论。所学的知识才印象深刻，掌握牢固，把别人的知识变成自己的知识。

（5）掌控课堂，灵活教学。灵活过渡，必要时采取有效的取舍，游刃有余是每位优秀教师应该具备的素质。

（6）平等原则。每个学生都希望得到教师的关注与重视。处于青少年阶段的初中生的这一要求尤其强烈。教师的一个眼神、一个微小的细节，也会引起学生的注意、联想，甚至触发他们的情绪，使自信心受到打击。

通过这一节课，笔者对如何备好课，吸引学生，启发学生思维，培养学生学习能力有了更进一步的认识，也深刻体会到了备课既要备教材，也要备学生的真正含义。

3. 第三课时

（1）成功之处。本堂教学是一堂阅读教学课，教学围绕“读前——读中——读后”的教学程序，完整地展现了阅读教学的应用模式，并穿插总结，教给学生两种阅读的基本策略：扫读（scanning）和略读（skimming），让学生很好地运用阅读策略完成了课堂任务。

（2）不足之处。本节课定位为读（reading）和写(writing)课程，但是在读写的过程中，笔者又把说的内容加在课程后面，虽然活跃了气氛，调动了学生的积极性，但却显得定位不明确。

（3）教学机智。关于阅读教学策略，学生在概念上比较模糊，但在运用上已经有很多经验，经过对教学策略的解读，使学生能够彻底地弄懂教学策略的实际并在实际中更灵活地运用，使理论与实际结合更紧密，达到相辅相成的作用。

（4）学生创新。在教学过程中，学生在写作和语言表达方面有很突出的表现，例如在描述故事情节时，不少同学都对情节进行了恰当的推测，而且能够在时间的描述上较完整地表达，例如他们很好地使用了one day，first，then，next，after that，finally等。

（5）教学设计。以“3P”教学模式引导的教学设计能够很好地演绎教学过程。在本堂课中，Guessing game 的设计很好地调动了学生的积极性，引起了学生的学习积极性，是个不错的方法；在教学过程中，根据学生的上课实际，临时调整教学的步骤有时候也是有必要的。例如，在本堂的阅读教学中，当发现课堂稍显沉闷时，教师在学生完成讨论和写作后，把写故事临时改为讨论故事，并以小组竞赛的方式来呈现，一方面活跃了课堂气氛，另一方面以说促写。

4. 第四课时

在我们的日常听力训练中，一般只是核对答案，就不再对听力材料做进一步的重复使用。其实后期的处理和讲解更能提高学生的听力能力。

（1）先把整套听力题听一遍，然后倒回来再放音讲解。放音讲解时一定要求学生逐字逐句重复。如遇到较长的句子，可在意群或从句处暂停，等待学生重复完前半句后再放后半句，让学生再跟着重复。教师可以采取学生单独重复、两人对话重复，甚至小组、全班重复的方式，促使学生积极参与。

（2）讲完一套听力题后，一定要从头至尾再放一遍录音。此时教师要引导学生不要把注意力过多地集中在答案的选择上，应把注意力更多地集中在录音内容上，心里跟着录音重复默念。虽然只放一遍，但此时学生已是心领神会，眼睛看着答案加深印象。这样，学生在不知不觉中对英语学习的兴趣逐渐培养起来，自信心也相应提高。

【总结性教学反思】

在体现任务型教学的课堂教学中，新课程标准倡导以任务为基础的教学，也就是引导学生通过完成具体的任务活动来学习语言，让学生为了特定的学习目的去实施特定的语言行动，通过完成特定的交际任务来获得和积累相应的学习经验。任务的设计就是要给学生提供明确、真实的语言信息，使学生在一种自然、真实或模拟真实的情境中体会语言、掌握语言的应用。我们在教学中的体会主要有以下几点：

（1）任务要真实。既要从学生的认知水平和生活实际出发，又要与社会生活紧密相连。

（2）任务要可完成。如果设计的任务不可完成，将在很大程度上妨碍学生主体水平的发挥。

（3）任务要由简到繁，由易到难，层层深入，构建由初级任务到高级任务，并由高级任务涵盖初级任务的循环，使教学阶梯式地层层递进。而在本课时的学习中，我们也遵循这项原则，符合学生的认知规律，让学生有兴趣和信心继续往下探索。

（4）要注意任务的合作性。任务的完成必须依赖学生之间的共同合作，每一个学生在执行任务的过程中，都担当不同的角色，都需要提供自己所掌握的信息，在共同完成任务的过程中培养合作精神。

在对教材的运用和整合方面，我们对教材的每个部分的内容都做了大胆的整合。根据对本单元分课时教学要解决的问题，我们把教材中的内容做了一些调整。根据我们对模块教学的把握，遵照从基本的词、短语到句子，到文段的输入和输出，我们把有些部分从Section A部分调到了Section B部分，有些又从Section B调到了Section A部分，更是大胆地删掉了教材上的部分内容，充分利用教材而又不拘泥于教材。所以，备课是考验教师的水平，考验教师对教材的把握。

以话题为单位，以一个单元为模块的教学，需要我们整合有关话题的字词句，还要有所拓展和输出。在本单元从过去经历的话题入手，熟悉自己生活实践中的基本情况，引入到自己安排设计有意义活动的概念，并从旅游中保护环境入手，引申到爱我们的家乡，爱我们的祖国，从而过渡到怎样去描绘自己灿烂的未来。这样，我们就不再是为了让学生学英语而死教没有生命的字词句，而是教学生在生活中学英语，把所学英语用于生活，真正地体现了学英语做事情的《新课程标准》。

（二）教学建议

本单元的教学对教材的整合达到了极致。在语言结构上，通过温故而知新由小学内容提升到初中新内容的学习，丰富了学生的语言积累。在语言运用能力上，既照顾了一般学生对基本语言的掌握，又让能力强的学生得到了提升。在情感目标上，让学生充分体会到过去的生活经历给其带来的影响，引导学生积极思考，善于安排个人时间，对以后的生活充满期望。在课堂教学的过程中，真正体现了任务型教学和分层教学，让各个层面的学生都得到不同程度的提高。在我们的分课时教学中，如果学生水平达不到，可以在听说部分的课时里多花点时间，而写的部分多采用机械模仿，以给学生学习英语的信心；如果学生水平高，可以接受，那么听写课时是一个很好的对学生可持续性发展的补充课时，对提升学生语言运用能力和培养学生道德情操和提高思想境界都是很好的。

本单元的课件呈现内容，为了体现单个的教学任务在基础的语言知识的操练上显得不够充实，尤其是最后两个课时为了强化阅读和写作功能，基本知识运用没有一次次地输入。如果学生的英语能力不是很好的话，建议教师在课前和课后要加强基础知识的复习和操练。同时本单元课件设计的模块上，对教学的练习和任务设置不够清晰，建议老师在备课前要有更周密的考虑，研究相关的任务型教学，使自己的教学流程更完美。阅读课作为提高学生英语能力的板块，在阅读教材如何选题和如何拓展学生的阅读视野，如何通过阅读完成学生文化层面上交流，应该是教师重点思考的地方。例如，本单元的阅读拓展如果可以通过前车之鉴，取长补短，积极安排未来的生活；引导学生养成写日记的习惯，培养向他人讲述故事的能力，这样更能体现英语教学的实用性和日常作用性。

在运用本课程时，具体地说，主要注意以下几个方面的问题：

（1）整合教学资源，构建教学内容，新旧知识交融，最佳化使用多媒体，突出课堂重难点。

（2）课堂实施时，把握好度，注意对显性问题（如Yes和No问题）和隐性问题（如内化问题）的把握。

（3）上完课后及时反思，写下教学后记，对上课教师会有很大帮助。

（4）一堂好课的标准：①目标是舵；②要有三维目标，包含情感态度，价值观和教师的上课激情；③善于设置和提出问题；④能正确处理学生的口头或笔头上的讲练关系；⑤及时点评是强化正确认知的有效途径，具体归纳有101条途径；⑥有拓展与创新，对于低年级要有举一反三和充满联想的拓展，对于高年级则需要多向课外拓展；⑦合理使用现代化教育技术，如幻灯、多媒体技术等。

案例2：GFI Unit 8 Have you read Treasure Island yet? B4

Topic: Literature

一、单元整合说明

（一）单元背景

英语作为全球使用最广泛的语言之一，已经成为国际交往和科技、文化交流的重要工具。学习和使用英语对汲取人类文明成果、借鉴国外先进科学技术、增进中国和世界的相互了解具有重要的作用。学习英语有利于学生更好地了解世界，学习先进的科学文化知识，传播中国文化；增进学生与各国青少年的相互沟通和理解，提供更多的接受教育和职业发展的机会。结合英语学科的核心素养，作为教师，我们要教会学生用英语做事的能力，这才有利于学生今后的自主学习和终身发展，与国际社会接轨。

中西方有很多优秀的经典名著，是人类的璀璨文化，但初中生对中国的名著比较了解，而对西方的经典文化作品鲜有所闻。学习一门外语，不仅要习得语言知识，还要了解它的文化背景。因为文化和语言相互依赖、相互影响。语言是文化的重要载体，了解文化有助于学生学习和理解语言知识。人教版 Go for it八年级下册“Unit 8 Have you read Treasure Island yet?”的话题 Literature（文学）可以作为一扇窗口，帮助学生拓展视野，以“话题”带出词汇，引出本话题需要掌握的经典文学作品的名称、内容及相关的语言知识；以“功能”带出句型，主要包括完成任务所需的带有“already”“yet”和“just”现在完成时的语言结构来谈论最近发生的事件和经历；以“结构”带出语法，将现在完成时语法分散在Literature话题中；以“任务”带出综合，如谈论是否“做过和还没有做过的事情”“我最近读的一本书的介绍”等，结合目标语言，突出用本话题所学语言去做事情。

除此之外，通过与文学作品相关的听说读写活动，让学生懂得如何去谈论所读书本，交流文化作品，引导学生对西方优秀文学名著逐步产生兴趣并激发出其阅读求知欲望，能认识到书本阅读对人的作用、对人生的影响，懂得阅读的重要性，并在对语言结构的运用中发现自己的阅读现状，从而体验思维拓展性，挖掘自身潜能，并得到相应发展，从而提升学生的英语语言能力、文化品格、思维品质以及学习能力的学科核心素养。

根据《英语课程标准》，语言技能包括听、说、读、写以及这四种技能的综合运用能力。听、说、读、写是人们通过语言进行交际的重要形式，是人类认识世界、获得知识、发展智力、交流情感的重要手段。听说能力、观察能力和读写能力都需要加以关注和提高，尤其是写作。由于词汇量匮乏、语法知识薄弱等问题，有不少学生不喜欢上写作课，将写作看作是负担，写出来的文章错误百出、枯燥无味。教师花费时间和心血批改的作文也很少有学生仔细阅读。学生的写作水平提高效果甚微，直接影响了中考英语成绩，因为中考写作有15分。为改变学生书面表达相对滞后的现象，我们教师借着精品课程的设计开发，研究初中英语教学中有效的写作教学模式，探索提高学生英语写作能力的途径和方法，激发师生的学习英语兴趣，提高教师的课程资源开发能力和教研水平，提升学生的英语语言能力、文化品格、思维品质以及学习能力。

（二）主要内容

人教版 Go for it八年级（下册）“Unit 8 Have you read Treasure Island yet?”的主要内容见表7–9：

表7–9 Topic and literature

Topic（话题）	Literature
Function（功能）	Talk about recent events and experience
Structure（结构）	Present perfect tense with already and yet
Target language（目标语言）	Have you read Little Women yet? Yes, I have./No, I haven't. Has Tina read Treasure Island yet? Yes, she has. She thinks it's fantastic. Have you decided which book to write about yet? Yes, I have. I've already finished reading it. It was really good
Key vocabulary（重点词汇）	Treasure, island, ship, sand, land, mark, gun, tool, introduce, full of, book, writer, read, fantastic, famous, popular, successful

结合本单元的主要内容、中考考试大纲和英语学科核心素养，我们大胆地整合教材，探索新颖、有效的教学模式，将本单元的话题、功能、结构、任务

有机地结合在一起，以“话题”带出词汇、“功能”带出句型、“结构”带出语法、“任务”带出综合，最终让学生能用所学话题和语言结构进行交际，提升学生的英语语言能力、文化品格、思维品质以及学习能力。

1.“话题”带出词汇，系统归纳本话题需要掌握的词汇

根据本话题，我们系统归纳了需要掌握的词汇。主要分为names of books（文学作品的名称）、past participle tense of verbs（动词的过去分词）、description words（描述性的形容词）、link words（连接词）、conclusion words（总结词）、other new words（其他新词汇）等6大词类进行归纳，共88个单词及短语。由话题进行的头脑风暴、发散性思维，林林总总的知识碎片变得有逻辑性，让学生把书读薄，轻松地跨过词汇关。

2.“功能”带出句型，主要包括完成任务所需的语言结构

这个话题的功能语是谈论最近发生的事，集中为是否做过某事，谈论书本内容等方面。主要有：

Have you read Little Women yet?

Has Tina read Treasure Island yet?

I have already finished reading it

What is it like?

How is it?

What do you think of it?

I think/It makes me …

What is it about? It is about…

It was written by…

3.“结构”带出语法，将语法分散在本话题中

现在完成时是一个很灵活、很常用的初中阶段必须掌握的时态。它的语言点分散于本书的第八、九、十单元，由此可见它的重要性和难度。本单元教师创设真实的语言情境，学生运用目标语言进行交际，体验和感悟现在完成时的结构 have/has done，现在完成时的意义是表示过去发生或已经完成的动作对现在造成的影响或结果和 already，just 和 yet 在现在完成时的运用。

4.“任务”带出综合，突出用本话题所学语言去做事情

一切教学的策略和手段都服务于学生对语言的综合运用。根据不同的教学内容需要，给学生设置相应的任务，让学生在做中真正掌握英语，也真正体现英语语言的工具性、人文性。设置本话题的任务如下：

（1）谈论四件自己是否“做过和还没有做过的事情”：是否听过金志文改编的《关关雎鸠》这首歌、是否去过香港迪士尼乐园、是否看过《哈利·波特》的电影、是否读过《愚公移山》这本书。

（2）《鲁滨孙漂流记》相关文段阅读的练习。

（3）关于Growing up with good books的写作指导。

（4）介绍自己最近读过的一本书，包括书名、作者、评价、内容介绍、是否推荐这本书给其他人看等。我们设置的任务由简到繁，层层递进，让学生学有所获。

（三）课程目标

1. 语言素养

（1）语言知识。

① 能掌握关于literature的词汇。

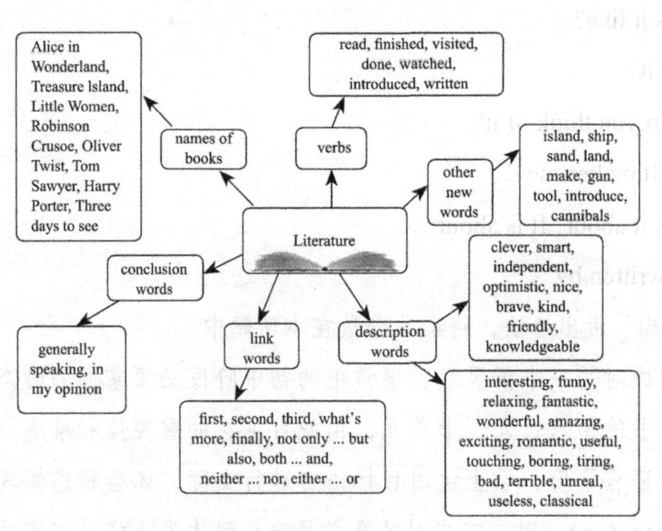

② 能掌握以下句型，并合理运用目标语言进行交际。

A: Have you read Little Women yet?

B: Yes, I have./ No, I haven't.

A: Has Tina read Treasure Island yet?

B: Yes, she has. She thinks it's fantastic.

I have already finished reading it.

A: What is it like?/ How is it? /What do you think of it?

B: I think it is wonderful.It makes me happy.

A: What is it about?

B: It is about a boy who goes out to sea and finds island full of treasures.

It was written by Daniel.

③ 语法。理解和掌握带有already，just 和 yet 的现在完成时，描述性形容词等，并合理运用目标语言表达自己对不同书本的阅读感受，谈话自己做过的事情、经历及发表个人观点。

④ 篇章和语用。掌握Growing up with good books, a book that I have read recently的写作。

（2）语言技能。

① 掌握预测听力内容、边听录音边记录关键信息的听力技能。

② 掌握略读、细读的阅读技能。

③ 掌握列提纲、自评、他评的写作技能。

④ 掌握大方、自信、准确的英语口语表达技能。

2. 文化素养

促使学生了解英美经典文学作品，能认识到书本阅读对人的作用、对人生的影响，懂得书本阅读的重要性。对待书本阅读的现状批判性看待，达到自如地运用结构语言对生活中的真实情境进行自由谈论。

3. 思维素养

（1）培养学生的批判性思维和创新思维，从新视角去思考问题，如课堂总结时，思考“What have you learned?” “What is interesting?” “What question do you have?”让学生突破常规思维，认真去思考问题，反思总结本节课个人所学的知识，而不仅仅局限于目标语言。

（2）培养学生的逻辑思维、系统思维，如系统归纳literature的词汇。

4. 学习素养

（1）掌握个性化的学习、合作学习、反思与实践、自主学习的学习策略。

（2）培养多元智能，如人际交往、逻辑表达、内省智能等。

（3）用英语思维的能力，如在完成任务时，运用目标语言去交流、写作，避免中式英语。

（四）教学重点

1. 对基本句型的掌握

A: Have you read Little Women yet?

B: Yes, I have./No, I haven't.

A: Have you decided which book to write about (yet)?

B: Yes, Little Women. I have already finished reading it.

2. 对目标语言的综合运用

从听、说、读、写四个方面整体提高学生对英语语言的运用能力，特别是对阅读技巧和写作技能的训练，最大限度地培养学生的语言综合运用能力。通过设计谈论四件学生是否"做过和还没有做过的事情"，"Growing up with good book"和"My favorite writer"的写作，逐渐培养学生用英语去做事的能力，与实际生活接轨，体现英语的实用性。

3. 情感目标的实现

学生能意识到通过谈论书本阅读、谈论做过和没有做过的事情，发现功能语言的结构并尝试使用继而灵活使用之。在对语言结构的运用中发现自己的阅读现状，对西方文学名著逐步产生兴趣并激发出自身的阅读求知欲望，从而体验思维拓展性，挖掘自身潜能，并得到相应发展。

（五）教学难点

（1）能否正确使用动词的过去分词等，能否通过总结带有already，just，yet现在完成时的用法，培养复习、归纳知识的意识，能否在生活中熟练地运用现在完成时的结构语言。

（2）在写作中，教师应给学生独立思考和完成任务的空间，完成后，教师要注意引导学生从信息的完整性、格式、目标语言的运用、书写规范性等方面进行评价，并让学生之间交换作文，根据教师的评价指导进行互评、修改，让学生在实践中习得写作的技能。

（六）教学策略和教学方法

（1）个性化的学习。

（2）“三P”教学法。

（3）项目学习。

（七）学情分析

本届学生大多数是外来学生，由于词汇量的缺乏和薄弱的语法基础，英语写作不理想。虽然本单元的话题“Literature”学生可能在这方面的信息储备不足，但教师可在教学中播放电影片段，采用多媒体教学，适当添加背景介绍，降低难度；而现在完成时虽然难懂，但本单元仅涉及带有already，yet现在完成时的结构，在任务教学中，加深学生对现在完成时的理解，用目标语言谈论是否“做过和还没有做过的事情”，联系跨文化意识，陶冶文学情操。

（八）整体规划

关于Literature和带有already，just，yet现在完成时的语言结构，本单元安排了三个课时。

1. 第一课时是话题下的听说课

首先，话题导入词汇，教师让学生看教师自制的画卷PPT课件展示，展示出优雅的中国画卷搭配高雅的古筝音乐，引入文学、书本话题，引导学生进行高尚的文学学习，激发其欣赏情趣，激活学生相关背景知识与体验。以词汇带动功能结构语言，教师利用学生所熟知的书本和单元新引入的书本名称，逐步引导学生学习，通过自己造句等方式来使用该功能语言。接着给出新的单元要求的书本名称，并在学生中开展调查，询问是否读过这些书本？感受如何？紧接着是听力练习及听力技巧渗透，引导学生分别听西方文学名著名称、听对话者谈论是否读过该文学名著、听句子的具体陈述并判断正误。再接着话题拓展，侧重语言表达，升华情感及反省。学生对四件贴近自己生活实际的事件进行讨论，自由发表观点，谈论是否做过，评价及感受如何。激发学生对英语语言文化的兴趣，学会如何与人探讨和交流文学作品，发表个人观点和看法，从而提高学生的文学素养和人文素养。

2. 第二课时基于阅读Section A 3a的写作课

通过*Robinson Crusoe*（《鲁滨孙漂流记》）两个节选片段的阅读，作为一扇窗户，打开学生对西方文学名著的认识和激发他们的阅读兴趣，并设计了四个不同的活动来帮助学生加深对两个片段的理解，教会学生从哪些方面来理解名著和阅读技巧的习得，为后面的写作做铺垫。例如，第一个活动的主旨句搭配，则告诉学生在篇章找主旨句理解文段，在写作中也有主旨句。第二个活动是猜测词意活动，训练学生根据上下文猜测词意，习得阅读技巧。第三个活动是鲁滨孙在孤岛中遇到了三个问题，他是如何解决的。第四个活动是排序，从而教会学生在赏析名著时，对人物的评价和他所做的事情联系起来，在写作中同样如此，性格的表现要和具体的事情结合起来，有理有据。通过设置对鲁滨孙这个人物的评价自然地引出阅读的重要性，“A good book is a light to the soul.”切入到写作任务。紧抓书本（books）这一中心词，接着发散思维，由词到句再到篇章，教师一步步给予学生写作指导，扫清学生在写作中可能遇到的障碍，树立学生的写作信心，让学生爱上阅读，学会赏析名著。

3. 第三课时基于话题“Literature”的写作课

由话题引出词汇，关于文学作品的名称，结合功能语言，“你是否有读过这些书籍？”呈现真实语境，加深学生对现在完成时的理解。接着又进一步讨论文学作品的内容，“你认为它如何？”引出描述性形容词和make sb. adj. / do的句型来讨论观点。再进一步深入，“这本文学作品是关于什么内容？”交流文化，由此拓展学生的文化视野，激发学生阅读欲望。接着展开调查，教师设计任务让学生相互介绍他们读过的一本书，它怎么样？它什么内容？采访2位伙伴，他们读过什么书？感觉如何？什么内容？然后学生汇报调查结果。介绍你最近读的一本书，如作品名称、作家、评价、主要内容等。培养学生的发散性思维，并合理运用目标语言带有already，yet的现在完成时进行书面写作。教师根据讨论，给出有用的表达方式，降低写作难度。学生独立写作，教师巡视加以指导，点评时渗透写作技巧。

（九）课程特点

（1）通过文学“literature”话题的层层深入，谈论中西方文学名著，谈论是否读过这些名著或故事书本以及感受如何，让学生了解一些基本的适合中学生的中西方文学名著的基本内容，激发学生的阅读兴趣。让学生懂得如何去谈论所读书本、最喜爱的作家，让学生感受阅读及书本在人们生活中的实际意义和对人类生活、交际、未来产生的重大影响。

（2）根据对本单元的教学内容的分析，结合本学校的学生特点及中考英语写作要求，我们进一步整合教材，分三个课时对本单元进行写作教学。第一课时为话题下的听说课，第二课时基于阅读Section A 3a的写作课，第三课时基于话题“Literature”的写作课，将本单元的话题、功能、结构、任务有机地结合在一起。“话题”带出词汇，引出本话题需要掌握的基本词汇；“功能”带出句型，主要包括完成任务所需的语言结构；“结构”带出语法，将语法分散在本话题中；“任务”带出综合，结合目标语言，突出用本话题所学语言去做事情。

（3）在教学中渗透英语学科的核心素养，提高学生的语言能力；培养学生的团队合作精神，对自己负责和关爱他人的文化品格；培养学生的批判性思维，如总结时让学生思考“What have you learned?”“What is interesting?”“What question do you have?”让学生突破常规思维，认真去思考问题，反思总结本节课自己所学的知识，而不仅仅局限于目标语言。

（4）两种不同类型的写作课均遵循了由输入到输出、从易到难的规律，不同的教学任务都让学生掌握词汇——句型——篇章。写作练习从半控制性到自由的过程性写作，层层递进，增强学生的学习信心，培养学生独立思考的能力，用英语完成任务。最后还拔高层次，授人以鱼不如授人以渔，引导学生从信息的完整性、格式、目标语言的运用、书写规范性等方面对写作进行评价，习得写作的技能。

（5）为提高学生的学习能力，教师设计的课堂趣味性强，方式新颖，生动有趣，激发学生的学习兴趣。在教学中，教师注重培养学生的学习策略，如个性化的学习、合作学习、反思与实践、自主学习、批判性思维，略读和细读的阅读技能，培养学生掌握写作的技能，如开头、中心段、结尾、连接词等。

二、教学设计

（一）话题下的听说教学设计

1. 基本信息

（1）教学内容。

① 教材内容。

②人教版八年级下册 Unit 8 Have you read Treasure Island yet? (Section A 1a-1c)。

③ 语言支架：话题、功能、结构、任务。

（2）学生：八年级学生，使用人教版教材。

（3）教师：广东省中山市小榄华侨中学。

（4）日期：2018年6月26日。

2. 教学内容分析

（1）听说教学内容。

① 话题知识内容：Literature（谈论文学）。

② 听力知识内容：听“西方文学名著名称”、听“对话者谈论是否读过该文学名著”、听“句子的具体陈述并判断正误”，穿插听力技巧渗透。

③ 语法知识内容：带有already、just和yet的现在完成时基本结构知识。

（2）听说教学技能内容。

①“话题”带出词汇，引出本话题需要掌握的基本词汇。

②“功能”带出句型，主要包括完成任务所需的语言结构。

③“结构”带出语法，将语法分散在本话题中。

④“任务”带出综合，结合目标语言，突出用本话题所学语言去做事情。

⑤通过听前、听中、听后的活动，渗透听力的一般性技巧。

（3）听说教学素养内容。

① 文化陶冶。通过文学（literature）话题的层层深入，以书本（books）为主线，谈论中西方文学名著，谈论是否读过这些名著或故事书本以及感受如何，让学生了解一些基本的适合中学生的中西方文学名著的基本内容，激发出学生的阅读兴趣。让学生懂得如何去谈论所读书本，让学生感受阅读及书本在人们生活中的实际意义和对人类生活、交际、未来产生的重大影响。

② 思维拓展。突出用本话题所学语言去解决口语交际的需求，展开相关话题的调查汇报以及利用功能语言自由谈论已经做过的事和还没有做过的事情。

③ 学习发展。用所学习话题和语言结构提升学生的英语语言能力，文化品格，思维品质以及学习能力。

3. 发展目标

（1）语言素养。学生几乎都能说出Section A中提出的六本西方名著的词汇，绝大多数能结合功能语言谈论自己是否已经读过或者还没读过该书以及自己读后对书本的评价，且语言结构正确，能正确使用already，just，yet。部分学生能表达自己对不同书本的阅读感受以及谈论自己做过的事情、经历及发表个人观点。

（2）文化素养。学生几乎都能认识到书本阅读对人起的作用、对人生的影响，懂得书本阅读的重要性。绝大多数的学生对待书本阅读的现状能批判地看待，部分学生能达到自如地运用结构语言对生活中的真实情境进行自由谈论。

（3）思维素养。几乎全部学生能意识到通过谈论书本阅读、谈论做过和没有做过的事情，发现功能语言的结构并尝试使用继而灵活使用。在对语言结构的运用中发现自己的阅读现状，对西方文学名著逐步产生兴趣并激发出自身的阅读求知欲望，从而体验思维拓展性，挖掘自身潜能，并得到相应发展。

（4）学习素养。学生几乎都能使用功能结构语言和文学名著词汇谈论是否阅读过书本，对用目标语言来谈论“已经做过和还没做过的事情”所使用的句型比较熟练，掌握了带有already、just、yet的现在完成时的基本结构，绝大多数的学生能通过语言表达的策略习得现在完成时的语法结构并自己造句。

4. 课时任务

（1）任务情境。现在完成时是一个很灵活、很常用的初中阶段必须掌握的时态。它的语言结构不难，难的是大量动词过去分词的变化。因此，在这节仅仅40分钟的课程当中，教师不要把这一部分当作需要克服的重点难点，而要更多地注重语言结构的使用和掌握。因此，结合本单元文学（Literature）这个话题，仅仅谈论“是否阅读过一些书本”这一谈资是远远不够的。而通过“文学”话题，再选择一些贴近学生生活实际的话题，就能够打开学生的思维，引导学生进行思考，也打开了他们的话匣子。随后，设置了谈论四件学生是否“做过和还没有做过的事情”，使该语言结构得到进一步使用。这四件事分别是：“是否听过金志文改编的《关关雎鸠》这首歌（have / haven’t heard the song）”，该歌曲旋律优美，意境深远，且是原诗歌歌词和改编后通俗歌词的合体，加上金志文歌手的深情演绎，向听众们包括我们十几岁的学生们传达了中国古典文学中最具有代表性的一首古诗歌的真实情意，使学生对它有了新的体验和感受，也是对我国正统文化的很好传承，更多要求学生去感受，能说到基本结构即可；“是否去过香港迪士尼乐园（have / haven't visited Hong Kong Disneyland）”，身处珠三角地区的中山市，离香港很近，我们十几岁的孩子要么小时候已经去过，要么因为是外来子弟一直都很想去，这个话题很适合他们；“是否看过《哈利·波特》这部电影（have / haven't watched the movie Harry Potter）”，现代娱乐休闲中，电影是不可或缺的，选择《哈利·波特》则是因为它风靡全球，且更是让青少年着迷；“是否读过《愚公移山》这本书（have / haven't read Yu Gong Moves the Mountains）”，本故事学生已在第六单元学过，包括对其中的精神挖掘，学生也是掌握了并能够表达的。因此，本次在四个事件基础上设置的Free Talk对学生来说很好表达，也容易做到“言之有物”，十分贴切。

积极思考所设置的情境，并运用所学表达不同和感想。

（2）任务行为。通过话题（Literature）引导学生谈论书本名称及评价—功能结构—目标语言操练—听力及技巧—拓展表达—情感发展，使学生有机地把本节课的语言目标（带有already、just和yet的现在完成时）与语言学习观中的社会建构主义相结合。

（3）任务成果。学生运用所学话题和语言结构，积极创新，善于运用语言结构进行积极拓展思维，发表个人观点并提出问题。

5. 教学用具

PPT课件、多媒体教学资源与设备。

6. 教学过程，见表7-10

表7-10　教学过程

阶段与环节	师生活动	教学目的	教学用具
课前	1. 与学生初次见面，彼此熟识； 2. 通过电影《哈利·波特》的同步影音音乐引起学生关注屏幕，进入新课状态	为学生热身（warming-up）、缓解新环境压力，准备进入教学	电脑

续 表

阶段与环节	师生活动	教学目的	教学用具
课中：话题导入词汇	1. 教师让学生看自制的画卷PPT课件展示，展示优雅的中国画卷搭配高雅的古筝音乐，引入文学、书本话题，引导学生应有高尚的文学学习、欣赏情趣； 2. 画卷中呈现“中西方文学”字样，初步引起学生关注	1. 激活学生相关背景知识与体验； 2. 通过生动形象的画卷和书本的出现，展现单元话题文学的特殊性质； 3. 任务引入，让学生了解本单元必备文学名著名称	PPT播放音乐搭配画卷设置动画
课中：词汇带动功能结构语言	教师利用学生所熟知的书本和单元新引入的书本名称，逐步引导学生学习，通过自己造句等方式来使用该功能语言	让学生学习带有already，just和yet的现在完成时的基本结构	PPT播放呈现各种书本的画面
课中：知识巩固，两两合作操练对话	1. 继续给出新的单元要求的书本名称，并在同学中开展调查，询问是否读过这些书本，感受如何； 2. 强化功能语言，巩固语言结构的使用并达到熟练	1. 强调语法知识和功能语言训练； 2. 培养思维、观察和模仿造句能力，发展语言素养、文化素养	PPT播放呈现各种书本的画面
课中：听力练习及听力技巧渗透	1. 教师选择单元听力中的一个进行听力题型的组织改编，设置一个听力材料听三遍，并由浅入深地设置问题，引导学生分别听“西方文学名著名称”“对话者谈论是否读过该文学名著”“句子的具体陈述并判断正误”； 2. 并通过听前、听中、听后的活动，渗透听力的一般性技巧	1. 关注学生认知规律，鼓励学生关注细节、注重策略； 2. 通过课堂训练，培养学生发现问题、分析问题和解决问题的能力	播放听力语音
课中：话题拓展，侧重语言表达，升华情感及反省	1. 学生对四件贴近自己生活实际的事件进行讨论，自由发表观点，谈论是否做过、评价及感受如何； 2. 学生也能自由表达其他相关话语，积极展示自己的丰富的思维，提升自己的语言表达能力； 3. 询问学生是否喜爱阅读；请学生思考书本对人生的意义，观看央视阅读公益视频； 4. 学生思考：这节课学到什么？你对什么感兴趣？你还有什么问题	1. 给学生思考、发现和表达的机会，引导学生积极联系实际、反思、表达自我； 2. 发展思维品格和文化品质素养，引导学生对文学和阅读的兴趣爱好，同时反思自己的阅读现状，引起自己对阅读的思考，对其实际生活起积极的引导作用	播放视频

续表

阶段与环节	师生活动	教学目的	教学用具
课后：作业	找出更多你感兴趣的文学著作，谈论自己是否已经朗读过，感受评价如何，对没有阅读过的，制订一个阅读计划	指向真实的生活，发展相关素养	

（二）基于话题下以读促写的教学设计

1. 教学内容：人教版八年级下册Unit 8 Have you read Treasure Island yet?［（Section A 3a）第二课时。］

2. 读写教学内容

Literature（谈论文学），阅读知识内容：阅读名著*Robinson Crusoe*（《鲁滨孙漂流记》）节选片段，略读文章，搭配主旨句、细读文章猜测词意、细读文章填空、细读文章排序；渗透阅读技巧。写作知识内容：由书本发散的词汇，句型，篇章写作，渗透写作技巧。

3. 读写教学技能内容

通过读前、读中、读后的活动，渗透阅读、写作的一般性技巧。

4. 读写教学素养内容

阅读名著*Robinson Crusoe*（《鲁滨孙漂流记》）节选两个片段，片段一中主人公鲁滨孙即使陷入了绝境，也不自我放弃，在孤岛上以种菜、打猎为生，等待有船靠岸拯救，可以看出鲁滨孙聪明、独立、乐观；片段二中鲁滨孙从食人者手中救出星期五，并教星期五英语，可以看出鲁滨孙友好、勇敢，有学问。由鲁滨孙个人的人格魅力，激发学生对名著的阅读兴趣。紧接着写作“Growing up with good books”让学生懂得书本的重要性，如何让书本成为我们的良师益友，突出用本话题所学语言去解决口语交际及书面表达的需求，展开相关话题的阅读和写作以及利用功能语言自由谈论阅读的重要性及如何评论自己最喜爱的书。

5. 语言素养

学生几乎都能读懂Section A 3a中涉及的词汇，绝大多数的学生能结合功能语言谈论自己是否已经读过或者还没读过*Robinson Crusoe*（《鲁滨孙漂流记》）以及自己读后对书本的评价，部分学生能表达自己对该书的阅读感受以及对主人公鲁滨孙的经历发表个人观点，能用目标语言完成阅读的重要性及我最爱的书的写作任务。学生几乎都能使用功能结构语言谈论是否阅读过*Robinson Crusoe*（《鲁滨孙漂流记》），通过四个不同的阅读任务，提升阅读中细读、略读的阅读技巧。用目标语言来谈论阅读的重要性，用目标语言完成“Growing up with good books”的书面写作，从而习得写作的学习策略，从中心词到句型、到篇章的有机结合。

6. 任务情境

本单元文学（Literature）这个话题对于初中生来说有点深奥，由于学生在这方面的信息储备不足，要把本单元设计的英语文学作品讲透更是不太现实。通过话题（Literature）引导学生谈论书本名称及评价—功能结构—目标语言操练—阅读及技巧—书面表达—情感发展，善于运用语言结构进行表达，完成关于阅读书本的写作，能积极拓展思维。

7. 教学过程，见表7–11

表7–11 教学过程

阶段与环节	师生活动	教学目的	教学用具
阅读前	1. 与学生初次见面，做适当的热身彼此熟识； 2. 通过播放电影《鲁滨孙漂流记》的节选片段引起学生关注，进入新课； 3. Free talk. 假设你是鲁滨孙，你的感受如何？你会如何做？进入名著阅读	1. 为学生热身（warming-up）、缓解新环境压力；准备进入教学； 2. 了解书本阅读的相关背景知识，激发学生阅读的兴趣	电脑，PPT课件播放电影
阅读中：略读文章，掌握文章主旨	1. 阅读文章，搭配主旨句； 2. 核对答案； 3. 总结阅读略读的技巧，在文段的第一句或最后一句找出主旨句，帮助理解文章大意	培养学生的略读技能，了解文章大意	PPT课件播放练习文本
阅读中：细读文章，寻找关键信息	1. 细读文章，猜测词义，并选择答案； 2. 读第一段，找出鲁滨孙遇到的问题以及他的解决方法，并评价鲁滨孙； 3. 读第二段，排序	1. 培养学生掌握根据上下文得猜测词义的技能； 2. 培养学生细读寻找关键信息的阅读技能； 3. 教学生如何赏析名著，了解名著对我们的重要性	PPT课件播放练习文本

续表

阶段与环节	师生活动	教学目的	教学用具
阅读后：相关话题写作，提高学生写作技巧和能力，提高综合语言应用能力	1.讨论书本想到的词或词组，由词组如何过渡到句型写作，介绍连接词的使用及范例； 2.完成“Growing up with good books”的写作，学生之间互评、修改，教师评价； 3.学生思考：这节课学到什么？你对什么感兴趣？你还有什么问题	1.培养学生的写作技能； 2.培养思维、观察和模仿造句能力，发展语言素养、文化素养； 3.通过课堂训练，培养学生发现问题、分析问题和解决问题的能力； 4.发展思维品格和文化品质素养，引发学生对文学和阅读的兴趣爱好，同时反思自己的阅读现状，引起自己对阅读的思考，对其实际生活起积极的引导作用	PPT课件播放呈现文本
课后：作业	找出更多你感兴趣的文学著作，谈论是什么、关于谁、什么内容、感受评价如何，写最喜爱的书评	指向真实的生活，发展相关素养	PPT课件播放作业文本

（三）基于话题下的写作教学设计

1. 基本信息

话题写作：以话题Literature（谈论文学）为主线，引出本话题需要掌握课标词汇，写作中需要话题拓展词以及行文需要的词。通过写前、写中、写后的活动，渗透写作的一般性技巧。最终，通过话题（Literature）引导学生谈论书本名称及评价—功能结构—目标语言操练—写作及技巧—拓展表达—情感发展。

2. 教学过程，见表7–12

表7–12 教学过程

过程	师生活动	教学目的	教学用具
课前	通过讲故事《老人与海》进入新课	准备进入教学	电脑
课中：话题导入词块及结构语	1. 教师引导学生思考：当提到文学的时候你会想到什么？我们经常想到：它的名字是什么？ 2. PPT呈现本单元结构语言	1. 呈现词块； 2. 通过PPT，展现单元话题结构语言，为写作做铺垫	
课中：写作前，引导学生写一些结构语言	逐步引导学生学习、自己造句，巩固语言结构的使用并达到熟练程度	让学生学习带有already、just和yet的现在完成时的基本结构，发展语言素养、文化素养	PPT播放呈现各种书本的画面

续 表

过程	师生活动	教学目的	教学用具
课中：调查报告	1. 教师设计任务介绍自己读过的一本书； 2. 学生面向全部汇报； 3. 渗透写作的一般性技巧	话题下写作。给学生思考、发现和表达的机会	PPT呈现调查表格
课中：评价	引导学生自评、他评及教师评	培养学生的思维能力及综合运用能力	PPT呈现范文
课后：作业	评价《老人与海》	引导学生反思再实践	PPT呈现作业

三、教学反思

（一）话题下听说课反思

本堂课为新课开课第一课时，设计为话题下的听说教学，以听前、听中、听后活动贯穿整体，最后以“三二一”的思维反馈结束课程。

1. 课堂靓丽的一面

（1）本课时以文学话题引入词汇，完成听说教学任务的同时，让学生对文学、对书本有新的、更生动的印象，能提出各种问题，能重新反问自己，审视自己对待书本的态度，引起了学生对书本阅读的兴趣，这是本课堂最大的收获。有学生在课堂上明确表示：“以前不喜欢看书，上完这堂课以后，决定以后要多看书。”

（2）学生通过听说练习，对基本句型和语法结构的掌握也比较好，对于现在完成时“Have / haven’t done”结构的运用把握较好。

（3）在Free talk环节中，学生对所提事件是否做过所发表的看法表达到位，语言结构精准，兴趣盎然，充分体现了他们对文化和文学的思维萌芽，对学生以后的生活和人生有一定的思想影响。

2. 不足之处

（1）课堂重视学生的思维反映，忽略学生之间的互动，在语言操练上，摒弃了以往的机械口头训练，但实际上也可以添加进去，使课堂更加活跃，使语言训练更加充分。

（2）可以鼓励更多的学生参与进来，表达自己的观点。例如在“三二一”环节，即使鼓励学生可以用中文来表达思维，依旧有很多学生没有发言表达。

是否有更好的激励方式来调动学生的积极性?

附上学生提出的问题，供以后改进:

1.《鲁滨孙漂流记》的作者是谁?

2. 我为什么没有像旁边的人一样积极举手发言?

3. 什么时候用过去分词?

4. 怎样在句子中用过去分词?

5. 看纸质书好还是电子书好?

6. 我们应该向鲁滨孙学习吗?

7. 为什么书是我们的好朋友?

8. 故事主要是关于什么的?

9. 鲁滨孙发生了什么?

10. 书对我们的重要性有哪些?

11. 如果我们的世界没有书，没有语言、文化、知识，那么这个世界会变成什么样?

12. 为什么书本中总可以学到更好的道理?

13. 我们现在的年龄段应该多读什么样的书? 对我们有什么好处?

14. 鲁滨孙在等待什么?

15. 汤姆·索亚历险记》讲的些什么?

16. 糖果屋的男孩、女孩最后得救了吗?

17.《小妇人》讲了什么?

18. 其他的书对我们有什么好处?

19. Have的用法有哪些?

20. 为什么鲁滨孙叫这个男人星期五?

21. 我认为我们应该有更多的时间让同学们展开讨论。

22. 我认为我们应该在看视频上花费更少的时间。

23. 为什么有许多书可以告诉我们一些很深刻的道理?

24. 为什么《金银岛》是一本很棒的书?

25. 我们如何阅读一本书?

26. 你最喜欢的书是什么?

（二）话题下以读促写教学反思

本节课是一节基于阅读的写作课，阅读的文段来自于课文，是Robinson Crusoe（《鲁滨孙漂流记》）的节选，结合本单元的题目和话题，写作就以“Growing up with good books”为题写一篇作文。整节课目标明确，层层推进，用简单的阅读技巧如（mind-map）来挖掘文本的内涵。课堂上学生能结合之前学过的知识，解决并回答问题。让笔者印象最深刻的是，看完小视频后，笔者问学生如果他们处于鲁滨孙的境况时，他们会怎么做？有一个学生说“I want to kill myself”，当时听了比较吃惊。经过阅读并分析鲁滨孙的人物性格之后，在最后“Thinking”的环节时，笔者再次问这位学生：“Would you kill yourself after reading the passage?”他很自信地回答：“No，I would try my best to solve the problems.”这是一个意外的收获。

写作环节中，笔者给出了范文，让学生在范文的基础上，用上本单元学过的句子和时态。学生能在第二段上增加自己阅读的经历，并举例子。通过这节课，笔者意识到自己在今后的教学中要注意以下几点：

（1）学生有无限的创造力和活跃的思维，教师的问题要尽可能开放，而且课堂必须要留出时间给学生思考和回顾总结。

（2）以读促写中的阅读，除了培养学生的阅读技巧，更需要教师挖掘文本的内涵。

（3）通过使用英语来掌握一门语言。写作就是产出。上完这节课后，笔者认为，只要阅读过程风卷残云，搞懂搞透，再结合一些简单的写作技巧，文章就自然而然出来了！只是到后面，时间有点紧，没有更多的时间来展示学生的作文。

在今后的教学中，教师应该更精准地把握教学目标，掌握好每个环节的时间分配，不断反思，以改进自己的教学。

（三）话题下写作教学反思

本节课是八年级下册第八单元的第三课时，设计的教学形式是话题写作。在这一堂课中，教师利用文学作品以图片导入新课，给学生直观的感受。借助图片，利用一问一答的形式呈现了现在完成时，充分调动了学生的学习兴趣。课堂中教师设计的学生互动包括对话练习、小组调查报告，这两个环节充分调动了学生的学习积极性。学生积极参与到整个活动中，成为整个环节的主导者。最后的写作设计中，教师设计了可参考的表达方式和句型，活跃学生的思维。整堂课以话题带动写作,以话题促进写作，层层递进，让学生轻松容易地进入写作环节。最后的思考部分，让学生反思反观自己的课堂，起到很好的总结和反思的作用，让学生学会总结，学会思考。

本堂课也有一些需要改进的地方，在扩展文学这个主题时，还可以适当增加内容，如：Who is the writer? How do you feel about this book? 等。在写作引导时，还可以更多地输入词汇或重要句型，让学生有话可说、有内容可写。

案例3：GFI Unit 3 Is this your pencil? B1

Topic: Things in the classroom

一、整合整体规划

（一）单元背景

随着我国对外开放的进一步发展，社会对英语人才的需求越来越迫切，这对学校英语教学提出了更高的要求。培养学生的英语口语、书面交际能力是整个初中阶段英语教学的目的之一。“写”是较高层次的信息系统，它要求学生具有较高的书面语言表达能力。教师应根据《新课程标准》的要求，根据现代现实生活的实际需要，培养学生较好的写作能力。

《英语课程标准（2011年版）》对中学生的写作能力做了如下要求：“能仿照学过的题材或话题，利用所给的范例写简单的书信、便条、通知等；能按要求笔头转述所听、所读的简要内容。”“能为图片提供简单的文字说明并能表达自己的观点。”从中可以看出国家教委对中学生的英语写作能力做了比较明确的规定，要求广大教师在教学过程中加强对初中学生运用英语能力的培养。写作可以最大限度地反映学生的综合英语水平。它不仅考察学生的词汇量，还包括对语法的运用和语言表达组织能力，在中考英语中，它的分值有15分，其重要性不言而喻。因此，在初中阶段重视对学生写作能力的培养是极其重要的。

目前初中英语写作教学中存在的普遍问题有：

（1）学生英语词汇量严重不足。词汇是写作的基础，词汇量的多少直接影响学生的写作能力的发挥。拥有丰富的词汇，学生写起来得心应手，反之，抓耳挠腮怎么都憋不出几句话来，词穷得让人着急。

（2）汉语式的英语表达频繁。由于中西方的语言表达方式上的差异，学生容易受汉语语言表达方式的影响，运用汉语书写的方法进行英语写作，有的学生甚至直接采用直译的方式直接将汉语翻译成英文，非常不地道。如，My family have four people.（我家有四人。）正确的表达方式是There are four people in my family.

（3）语法运用错误，体裁结构不清晰。在写作中，学生逻辑思维混乱，抓不住主旨，还有跑题的情况。对文章整体结构把握不清晰，格式有错，还伴随着很多语法错误。例如人称、数的使用，“她没有足球。”学生翻译成“She don't have a soccer ball.”忽略了第三人称单数的限定，应改为“She doesn't have a soccer ball.”这些语法错误就成了学生的失分点。

针对初中生写作中出现的普遍问题——词汇量不足、语法知识薄弱，要想提高学生的写作能力，就必须提高学生的词汇量和巩固语法知识。怎样才能高效呢？若是死记硬背去记英语单词，非但不能取得良好的效果，而且对学生来说也是极大的压力，倘若我们采用一些方法来巧记英语单词，那学生就会有事半功倍的效果。语法是语言知识的重要组成部分，假设我们在教学中过度强调语法，仅注重语言的形式，对学生进行一味地机械地模仿操练，忽视语言的实际运用，则会造成学生并没有真正理解掌握语法知识，在实际中不能准确和得体地运用英语进行口头表达，也写不出几句完整的句子，难以实现高质量的语言输出。

在听、说、读、写中，初中英语教学的书面表达相对滞后，学生的写作水平提高甚微，形成了“听到写作学生心烦，见到习作教师不愿”的现象。为了改变这一现状，我们老师想办法，出点子，借精品课程建设的契机，根据初中生的心理特点和知识水平，研究初中英语教学中有效的写作教学模式，探索提高学生英语写作能力的途径和方法，激发师生的兴趣，提高英语教学的实效性。

（二）主要内容

人教版《初中英语》Go for it七年级上册“Unit 3　Is this your pencil?”以“Things in the classroom”为话题，让学生学会谈论教室内常见的物品并能够就物主关系进行问答，能够正确使用名词性物主代词。掌握失物招领和寻物启事的目标语言写作，让学生在实际生活中学会使用目标语言，从而感知英语学习的重要性和实用性。

英语学科的核心素养包括语言能力、思维品质、文化意识和学习能力四个维度。语言能力就是用语言做事的能力，涉及语言知识、语言意识和语感，语言技能、交际策略等，而不是哑巴英语，只会做题、考试。基于核心素养的语言能力，我们教师决定打破传统教学，采用新颖的教学模式，将本单元的话题、功能、结构、任务有机地结合在一起。根据教学内容设计了第一课时基于话题“things in the classroom”的写作课和第二课时基于阅读Section B 2a-2c的失物招领和寻物启事的写作课，引导学生主动参与到课堂中，促进学生英语听、说、读、写能力的全面发展。

人教版Go for it七年级上册“Unit 3　Is this your pencil?”的主要内容见表7–13：

表7–13　Content

Topic（话题）	Things in the classroom
Function（功能）	Identify ownership
Structure（结构）	Possessive pronouns, Yes/No questions and short answers
Target language (目标语言)	Is this your pencil? A: Is this/that your… B: Yes, it is. It’s …/No, it isn’t. It’s… A: Are these/those your… B: Yes, they are. They’re …/No, they aren’t. They’re… This/That is a/an…It’s… These/Those are…They are…
Key vocabulary （重点词汇）	pencil, pen, pencil box, schoolbag, ruler, book, notebook, eraser, baseball, computer game, dictionary

（1）“话题”带出词汇，引出本话题需要掌握的基本词汇。“Things in the classroom”话题引出教室内常见物品的话题词汇“pencil，pen，pencil box，schoolbag，ruler，book，eraser，watch，bag，computer，notebook，dictionary...”等，这些词汇在话题的带动下，词与词之间有了关联，方便学生记忆，从而拓展了学生的词汇量，提高学生的思维品质，培养学生的发散思维

能力。

（2）“功能”带出句型，主要包括完成任务所需的语言结构。Identify ownership带出了本单元的句型。

A: Is this/that your…

B: Yes, it is. It’s …/No, it isn’t. It’s…

A: Are these/those your…

B: Yes, they are. They’re …/No, they aren’t. They’re…

设置不同的教学任务，学生在完成任务时就会自然而然地使用目标语言进行交际，有助于帮助学生在语境中掌握目标语言。

（3）“结构”带出语法，将语法分散在本话题中。本单元的重点语法结构是使用单复数的一般疑问句询问物主及使用不同的名词性物主代词进行回答。

A: Is this/that your …

B: Yes, it is. It’s mine. /No, it isn’t. It’s hers/his.

A: Are these/those your…

B: Yes, they are. /No, they aren’t. They’re hers/mine.

学生在不同的教学任务中对目标语言进行语言实践训练，让语法结构教学情境化和趣味化，从而得出以下结论：

① be动词与指示代词保持一致：this/that 用is, these/those 用are。

② 一般疑问句的基本结构：be 动词置于句首。

③ 简略回答用it代替this/that, 用they代替these/those。

④ 形容词性物主代词与名词性物主代词的不同：形容词性物主代词后需跟名词，名词性物主代词后不能再接名词。

（4）“任务”带出综合，结合目标语言，突出用本话题所学语言去做事情。本单元学习了指示代词和名词性物主代词，并不是只是为了做题拿高分，而是让学生知道在真实生活中，什么场景需要用到指示代词和名词性物主代词。第一课时在基于话题的写作课中，设计了“things in the classroom”的话题写作，在介绍教室的物品时，学生自然而然地在写作中用到和话题词汇等目标语言。

A: This/That is a/an …

B: It's mine/hers/his/Lucy's.

A: These/Those are …

B: They are mine/hers/his/Lily's.

第二课时在基于阅读的写作课中，设计了Lost和Found的写作。学生通过Discovery感知Found失物招领和Lost寻物启事的结构。

Found:

Some books are in Classroom One. Are they yours? E-mail me at Lilyyg@163. com.

Lost:

I lost my schoolbag. I must find it. Call me at 785-2375. Thanks.

在Lost 和Found写作任务中，学生很自然地把目标语言和话题词汇运用于写作中，做到用本话题所学的语言去做事情，突出了语言的实用性和交际性。

除此之外，在第二课时设计了阅读前、阅读中、阅读后的活动，渗透阅读的一般性技巧。阅读和写作是英语学习中的重要模块，对学生的英语综合素质有较高的要求。俗话说："读写不分家。" 阅读要求的是理解和领悟能力，写作要求的是运用和表达能力。阅读能力的高与低直接影响着学生的书面表达能力，而学生写作水平的提升也会对阅读理解能力有促进作用。在实际教学中，将二者有机地结合起来，在授课过程中兼顾读写，以读促写，以写促读，可以同时促进学生读写能力的共同提高。

（三）课程目标

1. 语言素养

（1）语言知识。

① 能掌握关于"things in the classroom"的词汇和结构。

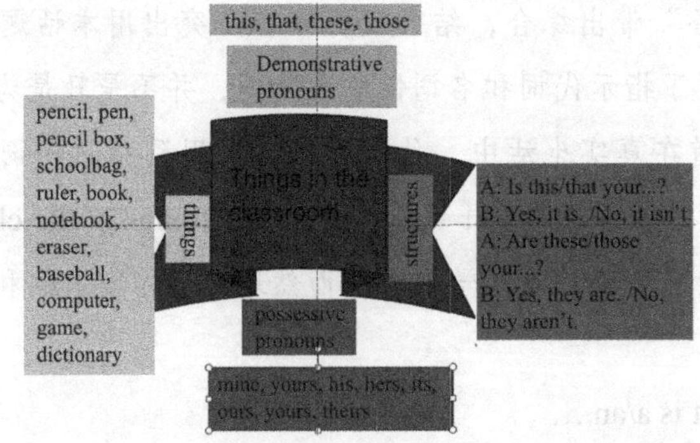

② 能掌握以下句型，并合理运用目标语言进行交际。

A: Is this/that your…

B: Yes, it is. It’s …/No, it isn’t. It’s…

A: Are these/those your…

B: Yes, they are. They’re …/No, they aren’t. They’re…

This/That is a/an…It’s…

These/Those are…They are…

③ 语法。理解和掌握名词性物主代词的用法，结合第二单元学过的指示代词，能熟练运用其来指认物品的所属关系。

④ 篇章和语用。掌握“Lost and Found”的写作。

（2）语言技能。

① 掌握略读、细读的阅读技能。

② 掌握列提纲、自评、他评的写作技能。

③ 掌握大方、自信、准确的英语口语表达技能。

2. 文化素养。

让学生进一步熟悉教室里的物品，从而更加热爱校园生活；在保管好自己物品的同时，乐于助人，帮助他人找回丢失的物品；在活动中增进同学情谊，培养跨文化意识，了解西方失物招领的小常识；能够了解电子邮件的基本常识。

3. 思维素养。

系统归纳“Things in the classroom”的词汇。

（1）掌握个性化的学习、项目学习、反思与实践、自主学习的学习策略。

（2）用英语思维写作。通过设计“Thing in my classroom”和“Lost”“Found”的写作，学生能介绍在学校所接触的常见物品，并能对物品的主人进行问答，通过物品来熟悉同学，了解同学，增进同学之间的情感，热爱校园生活。同时，促使学生学会保管好自己的东西，避免发生丢失的情况，学会对自己的东西负责；而对于别人丢失的物品能积极地帮忙找到主人，学会帮助他人地博爱精神。

（四）教学难点

能否正确地使用名词性物主代词，如mine，his等。通过总结指示代词和名词性物主代词的用法，能够熟悉身边的物品及主人，学会对自己的物品负责，不丢三落四。同时，也学会帮助他人，找回物品的失主，做一个负责、有爱心的学生。

（五）整体规划

关于写作课，本单元安排了两个课时。

1. 第一课时是基于话题的写作课

在第一课时中，主要是要学生了解本单元基本的语言目标，包括教室内常见的物品、名词性物主代词，使用一般疑问句确认物主关系并做简略回答，指示代词和be动词的正确使用。根据要解决的语言目标，我们把第一课时定位为说写课。通过反反复复地说，进行由浅入深地操练，掌握了基本的语言目标后，马上进行与本话题相关的写作训练。让学生通过“things in the classroom”中心词，学会发散思维，联想到教室里的物品，解决词汇问题，接着本节课所学的目标语言指示代词进而介绍物品的主人，由词过渡到句。那么，句子如何组织成篇呢？需要连接词，把文章有机地结合在一起。这就是文章的Body parts中心端。那么，如何写一篇高质量的文章？教师则要渗透写作技能，加开头topic sentence 和conclusion。然后学生根据教师介绍的写作技能，自己操练，当场就教室内的物品写一篇文章，然后互评、修改，运用目标语言完成此任务，巩固本节课所学的目标语言，提高话题写作的能力。

2. 第二课时是基于阅读的写作课

通过对第一课时中指示代词、教室内常见物品的复习，阅读前的教师的“What do you do if you lost things at school?”的问题巧妙地引出了跨文化背景知识，即什么是Lost and Found，为下文阅读和写作做好铺垫，拓宽学生的知识面和视野。接着通过层层递进的阅读任务，让学生掌握略读、细读的阅读技能。通过略读了解文章大意，细读有效获取信息，提高语言能力。这些阅读技能不仅帮助学生解决英语阅读的问题，对其他学科也有很大的帮助，它们能帮助学生读懂题目，找关键词。阅读中设计的Discovery让学生观察Lost和Found的语编结构、要点，要使用哪些目标语言，启发学生善于观察，培养学生自主学习的能力。紧跟着Lost 和Found的写作练习让学生把刚刚所学的语编结构等知识学以致用，让所学知识和中考挂钩。阅读后设计的是一个过程性写作训练，为帮助学生树立信心，扫清在写作中可能遇到的障碍，教师和学生总结出了写作中可能要用到的常用词汇和常用句型。首先，通过半控制的写作练习，要求学生选择相应的词汇补全两则启事，初步掌握失物招领和寻物启事的简单方法。其次，写作练习在第一个的基础上，由浅到深，按要求完成寻物启事和失物招领的写作，给不同层次的学生提供了展示的机会。最后，教师点评，学生之间互评修改、展示。失物招领和寻物启事非常贴近学生生活，这个写作任务让学生在实际生活中运用语言，从而感知英语学习的重要性及实用性。

（六）课程特点

（1）根据对本单元的教学内容的分析，分两个课时对本单元进行写作教学。第一课时是基于话题“things in the classroom”的写作，第二课时是基于阅读Section B 2b的Lost和Found的写作。将将本单元的话题、功能、结构、任务有机地结合在一起。

（2）注重东西文化的差异。如失物招领等跨文化交际方面的内容，如个性化的学习、合作学习、反思与实践、自主学习、批判性思维，如开头、中心段、结尾、连接词等。

二、教学设计

（一）基于话题下以读促写设计

【教学目标】

1. 语言知识目标

（1）掌握下列词汇：baseball, watch, computer game, ID card, notebook, ring, bag, library, lost, at, call.

（2）理解下列词汇：ask, lost, found, dictionary, e-mail.

（2）掌握下列句型。

What’s this? It’s a watch.

Is it yours? Yes, it is.\No, it isn’t. It’s hers\his.

Are they yours? Yes, they are.\No, they aren’t. They are hers\his.

（3）能够使用目标语言询问东西的所属，或者寻找物品的主人。

（4）能够读懂并能书写简单的招领和寻物启事。

2. 情感态度价值观目标

通过学习“询问物品所属”及阅读“寻物启事和失物招领”，既可以提高学生遇到类似情况时解决问题的能力，激发学生的主动性和学习兴趣，又能培养学生拾金不昧的精神和助人为乐、团结友爱的品德。

【教学重点】

（1）复习新词汇及询问这物品是属于谁的句型。

（2）通过听、说的训练让学生熟练掌握询问物品的所属或寻找物品的主人。

（3）阅读一些简单的失物招领和寻物启事，获得相关信息，并能根据信息写出寻物启事或失物招领。

【教学难点】

阅读一些简单的寻物启事和失物招领，并能根据相关信息写寻物启事和失物招领。

【教学过程】

1. Warming- up and revision

（1）Greet the Students and watch a video about possessive pronouns: mine, yours, his, hers, its.

（2）Review the school things we learned in Section A. Let Students say the school things they have, such as.

（3）Presentation

T: Look at the picture.

(Show students a picture of a ruler.)

T: What’s this in English?

S1:It’s a ruler.

T: Good. (Ask another student.) Is it yours?

S2: Yes, it is.

T: (Ask another student.) Is it yours?

S3: No, it isn’t. It’s his/ hers.

(Practice the other words “baseball, key, notebook and ID card” and the target languages in the same way.)

2. Guessing game

Ask the students put some of their school things into a box before the class.

(Teacher makes a model for the Students.)

T: I have many things in this box. But I'm sorry I don't know whose these are. Could you help me find the owners? Let's see who can find all the owners first and write the owners' names in the chart. You only have two guesses.

Language used for the task:

T: Is this your math book?

S1: Yes, it is. It's mine.

T: Is that your ruler?

S2: No, it isn't. It's hers. My ruler is blue.

T: Kim, is this your dictionary?

S3: No, it isn't. It's his.

T: Jim, are these your erasers?

S4: Yes, they are. They are mine.

T: Here you are.

S4: Thank you.

3. Free talk

(1) We all have many school things. We always lose some school things easily. Now discuss the school things you lose easily with your partner. Write them down on your workbook. Then report them to the class.

(2) Students work with their partners.

(3) Let some students report their things to the class.

(4) T: What do you do if you lost things at school? Have you ever picked up others' things or lost anything? How did you return or find them?

Ask students to discuss and share their ideas: ask for classmate, ask teacher for help and write a lost found.

4. Reading

(1) Introduce the culture background knowledge about Lost and Found notice to Students.

T: Here are four notices on the board. Read the notices and circle the lost things.

（2）Let some students say the answers.

（3）Read the notices again and write down the items. Then check (√) Lost or Found.

（4）Check the answers with the class. Found the target sentences in the notice.

① 第一条信息中，开头是Lin Hai，结尾是Mike，由常识可知是Mike给Lin Hai的留言条，关键句“Is it yours? ”故此条是Found条。

② 由第二条信息中的第一句话“Is this your watch?”，可知是John捡到的手表此条也是Found条。

③ 第三条和第四信息中明确有Found和Lost的关键词。

（5）Give a lost notice and found notice, then let the students discovery the structures of Lost and Found. Including four parts: Title, The lost thing, Ask if it is yours, Contacting ways and names.

5. Writing practice 1

（1）Review the words and target languages in lost and found notice.

（2）Here are two notices but some words in the notes are missing. Read the notices and complete the notices with the words or phone number in the box.

（3）Ask some students read the words in the box. One read them in English. The other read them in Chinese.

（4）Students read and complete the notices.

（5）Check the answers.

6. Reading and Writing practice 2

（1）Read a passage and then fill in the information card.

（2）Check the answers.

（3）T: Anna lost her ID card and a red pencil case. If you are Anna, what will you do?

Ss: … Write a notice and put up in the lost and found.

T: All of you are right. So we are going to write “Lost” or “Found” notice according to the information before.

T: OK. Now let’s try to write it. You may use the one in 2b or the one in 3a as a model.

(Students write their bulletin board notices and the teacher moves around the room offering language support as needed.)

(Ask one student to write it on the blackboard. And others to help correct their work.)

(4) Read a sample writing aloud together.

(5) Writing another lost and found notice according to the given information in Chinese and then check their writings.

7. Critical thinking

Ask students three questions about this class:

(1) What have you learned?

(2) What is interesting?

(3) What questions do you have?

8. Homework

Write a lost and found notice according to the given material.

(二) 基于话题下写作教学设计

Analysis of teaching target

Teaching aims	Language goals	1. To review the words about things in the classroom; 2. To review the sentence patterns about how to identify ownership; 3. To learn to write a short passage
	Ability goals	Developing students' abilities of writing
	Teaching strategy	Task-based teaching, cooperative learning
	Emotional goals	Enable the students to love the environment around them
Important points	This is a... That is an ... These are... Those are...	
Difficult points	Writing practice	

Teaching process

Activities	Content	Intention
Activity 1 warming-up	Sing with the chant and describe the things students watch in the chant	Attract students' attention Arouse interest
Activity 2 revision	Review words about things in the classroom and sentence patterns about how to identify ownership	Review words and sentence patterns
Activity 3 guessing game	Ask students to guess the owners of the things on PPT	Consolidate students' memory
Activity 4 writing strategies	Teach some writing strategies	Teach students how to write
activity 6 summary	Writing strategies	Consolidate new knowledge
activity 7 exercises	Write a short passage	Consolidate new knowledge
activity 8 homework	Write another short passage	Consolidate new knowledge

Teaching procedures

Steps	Students' activities	Teacher's help	Purposes
Warming-up	1. Greetings 2. Going over the words	Ask some questions about things in the classroom	1. Bring out the topic 2. Revise words about things in the classroom
Read aloud	Read out the words about things in the classroom	competition	Make students master the important words
Task 1 Identify ownership	Sentence structure	Show students sentence structures	Prepare for writing
Task2 Writing	Ask students to write a short passage	As a guide	Improve students' writing skills
Task 3	Evaluate your passage	As a guide	Enable students to evaluate their passage
Summary	Conclude writing strategies	Helper	Feedback
Homework	Correct your passage about things in the classroom	As a helper	Consolidation

Handwriting on the blackboard:

This is a pen.

These are pens.

That is a pencil.

Those are pencils.

（三）教学资源——课件

1. 以读促写课件

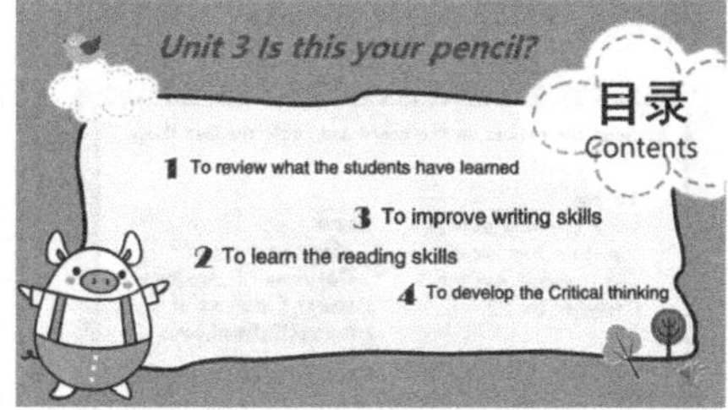

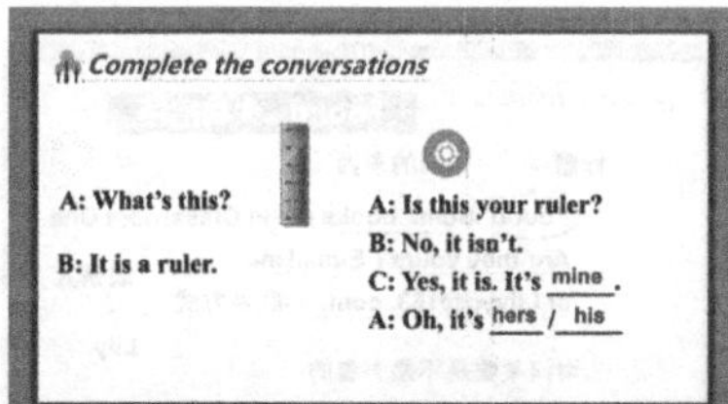

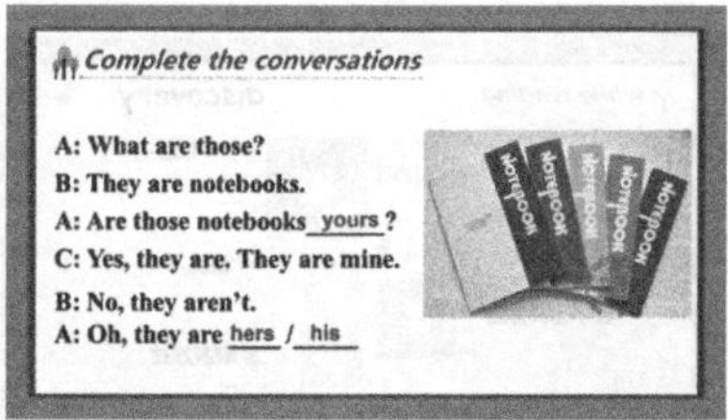

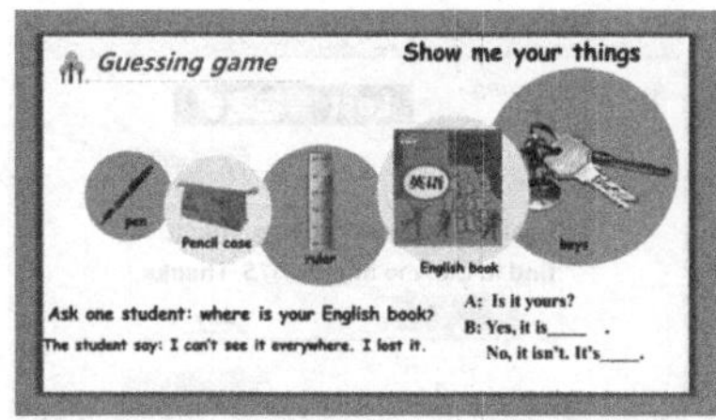

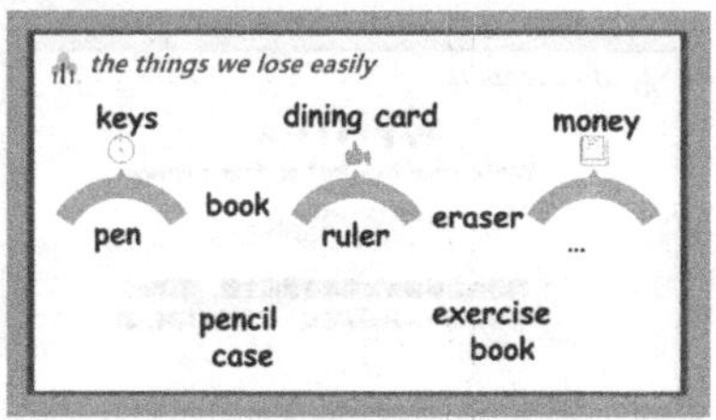

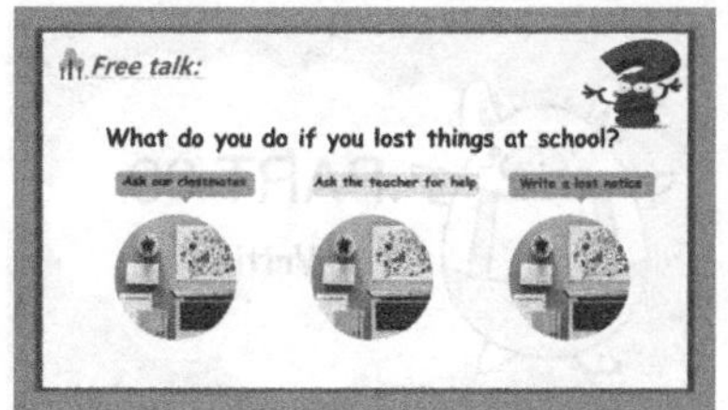

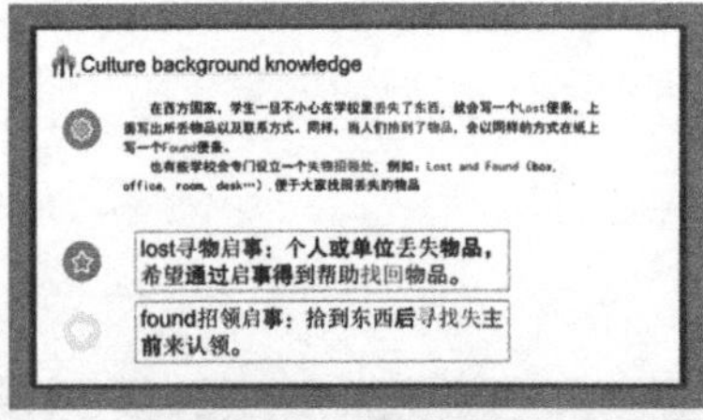
Culture background knowledge
lost寻物启事：个人或单位丢失物品，希望通过启事得到帮助找回物品。
found招领启事：拾到东西后寻找失主前来认领。

PART 02
Reading

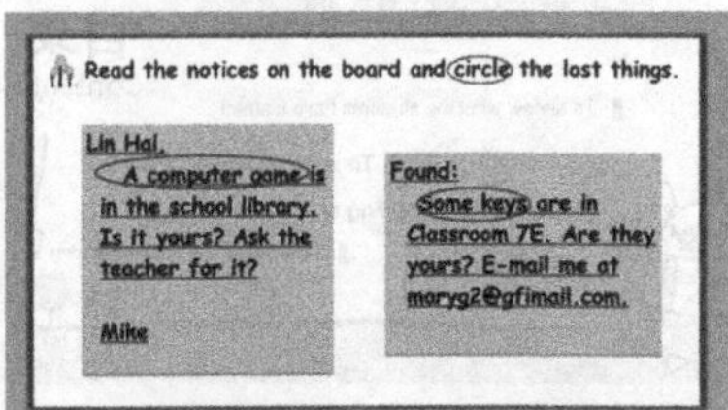
Read the notices on the board and circle the lost things.
Lin Hai,
A computer game is in the school library. Is it yours? Ask the teacher for it?
Mike
Found:
Some keys are in Classroom 7E. Are they yours? E-mail me at maryg2@gfimail.com.

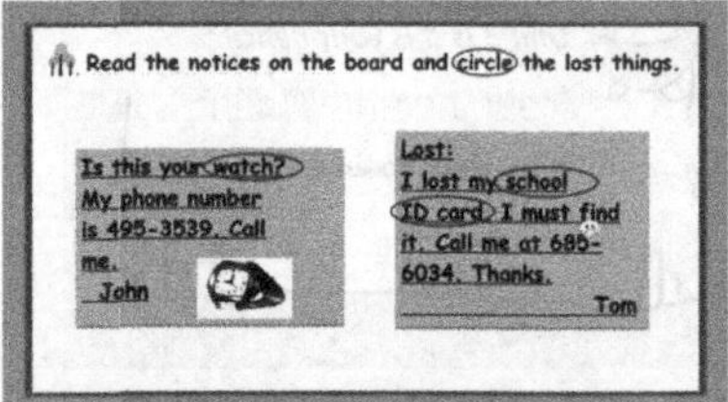
Read the notices on the board and circle the lost things.
Is this your watch? My phone number is 495-3539. Call me.
John
Lost:
I lost my school ID card. I must find it. Call me at 685-6034. Thanks.
Tom

while reading
1. Write down the items
•Number 1
A computer game
•Number 2
Some keys
•Number 3
A watch
•Number 4
A school ID card

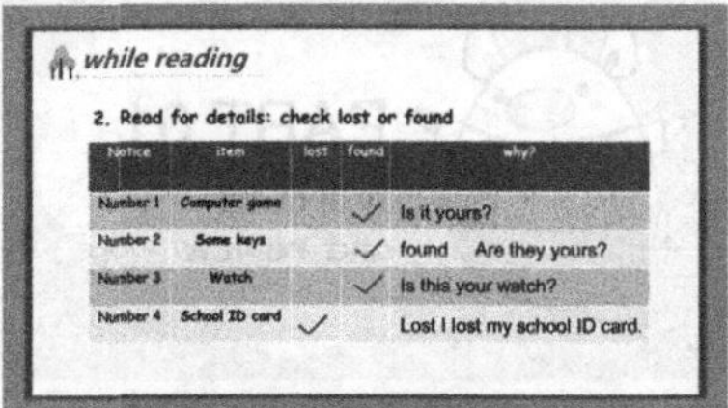
while reading
2. Read for details: check lost or found
Number 1 Computer game ✓ Is it yours?
Number 2 Some keys ✓ found Are they yours?
Number 3 Watch ✓ Is this your watch?
Number 4 School ID card ✓ Lost I lost my school ID card.

while reading
discovery
Found
1. 标题
2. 拾到的东西
3. 询问某物是不是失者的
4. 联系人
5. 联系方式

while reading
Found 失物招领
标题
拾到的东西
Found: Some books are in Classroom One.
Are they yours? E-mail me
at Lilyyg@163. com.—联系方式
联系人
Lily
询问某物是不是失者的

while reading
discovery
1. 标题
2. 丢失的东西及信息
lost
3. 丢失者的姓名
4. 联系方式

while reading
Lost 寻物启事
标题
丢失的东西
Lost: I lost my schoolbag. I must find it. Call me at 785-2375. Thanks.
联系电话
Jay
失者姓名

PART 03
Writing

after reading
Writing
Write your own lost or found notice
写作指导
1. 写寻物启事和失物招领要紧扣主题，写清物品名称、联系人及联系方式，要求表述明确，言简意赅。

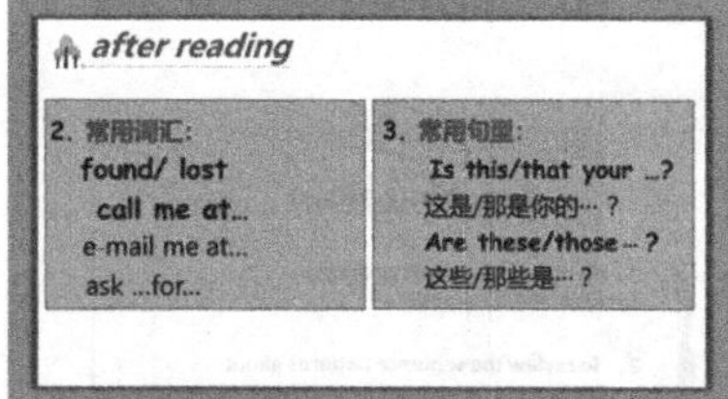
after reading
2. 常用词汇：
found/ lost
call me at...
e-mail me at...
ask ...for...
3. 常用句型：
Is this/that your ...?
这是/那是你的…？
Are these/those ...?
这些/那些是…？

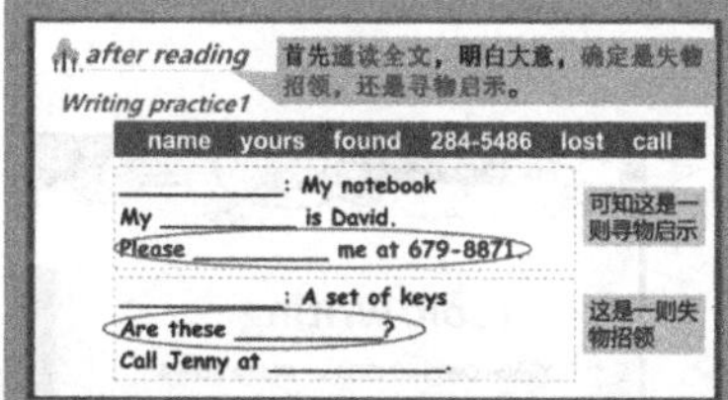
after reading
首先通读全文，明白大意，确定是失物招领，还是寻物启示。
Writing practice1
name yours found 284-5486 lost call
______: My notebook
My ______ is David.
Please ______ me at 679-8871.
可知这是一则寻物启示
______: A set of keys
Are these ______?
Call Jenny at ______.
这是一则失物招领

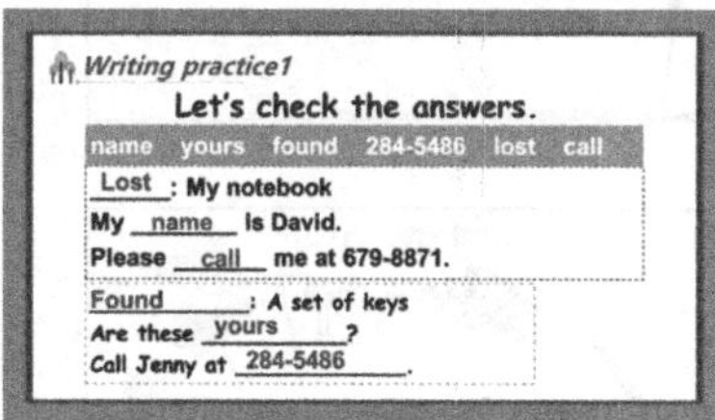
Writing practice1
Let's check the answers.
name yours found 284-5486 lost call
Lost: My notebook
My name is David.
Please call me at 679-8871.
Found: A set of keys
Are these yours?
Call Jenny at 284-5486.

Writing practice 2: 根据这个情境，写一个寻物启事
This is Anna Green. She's an English girl. She's eleven now. She's a good student. Her school is No.5 Middle School. She's in Class Seven. She likes her school very much. Her ID card number is 6695412238. Now her ID card is in her red pencil case, but she lost the pencil case in the school library. Her e-mail address is anna@tom.com.
Information Card
The girl's first name | 1 Anna
The girl's ID card number | 2 6695412238
The missing thing | 3 Pencil case and ID card
The color of the girl's pencil case | 4 red
The girl's e-mail address | 5 anna@tom.com

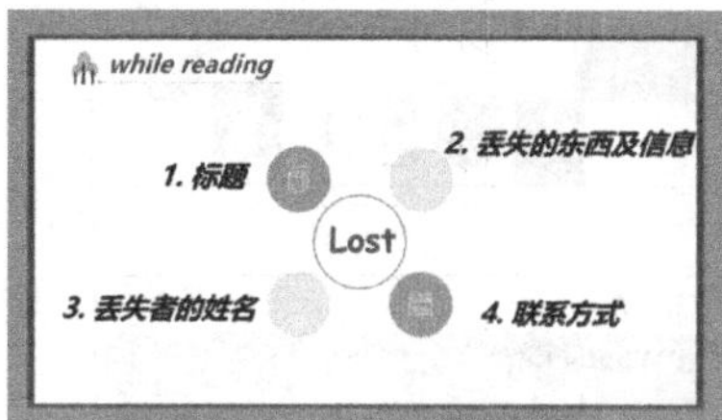
while reading
1. 标题
2. 丢失的东西及信息
Lost
3. 丢失者的姓名
4. 联系方式

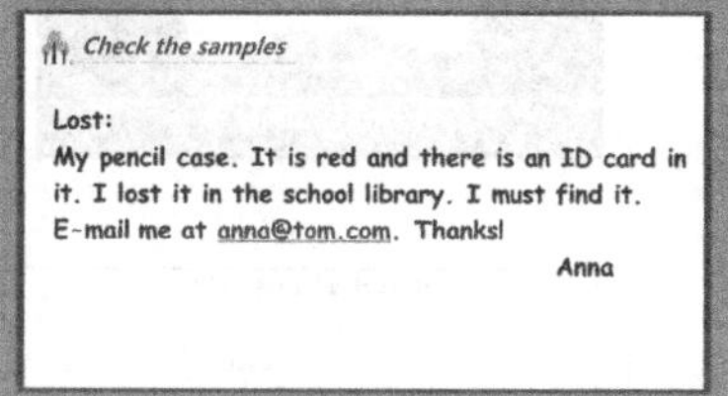
Check the samples
Lost:
My pencil case. It is red and there is an ID card in it. I lost it in the school library. I must find it. E-mail me at anna@tom.com. Thanks!
Anna

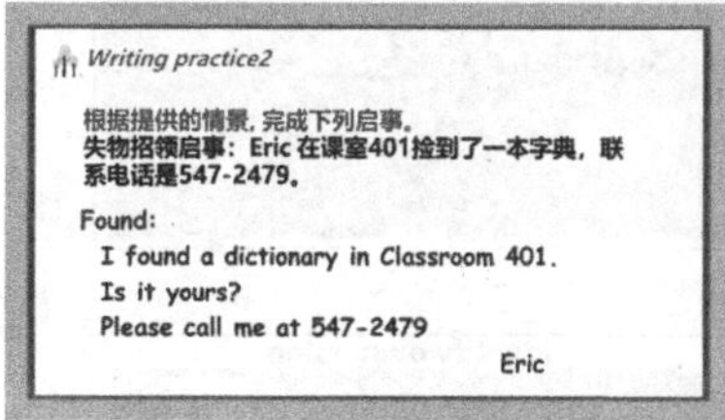
Writing practice2
根据提供的情景，完成下列启事。
失物招领启事：Eric在课室401捡到了一本字典，联系电话是547-2479。
Found:
I found a dictionary in Classroom 401.
Is it yours?
Please call me at 547-2479
Eric

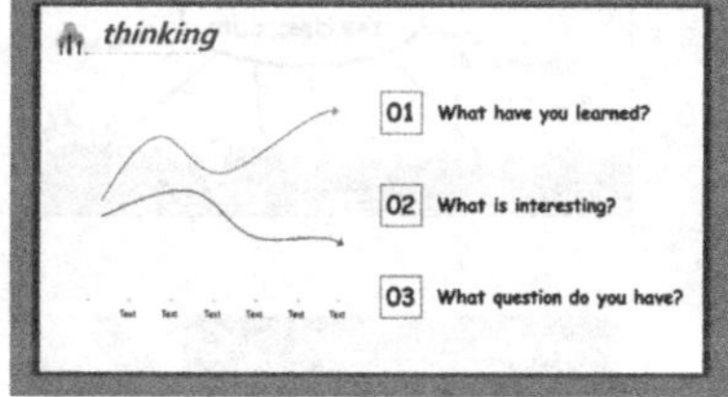
thinking
01 What have you learned?
02 What is interesting?
03 What question do you have?

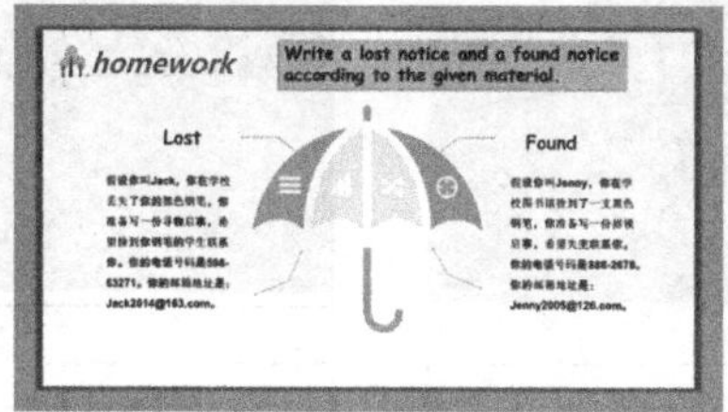
homework
Write a lost notice and a found notice according to the given material.
Lost
Found

2. 话题下写作课件

Topic writing
Xiaolan Overseas Chinese Middle School

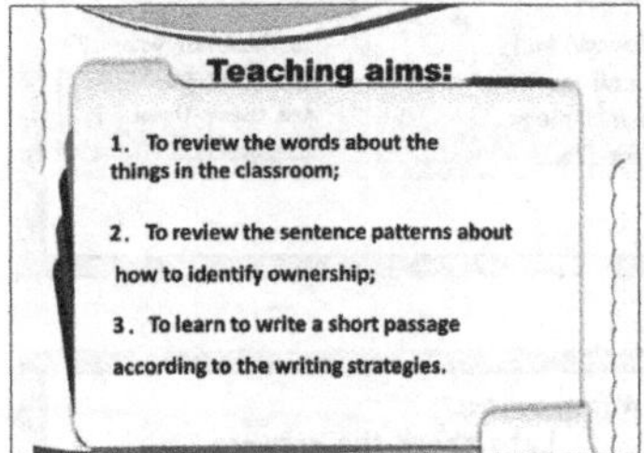
Teaching aims:
1. To review the words about the things in the classroom;
2. To review the sentence patterns about how to identify ownership;
3. To learn to write a short passage according to the writing strategies.

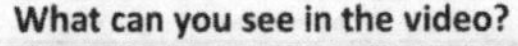
What can you see in the video?

What's this?

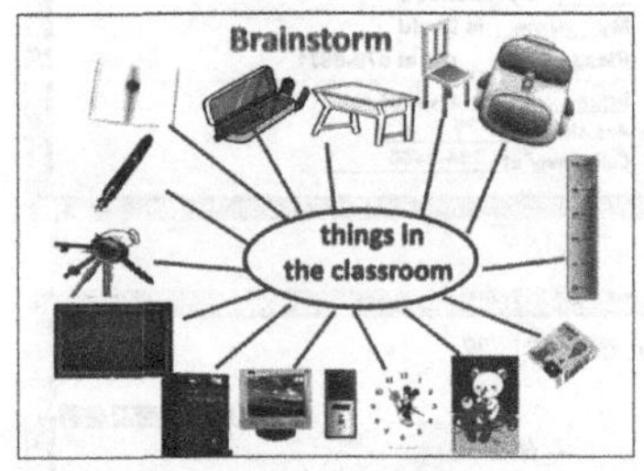
Brainstorm
things in the classroom

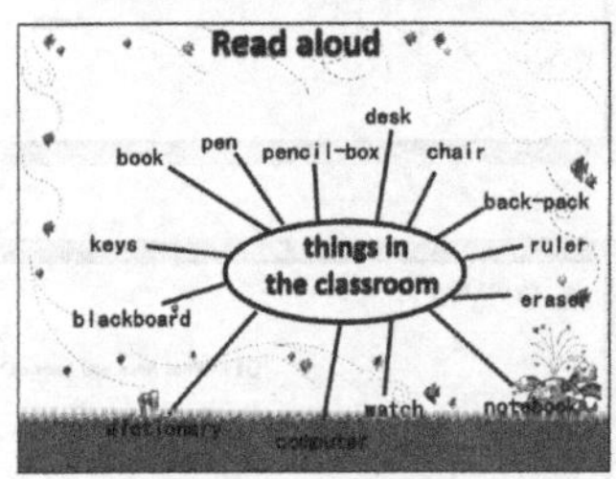
Read aloud
desk
book
pen
pencil-box
chair
back-pack
keys
ruler
things in the classroom
eraser
blackboard
watch
notebook
dictionary
computer

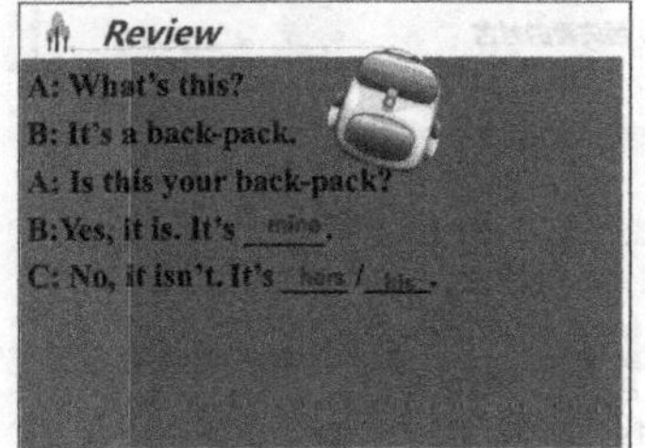
Review
A: What's this?
B: It's a back-pack.
A: Is this your back-pack?
B: Yes, it is. It's mine.
C: No, it isn't. It's hers / his.

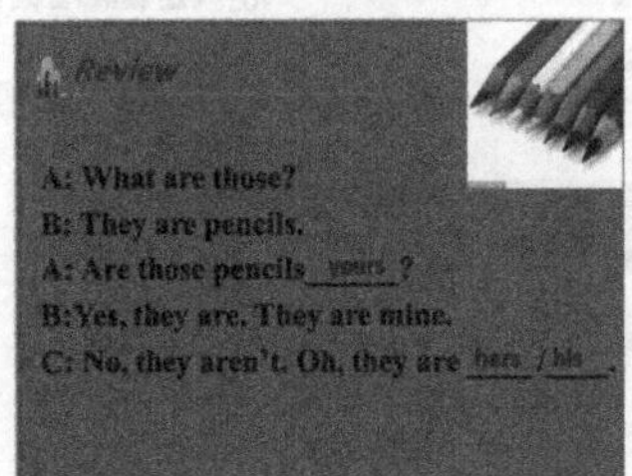
Review
A: What are those?
B: They are pencils.
A: Are those pencils yours?
B: Yes, they are. They are mine.
C: No, they aren't. Oh, they are hers / his.

Identify ownership
This is a pen. It's mine.
These are some pens. It's his.

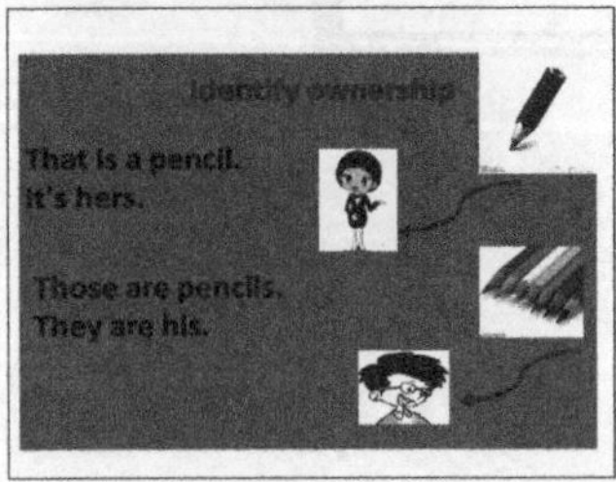
Identify ownership
That is a pencil.
It's hers.
Those are pencils.
They are his.

Identify ownership
This is a book. It's mine.
These are books. It's his.

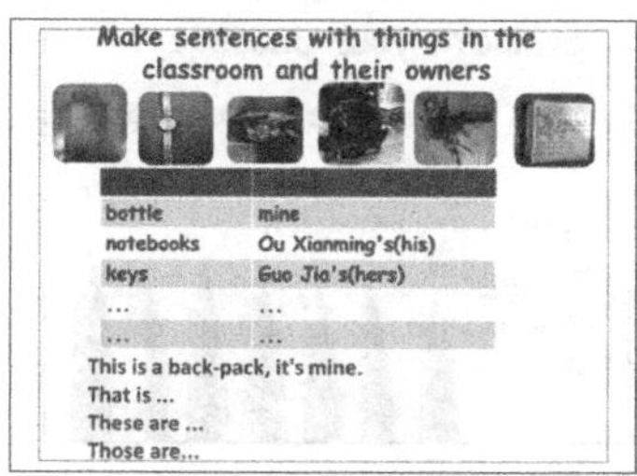

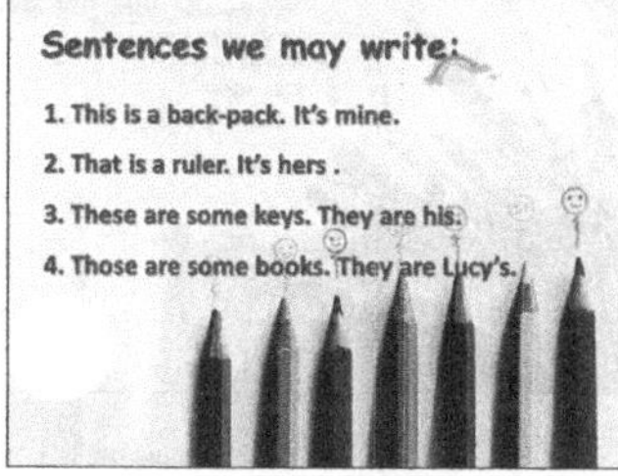

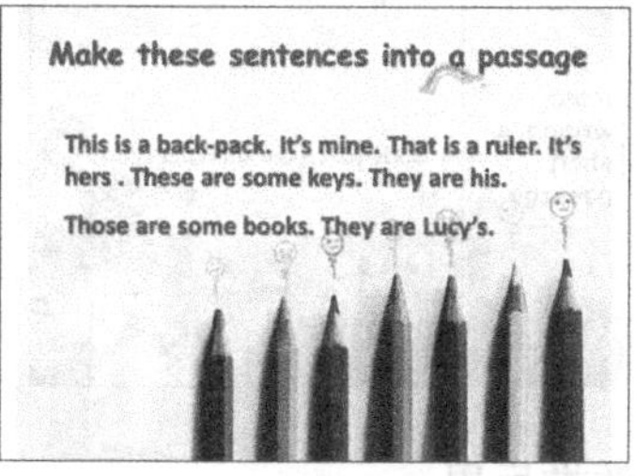

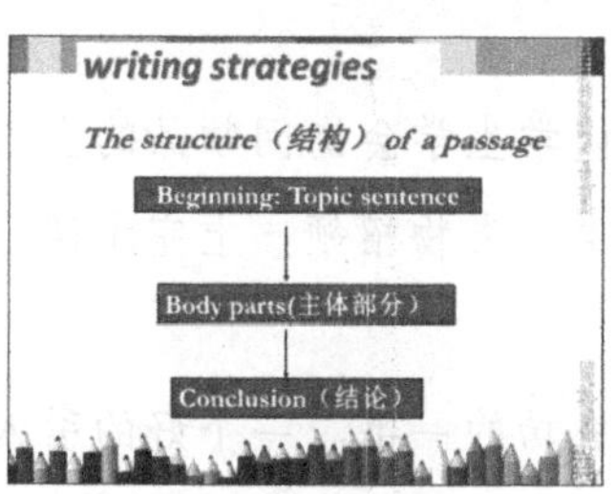

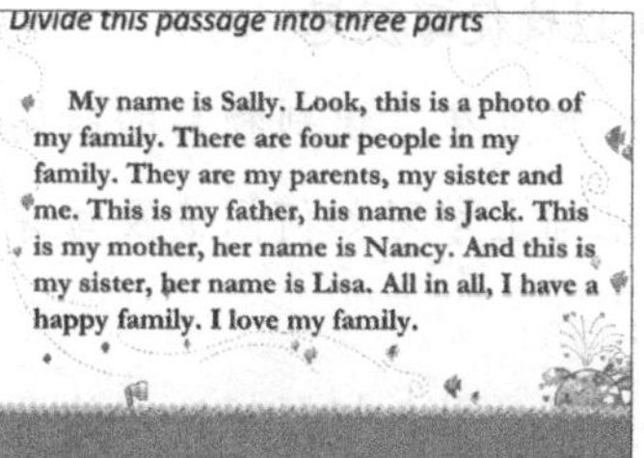

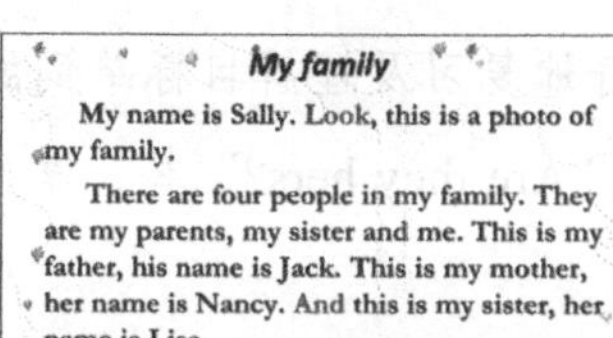

Strategy 策略提示

（一）三段式作文。

（二）我们在描述教室里东西的时候：

1. 要特别注意名词的单复数形式。

2. 可以用一些总结性的词如All in all, in a word...

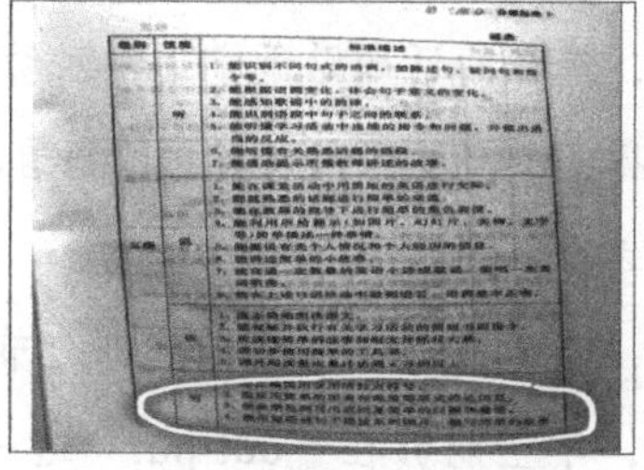

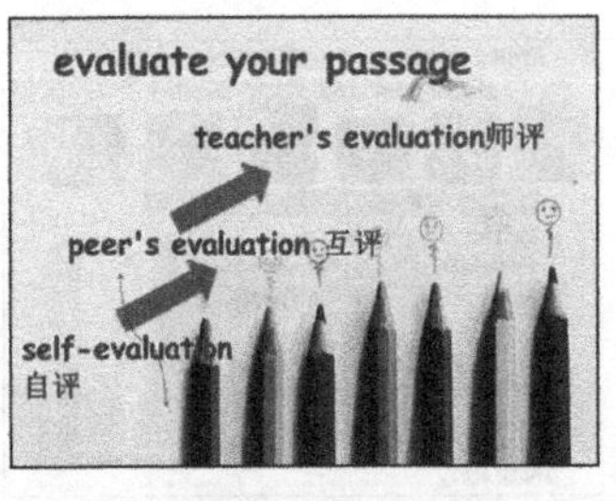

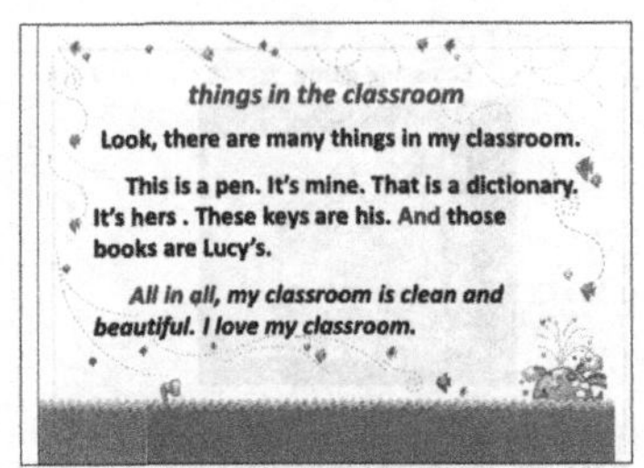

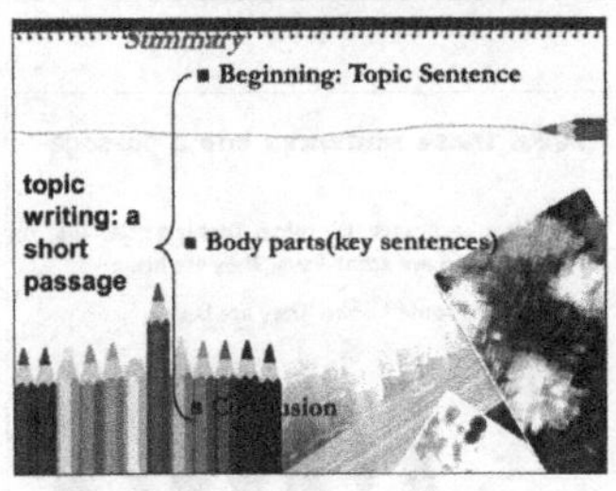

三、教学反思

（一）以读促写反思

本课时重点在“识别物品的所属”，使学生学会询问物品的主人的基本句型，在此基础上学习如何阅读及写寻物启事、失物招领。上完本课后，笔者有以下收获：

第一，课堂引入切题好！好的开头是成功的一半。一个好的引入能够让学生快速进入学习状态并参与基本的思考。本课时引入一段关于名词性物主代词的英语歌曲视频，让学生在听歌的同时很好地复习及理解目标单词的用法。随后，教师便提出相关的问题“Is it yours?” “Are they hers?”等，学生们也能给出正确的答案，而这些答案也正好切题。

第二，阅读及写作的技巧解读到位，配上及时快速的朗读，学习效果好！引导学生发现寻物启事及失物招领，并总结它们的文体要素，训练了学生的观察、总结及思维能力。

第三，选择的话题贴近学生，活动内容丰富。寻找课室物品的失主的游戏，学生热情高、参与度高，在自然的语言环境中充分练习了本节课的目标语言。

不足之处：

第一，教学设计在前面铺垫部分节奏有些缓慢，可以再快一点。

第二，学生能够在“out-put”这一阶段自由表述，但时间不够，如果老师多一些范围假设及时间，学生就有更多的机会展示自己，也能更好地调动学生的思维。

总之，本课时教学能够让孩子掌握基本的读写技巧去写寻物启事和失物招领，课堂上联系充分，自然过渡，是一堂能够让学生印象深刻的课。

（二）话题写作反思

这节课让学生围绕“教室里的物品”这个话题从单词到句子再到短文章，大多数学生都有话可说，较好地激发了学生的兴趣。同时，在课堂上知识点的呈现由浅入深，活动方式灵活多样，学生表现积极活跃，主动参与，做课堂的主人。但是，部分学生不喜欢开口说英语，胆量不够，口语表达能力仍然有所欠缺。教师应该关注到每一位学生，多鼓励和表扬，让学生在练习中体验到学英语的愉悦感和成就感。

【教学建议】

教师应该尽量多让学生开口说英语，多练习，多组织活动，安排任务。一定要由浅入深，循序渐进，引导学生,让学生学会用英语做事情。

第五部分　初中英语话题下教学介绍

（一）优化课堂教学，创建高效课堂

在提倡“减负增效”的今天，本专著针对不同课型探索了五种有效的教学策略：

1.词汇教学

（1）词汇教学要结合情境。

（2）词汇教学要利用语篇。

（3）词汇教学要培养策略。

（4）分层次、分阶段处理生词。

（5）流程：情境化—具体化—发现式—循环式。

2. 听说课教学

（1）要重视排除影响学生口语表达的主要障碍。

（2）听的技能训练要重视听力过程性训练。

（3）流程：pre-listening—while-listening (main idea, details, key words, extension）—post-listening。

3. 阅读课教学

（1）强化阅读过程，优化阅读活动设计。

（2）在课堂上充分利用图示阅读策略实施英语阅读教学。

（3）教学中通过语言知识增强学生的思想性、人文性。

流程：

① pre-reading（读前活动）：开阔学生视野，激发学生学习兴趣。

② while-reading（读中活动）：培养学生阅读策略，交互式阅读。

fast reading（略读）

skimming: 观察语篇特点，了解阅读任务。

scanning: 寻找关键时间点。

careful reading（精读）

finding details：根据时间点寻找相应的活动。

focusing on words, expressions or structures: 重难点解析。

③ post-reading（课后活动）：分享观点，发表见解，联系实际生活。

4. 语法课教学

在教学中增加开放性的任务型活动和探究性的学习内容，使学生有机会表达自己的看法与观点，使学生学会合作，发展与人沟通的能力。我们形成了自己的语法教学模式。

（1）语法教学的目标设计让学生学会用语言去做事情。

（2）语法教学过程设计要体现学生课堂学习的主体地位。

（3）在语法教学效果的检测中，重在交际，容忍错误。

流程：感知—发现—归纳—点拨—练习—活用。

5. 初三复习课模式

初三英语复习课堂中以任务带出综合复习，结合中考题型，突出用本话题所学语言去做事情。将《义务教育课程标准教科书英语（新目标）》的内容重新整合，按照任务型语言测试的思路设计。

（1）话题带出词汇复习，系统地归纳了本话题需要掌握的词汇。

（2）功能带出句型复习，主要包括完成任务所需的语言结构。

（3）结构带出语法复习，将语法分散在各个话题中。

流程：话题—结构—功能—任务的模式 。

在不同的课型中，以学生自主学习为主线，激发了学生的参与热情，实现“教得有效、学得愉快、考得满意、发展充分”的课堂教学效果，充分体现了语言工具性和人文性的有效结合。

第六部分　初中英语话题下案例展示

话题下语法教学案例

一、话题下的语法教学

1. 教学理念

重视语言结构的表意功能，倡导三维语法教学。

2011版课标：

五级	语法	1. 理解附录“语法项目表”中所列语法项目并能在特定语境中使用； 2. 了解常用语言形成的基本结构和常用表意功能； 3. 在实际运用中体会和领悟语言形成的表意功能； 4. 理解并运用恰当的语言形成描述人和物；描述具体事件和具体行为的发生、发展过程，描述时间、地点及方式；比较人、物体及事等

例：被动语态——被动语态常使用于非主观的文体。在非主观文体中作者不把自己和受话人置于语境之中，没有必要或故意避免强调动作的执行者，如科技文体、新闻文体、常见通知等。

2. 话题下语法板块的设计理念

增加了语法练习，强化语法训练，增强语法意识；体现语法学习的过程，从关注语言形式到关注语言意义，最后走向语言运用；渗透语法教学的体验式和发现式教学思想。第一层次：Form；第二层次：Meaning；第三层次：Use。

【案例】

话题下的初中英语语法课教学设计

GFI　Unit 9　I like music that I can dance to. B5

Topic: Music and movies

一、基本信息

1. 教学内容

（1）教材内容：人教版九年级第九单元——话题“music”中的语法项目：定语从句。

（2）语言支架：感知—发现—归纳—点拨—练习—活用。

2. 学生：中山市小榄镇华侨中学初三学生，使用人教版GFI教材。

3. 教师：广东省中山市小榄镇华侨中学，与该初三学生第一次教学。

4. 日期：2018 年10 月 21 日。

二、教学内容分析

1. 语法知识内容

（1）语法知识内容：定语从句（关系词 that 引导的定语从句）。

（2）话题知识内容：音乐music。

2. 语法技能内容：通过引导学生感知—发现—归纳—点拨—练习—活用，从话题学习素养内容。

3. 话题学习素养内容

（1）文化陶冶：通过音乐话题的层层深入，挖掘音乐在人类生活和交际中的重大作用。

（2）思维拓展：针对实际问题，使学生勇于思考，积极创新，善于表达。

（3）学习发展：用所学话题和语言结构解决生活中的实际问题。

三、发展目标

1. 语言素养

学生几乎能意识到各种音乐带给人们的不同感受，绝大多数学生能结合不同种类的音乐感受音乐的特性，部分学生能表达自己对不同音乐的喜好理由。

2. 文化素养

学生几乎能认识到人际交往中音乐所起的积极作用，绝大多数学生对音乐能批判性地看待，部分学生能达到自如地表达对生活中的音乐的喜好。

3. 思维素养

学生几乎都能意识到通过音乐可以治疗人们的心理问题，体验思维拓展性，并得到相应发展。

4. 学习素养

学生几乎能使用that关系词引导的定语从句表达自己对音乐的喜好，并了解定语从句语法规律，绝大多数学生能通过发现和练习的策略习得定语从句的语法结构并自己造句。

四、课时任务

1. 任务情境

（1）现代社会生活节奏很快，人们很容易患上各种身体疾病或心理疾病，例如考试前过度紧张、生活无聊没有目标、情感孤独、身心疲惫却不得不疲于奔命、考试不及格，各种担心纷至沓来，然而幸好有音乐的存在，音乐可以缓解这些问题。因此，请根据具体问题，向这些人们给出你认为最有效的音乐来解决他们的问题。

（2）积极思考并用定语从句表达所学、所感兴趣的东西和其他问题。

2. 任务行为

通过话题music引导学生感知—发现—归纳—点拨—练习—活用定语从句，使学生有机地把本节课的语言目标（定语从句）与语言学习观中的社会建构主义相结合。

3. 任务成果

学生用所学话题和语言结构，积极创新，善于表达，并解决生活中的实际问题。

五、教学用具

1. 学生用具（六人学习小组）。

2. 教师用具：PPT课件、多媒体教学资源与设备。

六、教学过程，见表7–14。

表7–14　教学过程

阶段与环节	师生活动	教学目的	教学用具
课前	通过网络平台调查学生喜欢什么类型的音乐及电影	1. 通过调查了解学校学生对本单元相关背景知识掌握情况； 2. 了解学生的认知状况，为教学设计做准备	手机、电脑

续表

阶段与环节	师生活动	教学目的	教学用具
课中：导入	1. 教师通过了解分组情况，对本节课的基本要求进行简单说明； 2. 教师让学生看一段有音乐的视频； 3. 教师通过思维导图让学生回忆他们所知的音乐种类	1. 让师生熟悉新的教学环境； 2. 激活学生相关背景知识与体验； 3. 引入任务，让学生熟知不同种类的音乐	PPT播放音乐视频
课中：感知	教师利用学生所熟知的音乐种类，逐步引导学生用that引导的定语从句模仿表达	让学生理解、感受that引导的定语从句基本结构	
课中：发现、归纳	教师利用媒体情境逐步引导学生用that引导的定语从句表达自己的音乐喜好	1. 借助媒体情景，让学生发现并归纳that引导的定语从句基本结构； 2. 关注音乐特征，发展语言素养、文化素养	
课中：点拨和练习	教师有针对性、量力性和典型性地让学生当堂训练	1. 关注学生的认知规律，鼓励学生求异思维； 2. 通过课堂训练，让学生学会发现问题、分析问题和解决问题	
课中：任务成果展示与反省	1. 学生用所学话题和语言结构，积极创新，就各种问题、心理疾病者分享提供音乐治疗的意见； 2. 学生思考：这节课学到什么？你对什么感兴趣？你还有什么问题	给学生展示的机会，发展思维和文化素养	
课中：评价	学生自评、他评和教师评	引导学生有理据判断，发展思维素养	
课后：作业	用that关系词引导的定语从句书面表达自己所感兴趣的东西	指向真实的生活，发展相关素养	

二、话题下语法教学课件

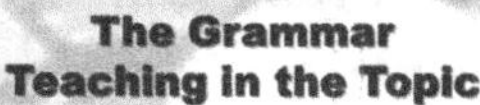

Function: express preferences
Topic: music
Structure: relative clauses with that
language goal:
Enable Ss to use relative clauses with *that* correctly.
Emotion Goal: get to know the important role of music in human life and communication.
Learning strategy: Discover and practice

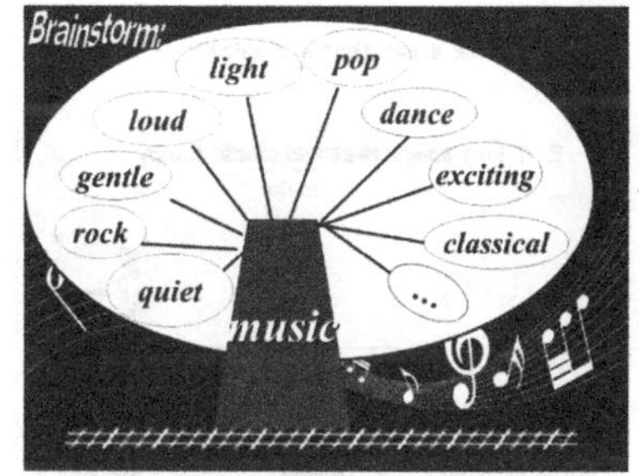

Brainstorm:

Kinds of music

classical music → music that is classical
pop music → music that is popular
loud music → music that is loud
quiet music → music that is quiet
light music → music that is light
dance music → music that you can dance to
…

Let's discover What do you think of the music?

active / popular/ smart
make me happy
dance to the music

A: What kind of music do you like?
B: I like music that is popular.
C: I like music that makes me happy.
D: I like music that I can dance to.

Let's discover

moving/ sweet/ exciting ;
make me surprised;

A: What kind of music do you like?
B: I like music that is moving/ sweet/ exciting.
C: I like music that makes me surprised.

Let's discover

soft/ beautiful/ quiet/ gentle/relaxing;
give me something to think about;

A: What kind of songs do you love?
B: I love songs that are soft/ beautiful/ quiet/ gentle/relaxing.
C: I love songs that give me something to think about.

Find out! that在定语从句中指代什么？

1. music → dance music → music that we can dance to
2. a song → a beautiful song → a song that is beautiful
3. a flower → a blue flower → a flower that is blue
4. things → interesting things → things that are interesting

which

Find out! that 在定语从句中的成份

1. I like songs that are popular.
(S-主语)
I like songs. The songs are popular.
(S-主语)

2. I love music that I can dance to.
(O-宾语)
I love music. I can dance to the music.
(O-宾语)

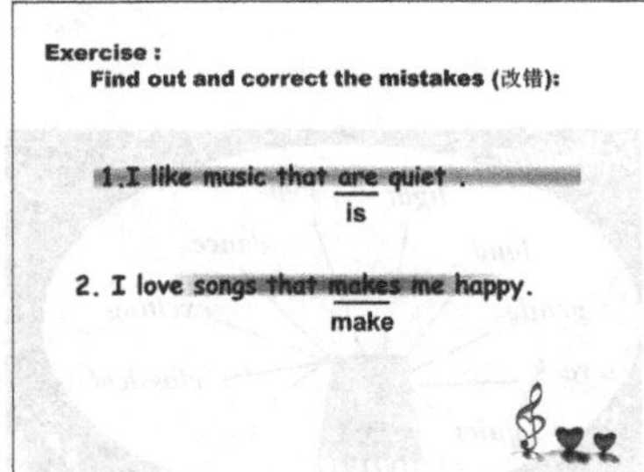

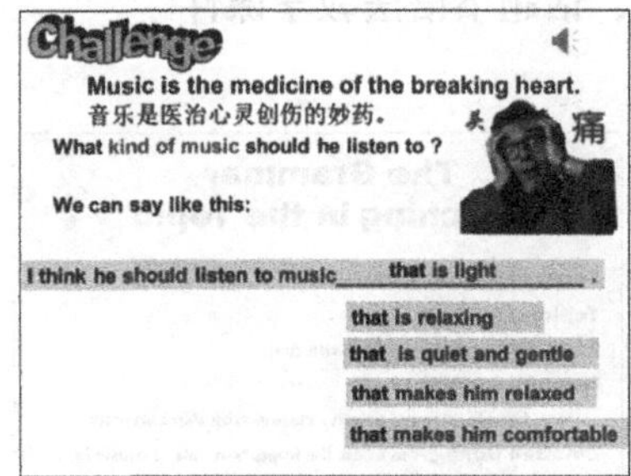

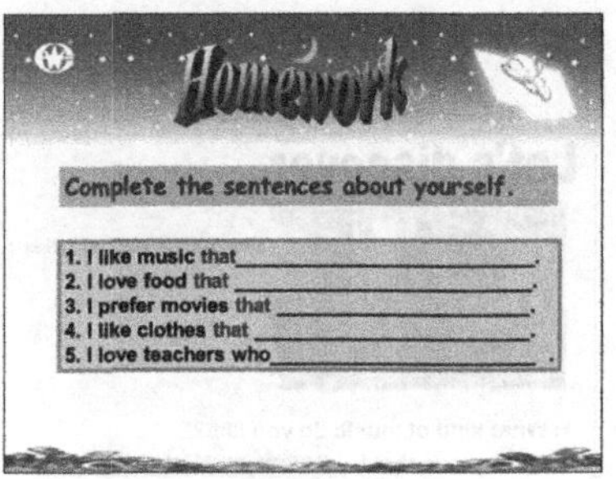

话题下初三复习案例

1. 教学理念

加强对教学过程的指导与帮助。现代外语教育注重语言学习的过程，强调语言学习的实践性，主张学生在语境中接触、体验和理解真实语言，并在此基础上学习和运用语言。语言学习的过程：Input—听，读；Presentation，Intake—语境，意义，刺激，思维；Internalization—不同层次的练习，知识整合与重构；Output—说，写，Use。因此，课堂教学要有效地把不同生命体之间的Communication，Interaction，Generation，Exchange，Problem-solving穿插起来，在课堂中充分关注学生、突出学生个性、启迪学生思维、促进学生发展；

在尊重、唤醒教学过程中，激励学生生命个体，体现教与学的过程。

2. 如何体现学习的过程性

在教学过程中，引导学生不仅要行为参与，更要思维参与；帮助学生实现在学习过程中的角色转换：由Language learner 变为 language user.

【案例】

初三英语话题复习教学设计

Topic: Personal Traits

结构语言：复习形容词

1. 基本信息

（1）教学内容。人教版——初三话题复习：Personal Traits

（2）任务行为。通过话题Personal Traits引导学生复习词汇—功能结构—语法复习—练习巩固—拓展表达—情感发展，使学生有机地把本节课的语言目标（形容词的比较级）与语言学习观中的社会建构主义相结合。

（3）任务成果。学生用所学话题和语言结构，积极创新，善于表达人与人之间不同之处。

2. 教学用具

教师用具：PPT课件、多媒体教学资源与设备。

3. 教学过程（见表7–15）

表7–15　教学过程

阶段与环节	师生活动	教学目的	教学用具
课前	通过微信了解更多学生的基本信息	1. 了解学校学生英语水平及学习情况； 2. 了解学生认知状况，为教学设计做准备	手机、电脑
课中：话题导入词汇	1. 教师让学生看一段有关人物性格特质的视频； 2. 教师通过轻松的相声和电影人物，结合思维导图让学生回忆他们所知的人物外形和性格的形容词	1. 激活学生相关背景知识与体验； 2. 通过生动形象的人物，展现个人性格特质； 3. 引入任务，让学生复习相关类型形容词	PPT播放经过剪辑的相声视频和电影视频

续表

阶段与环节	师生活动	教学目的	教学用具
课中：词汇带动功能结构语言	教师利用学生所熟知的形容词，逐步引导学生复习形容词比较级功能语言	让学生复习巩固所学过的形容词比较级和重要句型	
课中：知识小结与活用挑战	列出重点语法知识清单进行小结，强化功能语言，并利用创设的特别情境，让学生思考并对二者进行比较	1. 复习语法知识； 2. 培养学生思维、观察和对比能力，发展其语言素养、文化素养	
课中：拓展话题阅读	教师选择具有人物特征变化的短文阅读材料，训练学生的阅读技能和思维能力	1.关注学生认知规律，鼓励学生求异思维； 2.通过课堂训练，让学生学会发现问题、分析问题和解决问题	
课中：深入对比，升华情感及反思	1. 学生根据视频了解并对比力克·胡哲与自己的不同之处，反思自己； 2. 学生思考：这节课学到什么？我对什么感兴趣？我还有什么问题	给学生思考、对比和观察的机会，引导学生反思、表达自我，发展思维品格和文化素养，对其实际生活起积极的引导作用	
课后：作业	观察对比自己家人的外表和性格特征，记录下来并形成文字	指向真实的生活，发展相关素养	

4. 初三话题复习课件

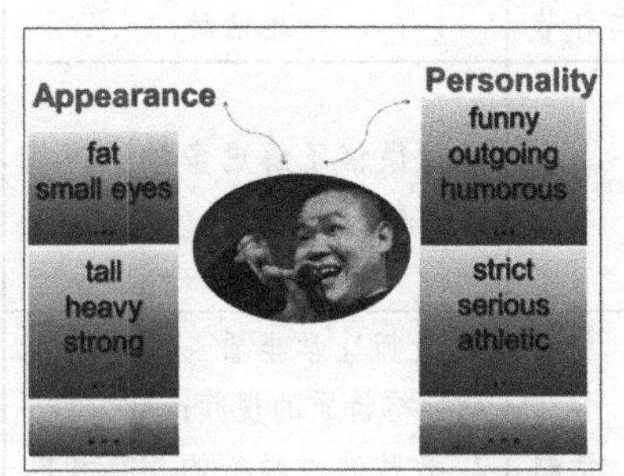

Yao is more athletic than Chou.

Yao is as popular as Chou.

Wang Junkai is more popular than Cai Xukun.

Cai Xukun is not as popular as Wang Junkai.

practice

Find out more differences between you and your classmates.

You can say like this（仿照如下）：

My **hair** is **longer** than **Jenny's**.

Jane is **smarter** than me.

I can play the guitar **better** than **Kate.**

Her **English** is **better** than **mine**.

Grammar **comparative degree 比较级**

(1) 形容词比较级（两种事物比较）
- taller, heavier, bigger... (er)
- more popular ... (more)

(2) 重点句型： A比B更……

eg.Yao is taller than Harden.

(3) 重点句型：as + 形容词原级 + as ... 和……一样
not as (so) +形容词原级 + as... 和……不一样

eg. Yao is as popular as Chou.
Cai Xukun is not as popular as Wang Junkai.

(4)表示程度的递增：比较级＋and +比较级（越来越…）

eg. My hometown is becoming more and more beautiful.

In the movie Dangal, the two sisters are changing step by step.

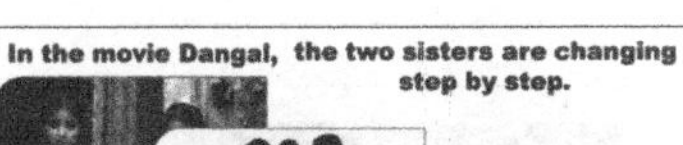

They are becoming stronger and stronger.
better and better
more and more popular

Reading **Jane is different**

Two years ago, Jane was a student. She had long hair. She got up at six a.m. And went to bed at 11:30 p.m. She played volleyball very well. She enjoyed telling jokes with her friends. She got along well with her classmates.

Now, she is a teacher. She is more hard-working and more serious. She has shorter hair. She is heavier, because she is busier and doesn't have any time to do sports.

	personality changes	appearance changes	the same
Two years ago	funnier more easygoing		
Now			

Reading **Jane is different**

Two years ago, Jane was a student. She had long hair. She got up at six a.m. And went to bed at 11:30 p.m. She played volleyball very well. She enjoyed telling jokes with her friends. She got along well with her classmates.

Now, she is a teacher. She is more hard-working and more serious. She has shorter hair. She is heavier, because she is busier and doesn't have any time to do sports.

	personality changes	appearance changes	the same
Two years ago	funnier more easygoing		
Now	more serious more hard working		

Reading **Jane is different**

Two years ago, Jane was a student. She had long hair. She got up at six a.m. And she went to bed at 11:30 p.m. She played volleyball very well. She enjoyed telling jokes with her friends. She got along well with her classmates.

Now, she is a teacher. She is more hard-working and more serious. She has shorter hair. She is heavier, because she is busy and doesn't have any time to do sports.

	personality changes	appearance changes	the same
Two years ago	funnier more easygoing	had longer hair thinner	busy
Now	more serious more hard working	heavier has shorter hair	busy

Watch the video and find out differences between you and him.

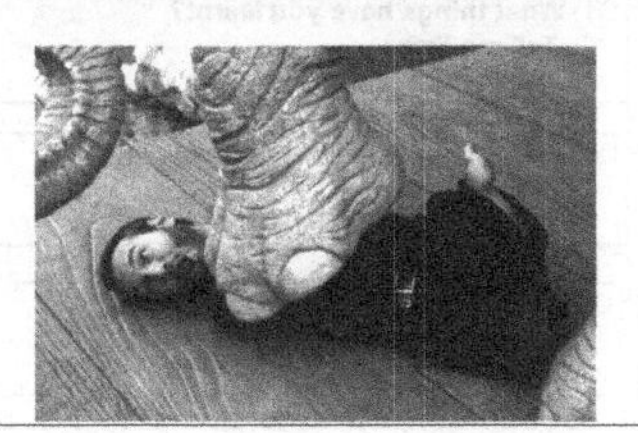

He can ...

surf

fish

We are ______ than him!

We can ______ better (faster...)than him!

BUT, he is ______ than us.

BUT, he __ better (faster...)than us!

We are taller than him!

We are healthier than him!

We can run more quickly than him!

BUT, he is more athletic.

BUT, he is more hard-working.

BUT, he is funnier.

BUT, he is more outgoing.

BUT, he is more famous.

Don't judge people by appearance!

不要以貌取人!

Don't care too much about your appearance!

不要过分关注自己的外表!

Inner beauty is more important!

内在美才更重要!

Thinking

Q1: What things have you learnt?
Tell me three.
(请你说出本节课学到的三点)

Q2: What things are you interested in?
Tell me two.
(请你说出本节课感兴趣的两点)

Q3: What questions do you still have?
Ask me one.
(请你说出对本节课还有什么疑问一个)

话题下听说课型案例

1. 教学理念

听说领先、读写跟上。

2. 问题

（1）教材听说板块是如何设计的？

（2）如何在听说教学中体现学习的过程与方法？

（3）Section A 2d 教什么？怎么教？

（4）学生学到了什么？

（5）考试/课程标准怎么达标？

《英语课程标准》要求听力技能与策略达到以下几点：听关键信息、听大意和主题、确定事物的发展顺序或逻辑关系、预测、理解说话人的意图和态度及评价所听内容。

3. 听前活动

热身活动、熟悉话题、熟悉相关词语和句型、接受背景信息、提出需要解决的问题及明确任务。

4. 听的活动

听信息，排顺序；听信息，列项目；听信息，补全文字；听并画图；听并制作；听并填空；听写；听并记笔记；听指令，完成系列动作；听并选择与听并匹配。

5. 听后活动

口头回答问题、小组讨论、模拟对话、复述或转述所听内容、做出书面回应、总结要点、改编所听内容及表达个人感受和观点。

【案例】

话题下的听说教学设计

Topic: Mysteries

GFI　Unit 8　It must belong to Carla B5

1. 基本信息

Unit 8　It must belong to Carla 第一课时

（1）听说教学素养内容。通过话题的层层深入，以神秘事件（mysteries）为主线，借助信息差(information gap)，让学生了解英语中如何进行推测、猜测，培养学生的逻辑思维能力，同时让学生懂得在生活中遇见实际问题和困难的时候，如何运用推测去合理分析问题、解决问题，帮助学生更好地体验生活细节，感受生活的不易和美好，并由此学会热爱生活。重点突破学生用自己的语言去表达"推测的理由（reasons）"，去回答"为什么(why)"，积极表达自己的逻辑推断，甚至鼓励在中文支持的情况下用简单的英文去表达思想。

（2）学习发展。学生几乎能说出Section A中提出的基本词汇，绝大多数学生能结合功能语言谈论自己对物品所属人的推测及理由，能正确使用must，could，might和can't. 部分学生能表达自己对神秘事件发生的深层挖掘，以及对自己没有见过或体验过的事情的猜测及发表个人观点、理由。学生几乎能认识到碰到突发事件或奇怪事件时要有自己的分辨能力，能够通过现象表层去推断、猜测事情的真相。绝大多数学生能够对突发事件或奇怪事件的现状批判地看待。学生几乎能意识到通过谈论神秘事件或突发事件发现功能语言的结构并尝试使用继而灵活使用之。在对语言结构的运用中发现自己的逻辑思维能力和对事物的分辨能力，学生几乎能使用功能结构语言must，can't，could，might和文学名著词汇谈论是否阅读过书本。

2. 课时任务

情态动词表推测是一个很灵活、很常用的初中阶段必须掌握的语言点。

3. 教学过程，见表7–16

表7–16　教学过程

阶段与环节	师生活动	教学目的	教学用具
课前	通过一首英语歌进入新课	准备进入教学	电脑
课中：引出话题	通过猜动物引出本单元的结构语言	让学生感知本单元的词汇和结构语言	PPT播放
课中：呈现结构语言	通过图片逐步引导学生使用结构语言	让学生发现本单元的词汇和结构语言	PPT播放不同的图片
课中：听前准备	巩固语言结构的使用并能熟练运用	1.让学生运用本单元的词汇和结构语言； 2.逐步培养学生的思维、观察和模仿造句能力，发展语言素养、文化素养	PPT播放各种书本的画面
课中：听力练习及听力技巧渗透	对教材1b、2a、2b进行整合，对教材中的听力题型进行改编，引导学生围绕一次“野炊”，猜测图片中呈现的东西可能是谁的，并且渗透听力的一般性技巧	1.关注学生个性发展，鼓励学生在听材料时，关注细节、注重听力策略指导； 2.让学生学会发现问题、分析问题和解决问题	播放听力语音
课中：听后拓展，引导学生围绕本节课主线“Mysteries”，借助表推测的情态动词进行陈述和升华情感及反思	通过音频、视频让学生推测可能是什么、为什么	在注重双基基础上，突破学生思维发展及实践运用	播放视频
课后：作业	围绕自己日常生活中一个问题，说明可能引起其的原因及解决方法	指向真实的生活，发展相关素养	

4. 话题下听说课件

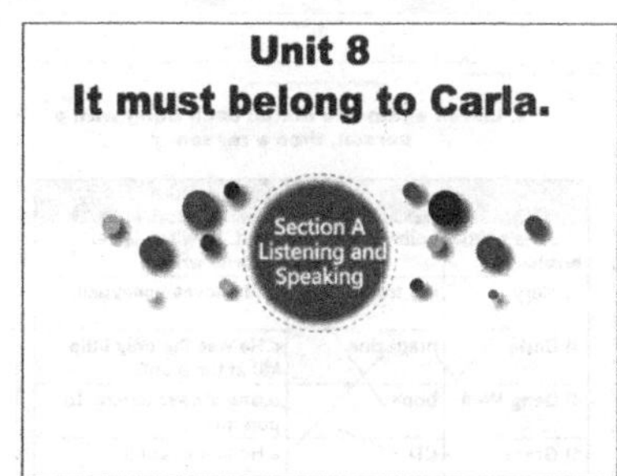

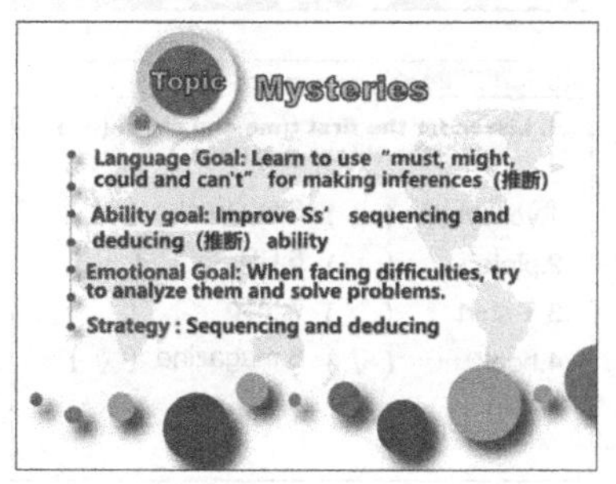

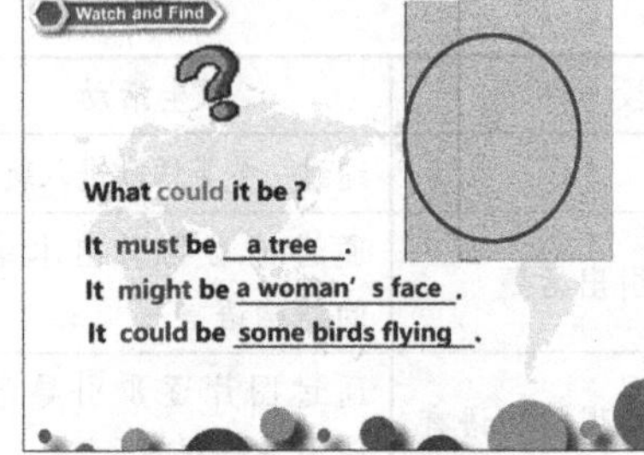

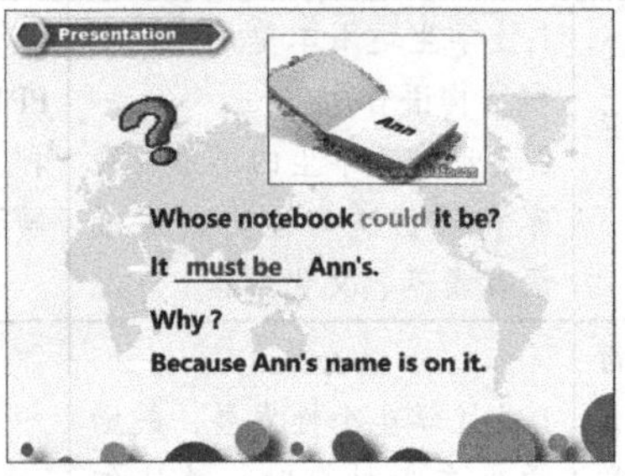

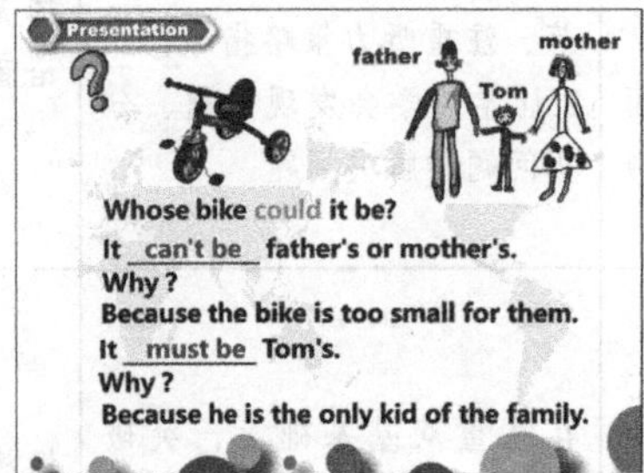

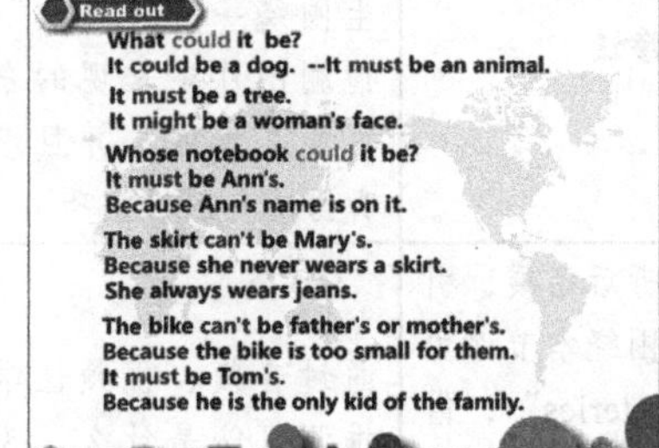

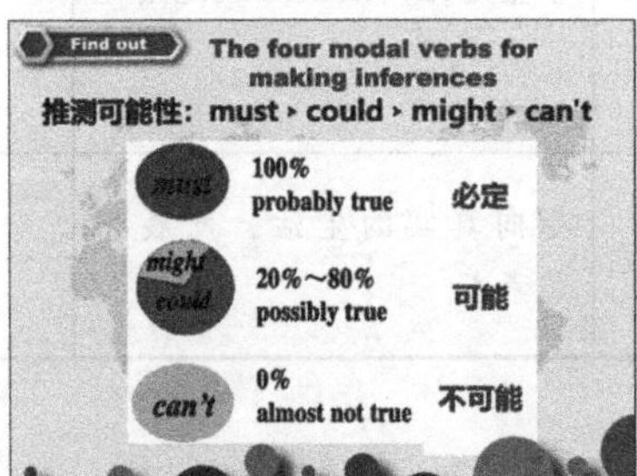

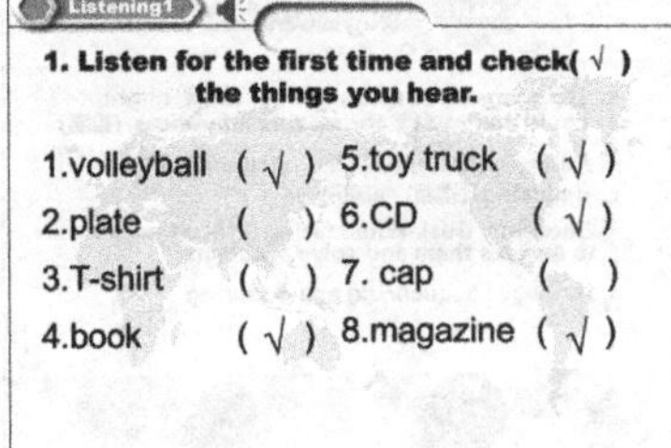

Listening1

2. Listen again and match each thing with a person, then a reason.

Person	Thing	Reasons
1) Jane's little brother	volleyball	a.J.K. Rowling is her favorite writer.
2) Mary	toy truck	b.She loves volleyball.
3) Carla	magazine	c.He was the only little kid at the picnic.
4) Deng Wen	book	d.She always listens to pop music.
5) Grace	CD	e.He loves rabbits.

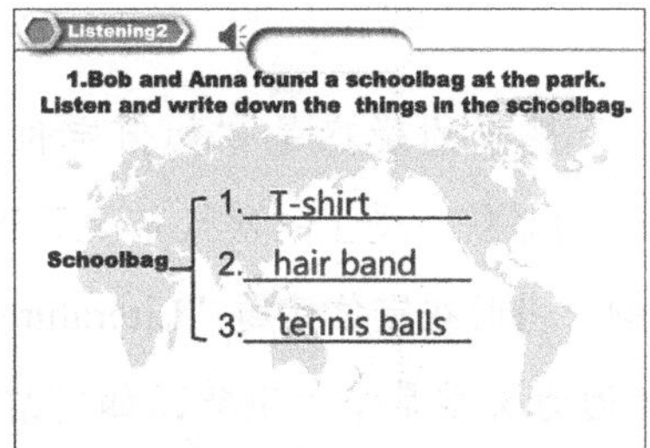
Listening2
1.Bob and Anna found a schoolbag at the park. Listen and write down the things in the schoolbag.
Schoolbag
1. T-shirt
2. hair band
3. tennis balls

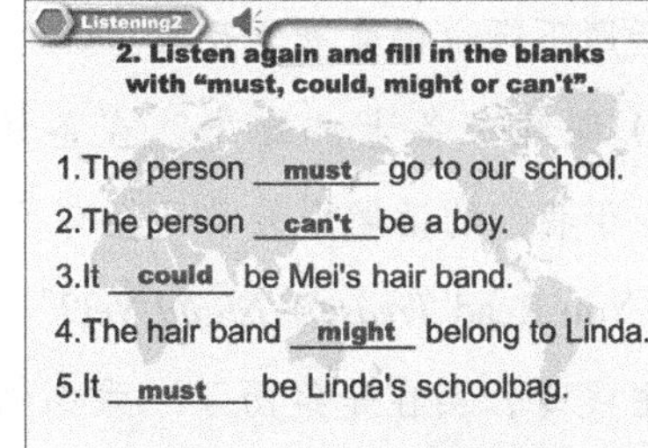
Listening2
2. Listen again and fill in the blanks with "must, could, might or can't".
1.The person must go to our school.
2.The person can't be a boy.
3.It could be Mei's hair band.
4.The hair band might belong to Linda.
5.It must be Linda's schoolbag.

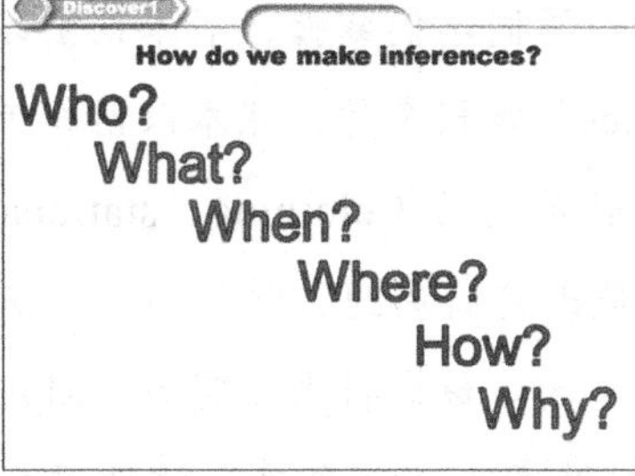
Discover1
How do we make inferences?
Who?
What?
When?
Where?
How?
Why?

Free Talk
Who could he be?
1
He can't be ____.
He could/might be ____.
He must be ____.

Free Talk
2
Who could he be?
A.Wang Feng B.Deng Ziqi
C.Hua Chenyu D.Yang Zongwei
He can't be ____.
He could/might be ____.
He must be ____.
Who? What? When? Where? How? Why?

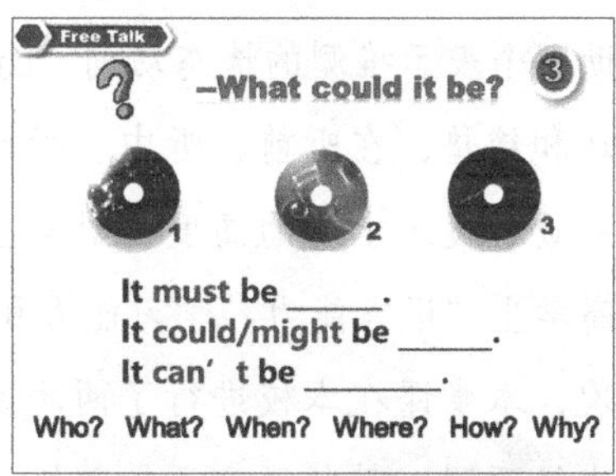
Free Talk
–What could it be?
3
1 2 3
It must be ____.
It could/might be ____.
It can' t be ____.
Who? What? When? Where? How? Why?

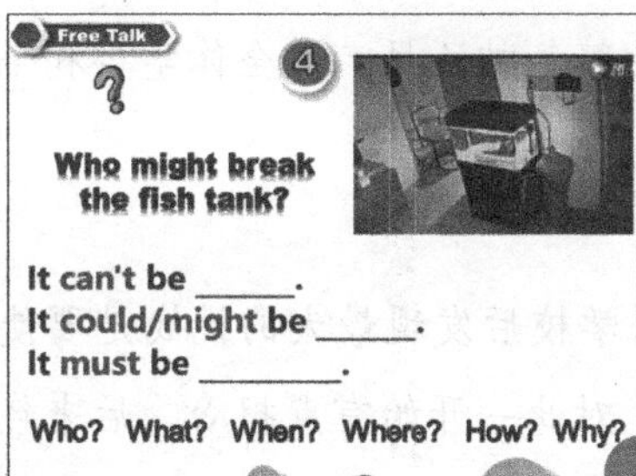
Free Talk
4
Who might break the fish tank?
It can't be ____.
It could/might be ____.
It must be ____.
Who? What? When? Where? How? Why?

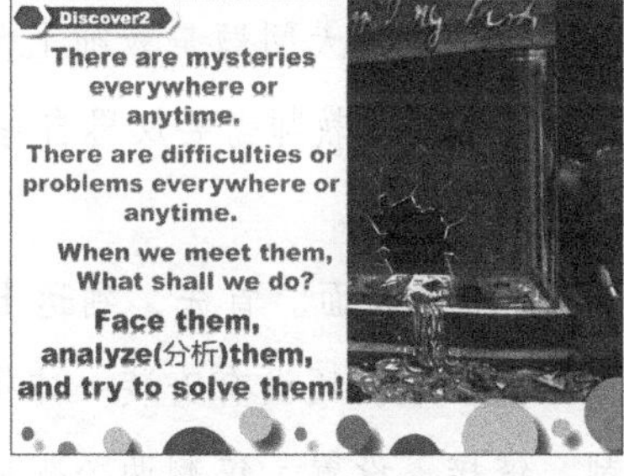
Discover2
There are mysteries everywhere or anytime.
There are difficulties or problems everywhere or anytime.
When we meet them, What shall we do?
Face them, analyze(分析)them, and try to solve them!

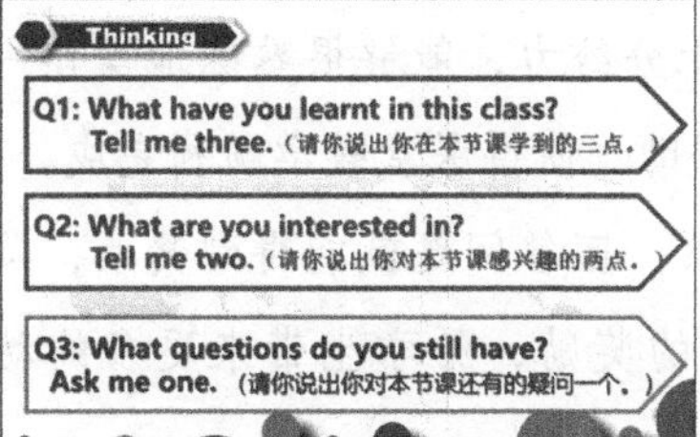
Thinking
Q1: What have you learnt in this class? Tell me three.（请你说出你在本节课学到的三点。）
Q2: What are you interested in? Tell me two.（请你说出你对本节课感兴趣的两点。）
Q3: What questions do you still have? Ask me one.（请你说出你对本节课还有的疑问一个。）

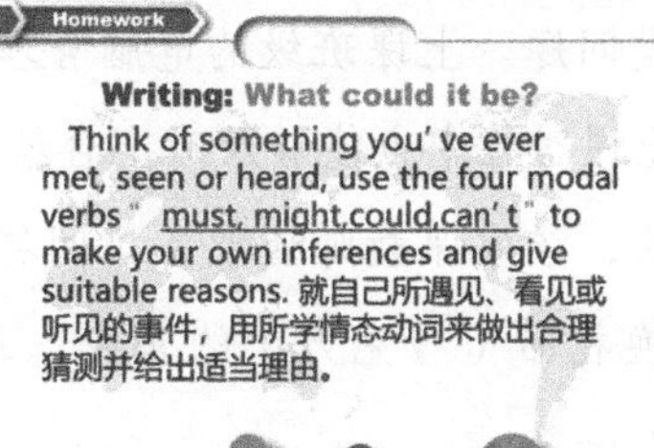
Homework
Writing: What could it be?
Think of something you' ve ever met, seen or heard, use the four modal verbs " must, might,could,can' t " to make your own inferences and give suitable reasons. 就自己所遇见、看见或听见的事件，用所学情态动词来做出合理猜测并给出适当理由。

5. 话题下听说课堂教学反思

（1）课程准备上。首先，在备课时，最大的疑惑是“如何定位话题主线”。由于我们的话题下教学已经有了自己的系统，受上一次八年级下册“Unit 8 Have You Read *Treasure Island* Yet?”影响，当时在定位话题“Literature”应当以何为主线时，实在是经历了一番纠结，因为文学是个大范畴，如何结合书本内容进行课堂整合，定位课堂主线是关键，最终确定为“books”，因为书本中出现了很多西方文学名著的书本名称，需要同学们掌握，书本词汇即是话题带出的词汇；而本单元的话题是“Mysteries”神秘事件，课本以话题带出“猜测身边的物品可能所属”活动的词汇是身边的物品（clothing，stationary，fun things，kitchen things等），这些词汇都是比较简单的、学生们已经掌握的词汇，如果以此活动为主线带出词汇，意义不大。最后将主线定为“Mysteries”本身，选择了学生感兴趣的话题，选择能够产生“信息差”的话题，由易到难，借助四个表示推测的情态动词“can’t，might，could，must”建构语言结构进行陈述和铺垫，在听前、听中、听后活动中一以贯穿，效果十分明显，达到了前后一致、逐步上升的高度，对学生的思维引领起到了很好的拓展作用，体现了提高学生“语言能力、学习能力和思维品质”的素养要求。

其次，本堂课在本校进行了两次试讲，第一次试讲时，其他教师认为最大问题是主线不明、教师语言不够精练；第二次试讲时，课件已经提升质量，可以拿出去上课，但最大问题是教师上课的精气神不足，对全体学生和个别边缘学生的关注度不够，教师需要反思自身。

（2）上课过程中。

① 教师准备方面。首先，到达上课学校后发现最大的挑战是要使用一体机来上课，由于本校还没有安装一体机，对此一开始有点担心，后来经过课件重新复制、链接、设置，仅剩两个视频没能链接上，经过反复几次操练，上课基本不是问题。上课班级的电脑管理员十分给力，能够很熟练地操作一体机，并且在上课过程中也能够及时上台给予帮助，使得课堂教学顺利完成。

其次，该堂课教师还准备了问答奖票，回答问题就能得到奖票，奖票多少决定兑换礼品（巧克力）的多少。适当的奖励，给学生带来更多的动力和积极性。

再次，教师在课前与学生见面时，先是带着微笑与学生问好，或积极回答或主动询问，与学生建立起初步的互动；在课堂开始前十分钟，结合单元话题“Mysteries”，教师利用学生对新教师的好奇，让学生猜测教师的姓名、来自哪所学校等，和学生建立起了初步的认识，让前来听课的教师甚至以为师生之前做过互动。

然后，教学的每一个环节转换需要教师始终带着微笑并给予学生极大的鼓励，用精练的语言带领学生进入下一环节。例如：

“The results are not very important. I just hope that you could be active and take part in it and then enjoy this class, ok?”

“I think you did a good job in guessing. But are you good at reading? ”

“Wow! You’re so smart! I believe you can do the following very well.”

“Is this funny? Now I’m showing you a even funnier one.”

“Is that easy? Now I have a difficult one for you. I believe you are good at it!”

“Please challenge yourselves!”

“Let’s give her some applause because she’s so brave to stand up.”（当学生起立但又回答不出问题时。）

“Don’t worry. It doesn’t matter.”（当学生回答不出问题时。）

“Do you like it? ...Yes? Yes!... Then you can say ‘Wow!’or ‘Amazing!’Let’s try:‘Wow!’ ‘Amazing!’”(with actions!)

“Boys and girls, I think you are really really great students! I love you so much! And thank you so much!”

最后，真正做到关注全体学生，能够用眼神关注全班每一名学生，能够关注不举手的学生，没有学生举手时不能慌忙着急，可以点名一些学生起立，没有回答出来也要鼓励学生下一次有机会再举手；鼓励学生用中文提问或回答；如有打瞌睡的学生要给予特别关注（起立、握手等），努力创造和谐而又热烈的课堂氛围。

② 学生方面。学生初见教师时，带着极大好奇心，基本上人人都能够主动向教师问好，体现了很好的交往素养。

课堂中绝大部分学生能够认真听课、跟上课堂节奏，近半数的学生能够积极举手回答问题。

绝大多数学生能够对教师的课堂产生兴趣并进行思考；部分学生的听力技巧和听力效果一般。

少数学生课堂有难度，能够尽力思考，例如前面提到的班级的电脑管理员，尽管英语听力跟不上，但或许是因为和教师做过了交流，他在课堂上也很积极地举手回答问题。

在表达时，遇见不会的表达，能够及时在教师的提示下用中文表达。

③ 教学策略上。首先，严格课型定位，将一堂40分钟的课划分为4个部分，即听前引入陈述、听中听力训练、听后活动拓展和总结反思部分。

其次，教师语言要简洁明了、指令清晰，语气抑扬顿挫，能充分引起学生的兴趣和关注，调动学生的积极性。

最后，关注学生整体，关照个别特殊学生，不放弃每一名学生。

④ 课堂效果上。考虑到听说课型有听力，借助多媒体，在课前进行“Warming-up”、播放视频、音乐等，可以让课堂活跃气氛。注重互动，关注学生情绪，引起学生的好胜心和求知欲。

总之，一堂课，定位课型和主线是关键；前后一致，由易到难设置是保证；全面关注、调动学生，充分吸引学生是锦上添花；气氛美好和谐，学生积极向上、对老师期待崇拜则是高层次追求！

话题下阅读课案例

1. 教学理念

阅读教学的本质是增加学生的可理解性输入，培养学生的语感。语言知识教学只是阅读教学的一部分，不是阅读教学的全部。

2. 关于英语阅读教学的几个问题

Question 1: Why do we read?

A. Reading for information.

B. Reading for learning the language.

C. Reading for learning cultures.

D. Reading for writing.

E. Reading for pleasure.

Question 2: What are the academic purposes for reading?

A. For general comprehension.

B. To search for information.

C. To learn new information.

D. To synthesize and evaluate information.

Question 3: What is the main focus when you teach reading?

A. To teach the important language points.

B. To teach reading strategies.

C. To test students' reading comprehension.

Question 4: What is the major activity of the reading lesson?

A. Check the students' understanding.

B. Let students talk about the reading.

C. Have students read the text.

D. Explain the language points.

E. Let students use the language.

Question 5: How many times are students supposed to read the passage?

A. Once or twice, from the very beginning to the end.

B. At least three times, but not necessarily the whole passage.

C. It depends on how many reading activities you have to do during the lesson.

D. It all depends.

Question 6: What level of reading competence are students required to achieve?

《义务教育英语课程标准（2011年版）》关于阅读技能的五级目标表述。

五级读技能学生必须达到以下要求：

（1）能根据上下文和构词法推断、理解生词的含义。

（2）能理解段落中各句子之间的逻辑关系。

（3）能找出文章的主题，理解故事的情节，推测故事情节的发展和可能的结局。

（4）能读懂相应水平的常见体裁的读物。

（5）能根据不同的阅读目的运用简单的阅读策略获取信息。

（6）能利用词典等工具书进行阅读。

（7）课外阅读量应累计达到15万词以上。

Question 7: What are the common reading strategies that can be taught to students?

Reading strategies that can be taught:

“Activating Prior Knowledge;

Predicting;

Skimming;

Scanning;

Guessing meaning of unknown words;

Recognizing text types;

Identifying topics and main ideas;

Word recognition exercises.”

——弗雷尔（homas S. C. Farrel）《阅读课的设计》（Planning Lessons for a Reading Class）

Question 8: What kind of activity do you usually use during a reading class?

Do you usually use the following activities when you teach reading?

True or False;

Multiple choice;

Ask and answer questions;

Fill in the table;

Put the events in order.

Do you usually encourage your students to:

guess the meaning of unknown words?

predict what the passage might talk about?

predict how the story might end?

think of a title?

describe the author's viewpoint/attitude?

find the topic of a paragraph?

identify the main idea of a passage?

create a mind map based on the passage?

use their own words to retell the story?

“在具体的阅读过程中，由于阅读内容的不同，作者所采用的表达思想、陈述内容的方法也不同，而读者本身语言水平、认知能力和阅读目的也有所区别，因此阅读的方法也不尽相同。”

——《英语阅读教学》(Developing Reading Skills) 导读

因此，在阅读教学前有必要对教材文本解读与阅读策略培养充分考虑，要对单元背景、阅读活动、语篇特点、教学重难点进行分析。

单元背景分析要点：

（1）单元目标：话题，功能，结构，词汇。

（2）板块联系：先前所学，后续任务。

语篇特点分析要点：

题材、体裁、篇章结构、语言特色、文化内涵、人文素养等方面。

3. 话题下教材文本阅读课件

Goals

Who's got talent?

Go for it Book3 Unit 4 SB 2b 2e

1. Learn and talk about four elements(基本部分) for a talent show.

2. Come up with ideas for our grade's talent show.

Activity 1 Skimming

Skim the first paragraph and find out <u>three talent shows.</u>

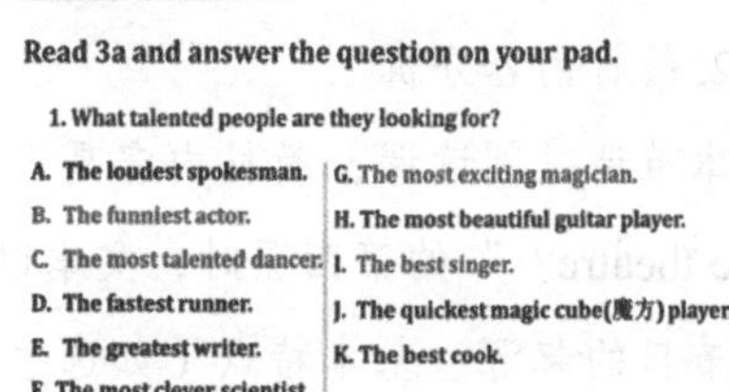

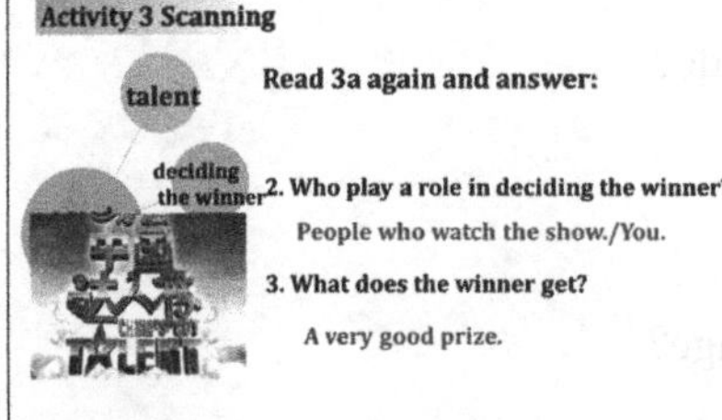

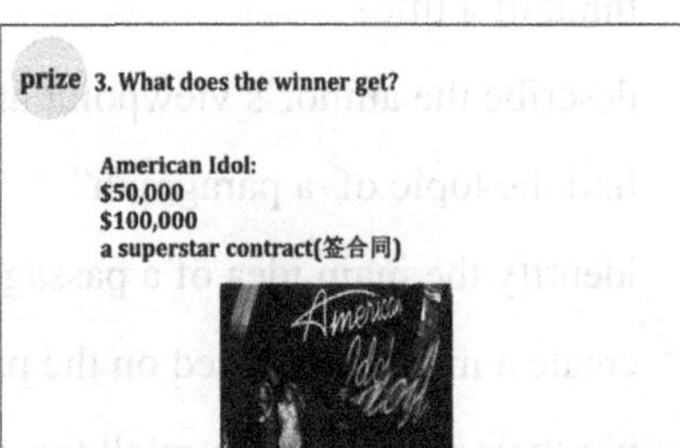

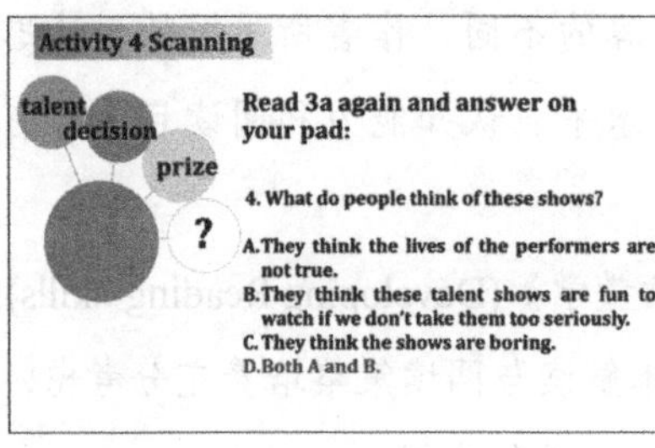

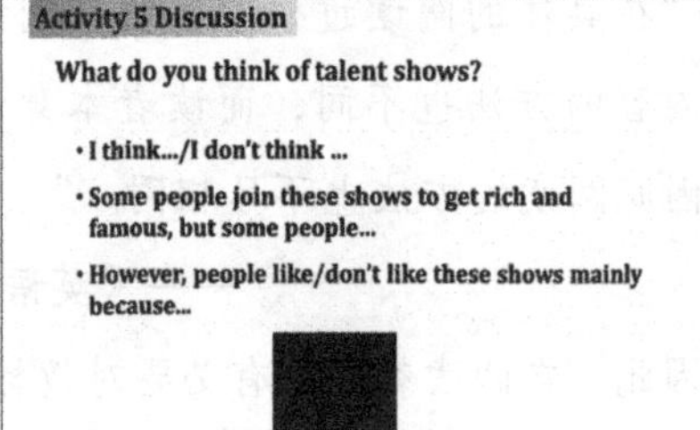

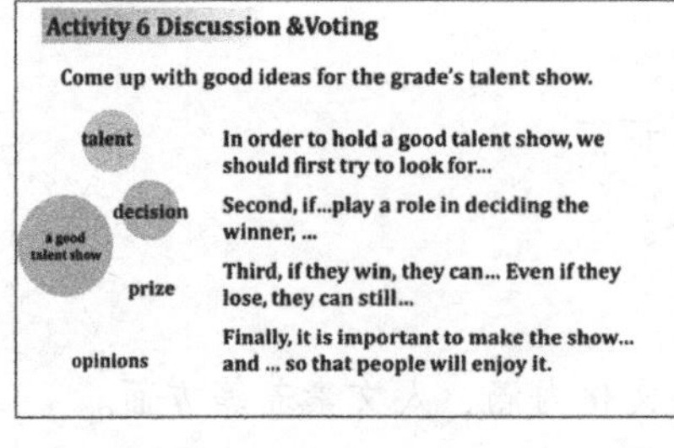

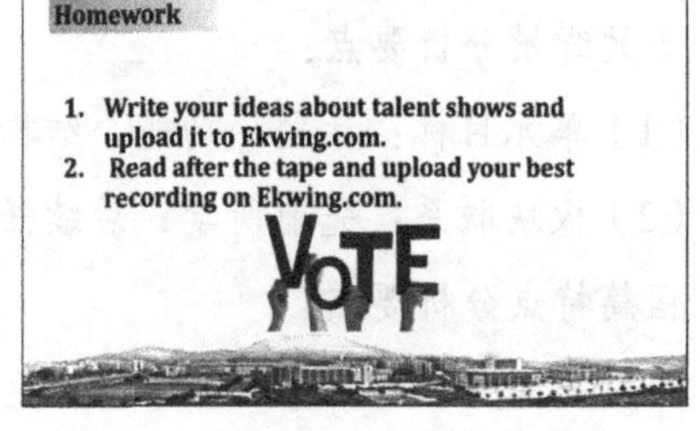

【案例】

话题下教材文本阅读教学设计

GFI Unit 4 What's the best movie theatre? B3

Topic: Talent shows

1. 基本信息

人教版八年级上册“Unit 4 What's the best movie theatre? Section B 2b-2c—Who's Got Talent?”

2. 教材内容分析

本节课是阅读课，教材内容是人教版八年级上册“Unit 4 What's the best movie theatre?”的第四课时，文本以“talent shows”为主线，主要学习“达人秀”节目的起源、基本特点（如选手类型、评选规则、奖项）以及人们对此类节目的不同看法。文章末尾，作者表达了个人对“达人秀”这类节目的观点，认为它们为人们提供了一条实现梦想的道路。最后，学生可以讨论对选秀节目的看法，学会辩证地看待问题。

3. 教学目标

（1）能够获取文本主要信息，即文本中关于达人秀节目的主要内容。

（2）能够运用跳读策略，快速找到三个选秀节目的名字。

（3）能够快速获取有关选秀节目选手、评选规则、奖项、人们观点四方面的细节信息。

（4）能够表达个人观点，判断是非，形成正确的价值观和批判性思维。

（5）能够运用文本中关于选秀节目信息为学校选秀节目提出建议。

4. 基本教学过程，见表7-17

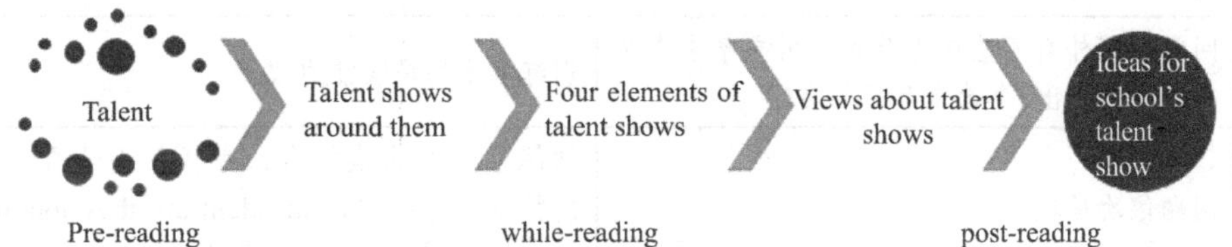

表7-17　基本教学过程

课前学习任务（课前一天）
学生在网上观看一个有关美国偶像的视频剪辑； 学生在翼课网上模仿朗读，朗读一篇有关选秀节目的文章； 学生在翼课网上阅读一篇有关中国达人秀的文章，并完成阅读理解练习
课前：话题导入与任务呈现
教师通过翼课网平台反馈课前任务的完成情况； 学生进行头脑风暴活动，说出教师和身边同学的才艺； 学生观看中山一中形象之星风采大赛视频剪辑
课中：阅读任务呈现
学生从文本中迅速找到3个“talent show”的名字； 快速阅读3a后，学生在翼课网上回答有关选手类型、评比规则、奖品设置、人们的观点等问题
课中：读后拓展任务
学生分享他们对“talent show”的看法； 学生从选手才艺、奖品设置、选手心态、意义四方面进行讨论，为学校的“talent show”提出好点子和建议，并投票选出最佳点子小组

续 表

课后
学生写下学校才艺节目建议书，上传到翼课网上； 学生在翼课网上跟读课文，并上传他们最满意的课文朗读录音

5. 具体教学过程，见表7-18

表7-18 具体教学过程

Activity活动	Motive活动目的
课前：通过本周日的文艺表演图片询问班里学生有什么才能，学生观看一中高中部的才艺表演	使气氛活跃起来，Is your talent show this Sunday a good one? Why? Is that one a good one?
教师给予学生本节课任务：了解一个选秀节目成功四要素，学生抢答他们所知道的国内选秀节目的名字	定义"what is a talent show"，激活已有背景知识，给予学生阅读文章和使用语言的情境
问学生国外有哪些选秀节目，引导学生在文中跳读，找出3个选秀节目的名字	训练学生的跳读能力
问题依次呈现： Answer the questions on your pad. ● What talent are they looking for? ● Who play a role in deciding the winner? ● What prize can the winner get? 学生猜测从这些选秀节目中可以看到什么才艺，学生速读验证，在翼课网上回答，回答后教师再问："What about other talent? Can Einstein join the show?"	训练学生的速读能力，寻找关于选秀节目的特定信息："What talent are they looking for?"同时拓展思维，思考talent的多样性 翼课网给出选择题（文字/图片） PPT逐步呈现选秀节目成功要素的三要素 Talent show •talent •deciding the winner •prize
备选：若时间应该，还可以让学生回到"who's got talent"的话题，即使他们设计了这么好的节目，其实社会上还有许多其他的才艺，如good memory，good hearing，good eyesight，如果挖掘到潜力可以给社会带来哪些贡献	进一步提升学生对talent这个定义的广泛理解，不仅仅局限于唱歌跳舞，人的才能有很多

续表

Activity 活动	Motive活动目的
学生预测“who can decide the winner”，在文中验证，口头回答教师；学生口头回答最后一个问题“what prize can they get”，教师补充具体的“prize”	训练学生的速读能力，找关于选秀节目的特定信息；教师给予美国偶像的奖项为例子（top 12 \$50,000; top 10 \$100,000, sign a superstar contract）
问学生，这样他们就可以设计好节目了吗，观众其实怎么看待这些节目的呢，再次阅读，在翼课网上回答有关人们观点的问题	训练学生的速读能力和概括总结的能力
教师再深一步询问，学生小组3分钟进行辩论准备，每组派出2人谈论他们对选秀节目的看法，在翼课网投票选出最佳观点组PPT： Work in teams and share your thoughts You can say it like this: • I think.../I don't think ... • Why do people join these shows? To get famous? To get rich? Well I think they can also... • However, people like/don't like these shows mainly because... • So, a good talent show should follow these four important rules: ...	总结学生能够从文中获取到的信息，帮助他们从4个方面考虑应该怎么设计一个好的才艺节目。帮助学生从服务社会、实现自我价值的角度思考选秀节目的社会意义和价值 Talent show • talent • deciding the winner • prize • meaning
备选：若还有时间，还可以问学生“Winner can get a lot, what about the losers? Can they also learn something? ”	围绕Meaning再继续挖掘，“talent show is not just fun, it can help people grow”，引导学生以积极心态面对输赢
布置作业： ①写一篇议论文，谈论他们对选秀节目的看法。拍照上传到翼课网上，投票选出最佳作文。 ②在翼课网上朗读课文	帮助学生再次深化思考，表达观点

话题下以读促写案例

1. 教学理念

运用思维导图锻炼学生的分析、综合、比较、概括、判断等能力，培养了学生的逻辑思维、直观思维、形象思维等多元思维的能力，使其能理性表达自己的观点。

2. 设计理念

为了把核心素养渗透到本模块中来，突出教学重点，突破教学难点，我们将运用多媒体教学，为学生创设生动、活泼的教学情境。运用任务型教学，围绕本模块的主题（weekend activities），设计各种与学生的实际生活和学习息息相关的教学任务。运用思维导图，培养学生的思维能力。增加自评、他评、互评等方式，为学生创建相互学习、相互帮助的平台，与同伴分享学习上的得与失，提高学习能力。同时，学生也相应地采取自主、合作、探究的学习方式，在教师的引导下，通过完成各种任务，来学习和巩固本单元的内容，从而达到语言综合能力的培养和提高，促进核心素养的发展。

围绕着本模块的话题“weekend activities”、本模块的教学目标重点难点，针对学生的具体情况，创新设计了一些教学情境和教学任务，如竞赛活动、猜词活动、故事接龙活动、展示活动等。

【案例】

话题下以读促写教学设计

GFI　Unit 12　What did you do last weekend? B1

Topic：Weekend activities

（一）教学目标

1. 语言知识和语言技能目标

（1）读懂文章，并能从文章中获取信息，培养阅读技巧。

（2）以读促写，能运用所学知识描述本人经历。

2. 情感态度和学习策略目标

（1）在生活实践中掌握生活小技巧，学习生存技能。

（2）在小组合作中积极参与，培养团队精神，共同完成学习任务。

（3）学会运用思维导图进行学习。

3. 文化意识

比较中西方周末活动，宣扬中国的传统文化，如敬老、孝亲等。

（二）教学重点

（1）读懂文章，并能从文章中获取信息，培养阅读技巧。

（2）以读促写，能运用所学知识描述本人经历。

（三）教学难点

以读促写，能运用所学知识描述本人经历。

（四）教学方式

mind-map，任务型教学法，多媒体辅助教学等。

（五）教学过程，见表7–19

表7–19 教学过程

步骤	目的	教师活动/方法	学生活动/学法	条件/手段
1. 热身（warming-up）	激发学生的兴趣，活跃课堂气氛	教师播放一段有关露营的视频和图画，并提问：What did they do last weekend	学生观看视频和图画，并根据视频和图画回答教师的问题：They went camping	多媒体视频和图画
2. 读前 Pre-reading	以思维导图引入与阅读材料相关的内容，拓展学生的思维，训练记忆和应用的思维品质	教师从记叙文的五要素“when, where, who, what, how”拓展与阅读材料相关的词汇	学生进行大脑风暴，在教师的引导下尽可能地说出更多的词汇： When: last weekend, National Day, summer holiday... Where: in the mountain, in the forest, on the beach... Who: classmates, friends... What: went camping... How: vehicles, feelings...	小组竞赛
3. 读中（While-reading）	读懂文章，从文章中获取信息，训练理解的思维品质	教师设置阅读任务 1. Guess where/what/how from the picture; 2. Detail reading: finish a mind-map	1. 学生根据书中图片猜测Lisa周末去了哪里、干了什么、看到蛇后的感受？ 2. 学生带着问题阅读文章并完成思维导图，小组内分享思维导图	小组合作
4. 读后（After-reading）	进一步理解文章，为写作做准备，训练学生的记忆、理解、分析等思维品质	根据完成的思维导图复述文章	学生复述文章	多媒体小组合作

续 表

步 骤	目 的	教师活动/方法	学生活动/学法	条件/手段
5. 写作（Writing）	培养学生的写作能力、训练应用、分析、创造等思维品质	要求学生分享自己的经历，先画思维导图，再根据思维导图写作文	画思维导图，写作文	教师指导写作方法，学生小组合作
6. 评价（Assessment）：	通过自评、他评、互评培养学生评价、创造等思维品质	展示学生的作文，对作文进行评价，并要求学生对本节课的整体表现进行评价。教师进行思想升华：It's important to keep safe wherever we go	学生看教师分析作文，小组内互相阅读作文，并进行自评与他评	多媒体
7. 作业布置（Homework）	巩固和拓展所学知识			

3. 话题下以读促写课件

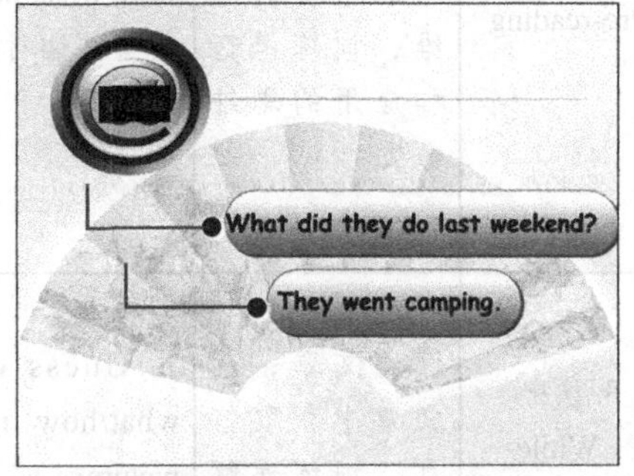

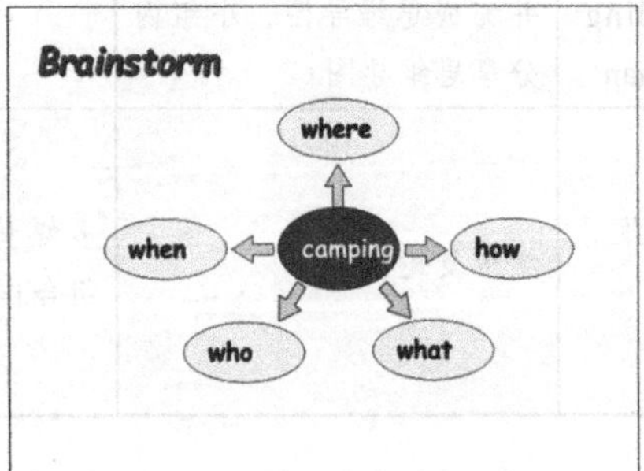

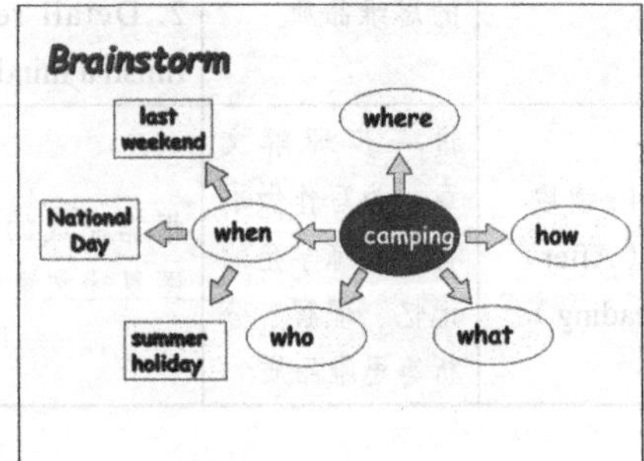

Group competition
where
in the mountain
in the forest
on the beach
by the lake
in the countryside

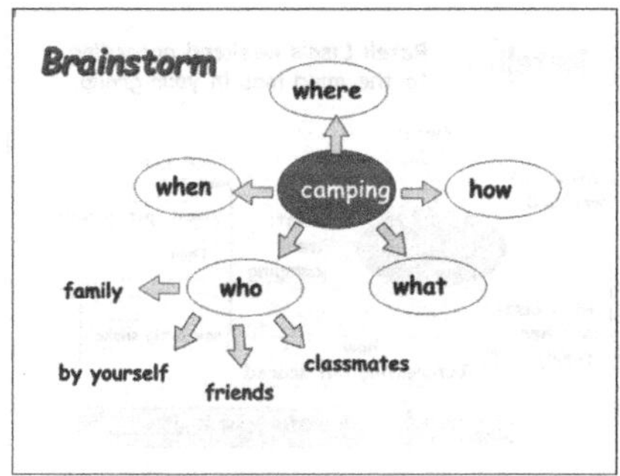
Brainstorm
where
when
camping
how
family
who
what
by yourself
friends
classmates

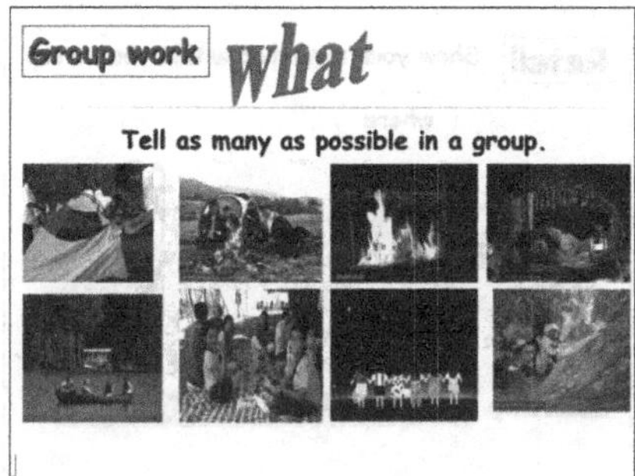
Group work
what
Tell as many as possible in a group.

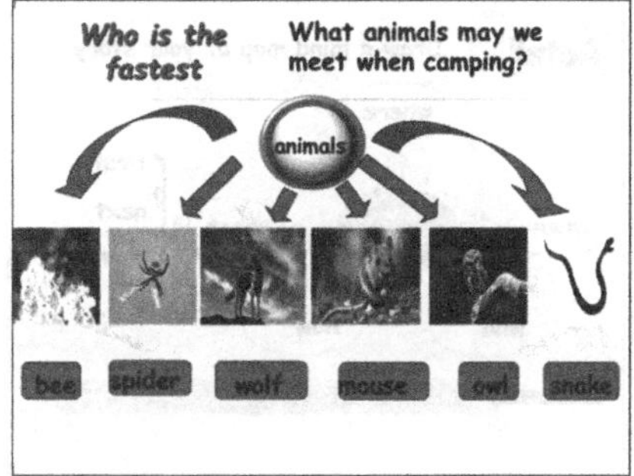
Who is the fastest
What animals may we meet when camping?
animals
bee
spider
wolf
mouse
owl
snake

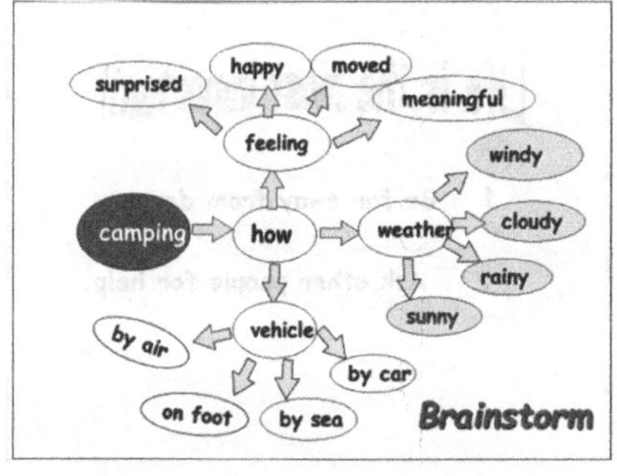
surprised
happy
moved
meaningful
feeling
windy
camping
how
weather
cloudy
rainy
sunny
vehicle
by air
by car
on foot
by sea
Brainstorm

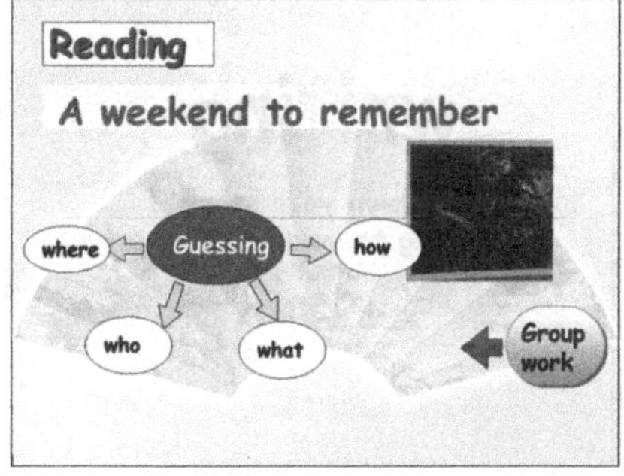
Reading
A weekend to remember
where
Guessing
how
who
what
Group work

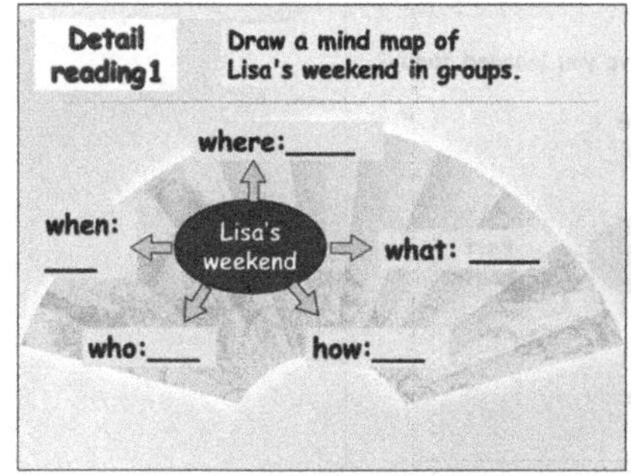
Detail reading1
Draw a mind map of Lisa's weekend in groups.
where:_____
when: ___
Lisa's weekend
what: _____
who:____
how:____

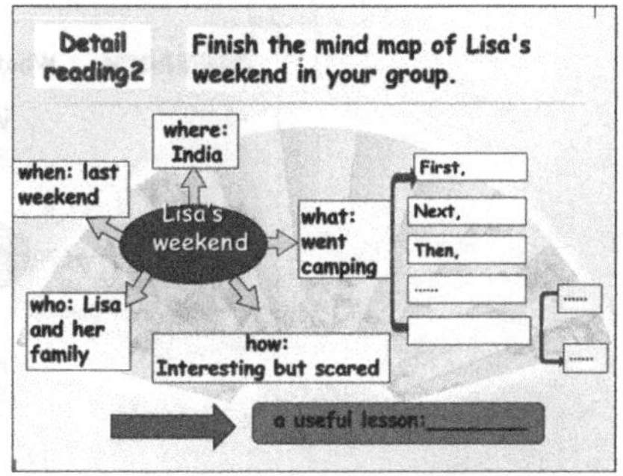
Detail reading2
Finish the mind map of Lisa's weekend in your group.
where: India
when: last weekend
Lisa's weekend
what: went camping
First,
Next,
Then,
who: Lisa and her family
how: Interesting but scared
a useful lesson:________

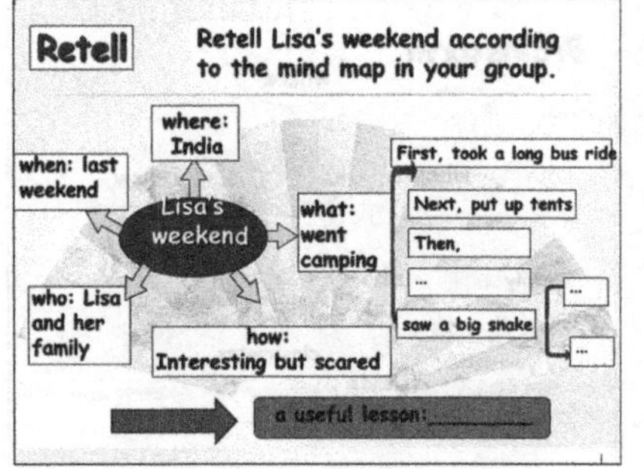
Retell
Retell Lisa's weekend according to the mind map in your group.
where: India
when: last weekend
Lisa's weekend
what: went camping
who: Lisa and her family
how: Interesting but scared
First, took a long bus ride
Next, put up tents
Then,
...
saw a big snake
...
...
a useful lesson:

难忘的
Did you do something unforgettable last weekend? What did you learn from it? Tell us your story.

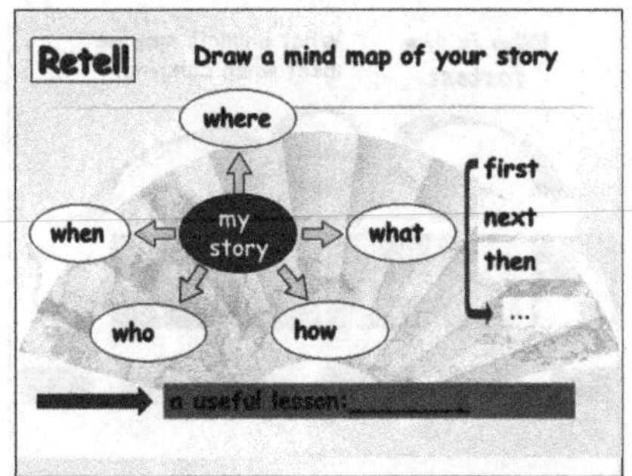
Retell
Draw a mind map of your story
where
when
my story
what
who
how
first
next
then
...
a useful lesson:

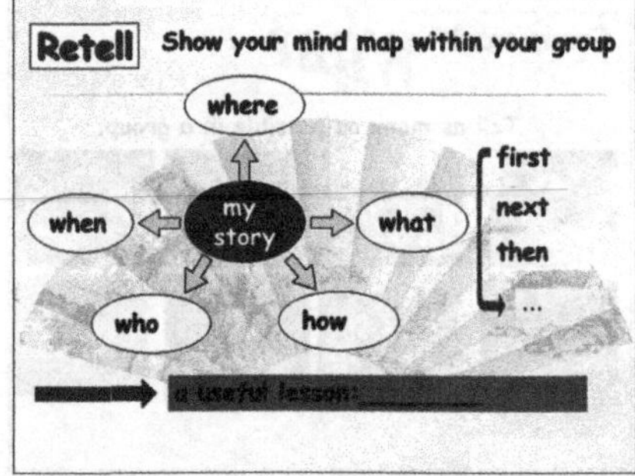
Retell
Show your mind map within your group
where
when
my story
what
who
how
first
next
then
...
a useful lesson:

writing
Write down your story according to your mind map.

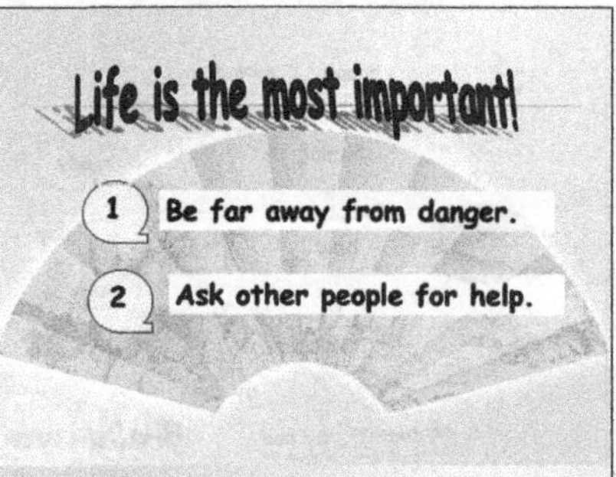
Life is the most important!
1 Be far away from danger.
2 Ask other people for help.

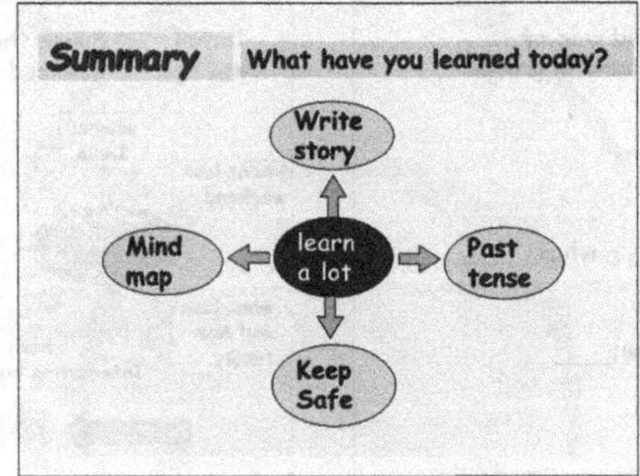
Summary
What have you learned today?
Write story
Mind map
learn a lot
Past tense
Keep Safe

4. 话题下以读促写教学反思

根据《新课程标准》精神和以培养学生核心素养为目的的教学原则，笔者认为，在设计一节课时，应该注意以下几点：

（1）充分利用现代化的教学手段，有创意地设计每一节课，激发学生的学习积极性和自信心，提高教学效果。

本课一开始，笔者就播放了有关露营的视频。学生被视频中有趣的活动情节所吸引，瞬间将学生的注意力全都拉回课堂，达到课堂开始的小高潮。

（2）所设计的任务一定要真实、有趣、有意义、有时代感，符合学生和教学的实际情况。

根据教学和学生的实际情况，笔者将本节课分为Pre-reading，While-reading，After-reading和Writing四个部分。

① Pre-reading利用概念图式将记叙文的五要素展示出来，帮助学生回顾并拓展相应词汇，为阅读扫除障碍，为写作做铺垫。

② While-reading中设置了两个任务，一是根据图片蛇猜测Lisa周末可能去了哪里，看到蛇后是怎样的感受。这个任务能激发学生的兴趣，发挥想象力，培养学生逻辑推理的思维品质。二是设置完成思维导图的任务，让学生进行细节阅读，这个任务旨在帮助学生理解文章，培养学生理解分析的思维品质。

③ After-reading让学生根据思维导图复述文章，培养学生的记忆理解和创造的思维品质。

④ Writing部分让学生小组讨论设计思维导图，描述各自的经历，旨在培养学生的应用与创造的思维品质。

⑤ 教师要求学生小组内进行他评与自评。

实践表明，这几个活动很符合学生的实际和兴趣，真实、有趣，既激发了学生的学习积极，又锻炼了学生的听、说、读、写的能力，还培养了学生的自信及合作精神。

（3）在教学过程中，不失时机地渗透思想教育和跨文化意识的培养。在学习其他国家文化的同时，更要了解学习并弘扬本国的文化，树立文化自信。

整堂课都以小组合作的方式进行，笔者一再强调小组合作的重要性，培养学生的合作精神。学生互相帮助、互相学习，既有效地提高了学习效果，又培养了学生合作互动的思维品质。

上完课后，笔者静静地思考，总结有以下困惑：

① 如何在有限的时间内，有效具体地实施分层教学？

② 如何更有效、更具体地提高学生的阅读理解能力？

③ 如何在阅读教学中更好地处理语法的学习和阅读能力的培养的关系？

④ 如何持续有效地激发学生的学习积极性、自觉性？

5. 话题下以读促写教学建议

这节基于阅读的写作课，教师引导学生将思维导图运用于阅读与写作中。首先，思维导图有助于激活学生原有的知识并调动他们阅读的兴趣。教师在文本阅读前通过引导学生对标题、图片和引言的扫读把握文章的主题，利用思维导图开展以主题为中心的头脑风暴，充分调动学生原有的知识，同时激发学生阅读的动机。其次，思维导图能促进学生对阅读文本的整体理解。在阅读教学中，教师通过问题的设计引导学生快速扫读全文，了解文章的体裁、基本结构和段落大意，并共同完成思维导图的中心主题和一级分支。然后，教师针对每个段落设计不同的练习，帮助学生理清文本各部分的重要细节，从而完成思维导图的二级、三级等分支。该过程有助于学生把握文章主要信息，剔除冗余信息，提高他们获取信息和处理信息的能力，培养学生记忆、理解、应用、分析和创造等思维品质。最后，运用思维导图帮助学生构建写作结构与思路，降低了写作难度。

让思维导图更多地走进我们的阅读写作课堂，有效地走出阅读教学中过分注重语言点讲解的误区，引导学生整体把握阅读文本，结合扫读和略读技能，了解文本的体裁，搭建文本的基本结构，并在不同练习的指引下提取相关主题的关键信息完成对文本的理解。将思维导图引入，帮助学生构建写作结构，能切实有效地帮助学生降低写作难度。从长远来看，可以提高学生的阅读写作能力与技巧，培养学生分析、归纳、创造的思维品质。

第八章
话题教学之意义

话题下的教材整合及话题下英语教学有效地拓展英语学习的广度与深度，从两个维度因材施教，分层教学，各有所得。对于能力强的学生而言，能够更加拓展自己的思维以及词汇量，对于基础弱一点的学生而言，可以适度提高自己的词汇量，依据自己的基础掌握一定的词汇。加大词汇出现的频度，反复见，循环用，即使不会也能感知到词汇的运用。同时，有效地培养学生的逻辑思维，分门别类，总结归纳，把书读薄。切实地提高学生的语言运用能力，由浅入深，层层递进，提升语言的综合运用能力。利用思维导图发散词块、功能语，把功能语组合在一起，形成了对话，这样对英语听说考试的情境对话产生潜移默化的影响，由功能语的答语连在一起，就形成了文段，为听说考试的口头作文以及笔试中的书面表达部分，充分积累了语言素材，也为终身学习奠定了良好的基础。具体表现在以下几点：

（1）初中学生现有的知识背景为“话题教学”提供了宽广的信息源。新目标英语教材的话题也是学生感兴趣、关注的话题，这使学生的学习目的更加明确，使语言学习和语言交际更富有真实意义。

（2）“话题分类复习”的核心任务是“话题讨论”，有利于充分挖掘学生的知识潜力，提高语言实践能力，增强学习效果。

（3）话题分类复习能帮助学生在复杂的英语学习中找到一个较合乎学生学习实际的切入点，使他们感到英语不难学，有一定的规律可循，从而消除学生学习英语的心理障碍。

（4）初中英语话题教学能有效地提高学生文化品质。文化（culture）是人类所创造的物质和精神财富的总和，多指社会意识形态。《义务教育初中英语课程标准（2011年版）》提出课程总目标是“通过英语学习使学生形成初步的综合语言运用能力，促进心智发展，提高综合人文素养”。课程从五个方面设计：语言技能、语言知识、情感态度、学习策略和文化意识，并提出“语言知识和语言技能是综合语言运用能力的基础，文化意识是得体运用语言的保证”，可见文化意识对英语学习的重要性。

语言离不开文化，文化依靠语言。通过英语学习，学生应对一些主要英语国家的文化有初步的了解，对中外文化的异同有所关注，并能“激发学习英语的兴趣，进一步接触外国文化，拓展视野，从而形成开放、包容的性格，发展跨文化交流的意识与能力，促进思维发展，形成正确的人生观、价值观和良好的人文素养”。缺乏文化交流与思想碰撞的课是乏味、缺少内涵的，也难以激发学生的学习兴趣。同时，如果教师忽视语言所含的文化或背景知识，会造成学生在接受信息或理解上的困难。因此，英语课堂不仅要学习语言知识，培养语言技能，还应是有文化的课堂。

Go For It 初中课本涉及的文化话题主要有：

（1）历史地理（history and geography）。学习英语，当然要了解英语国家历史、地理概况，但有的学生知识面窄，甚至对英国、美国的地理位置一无所知。上“感恩节”一课，笔者准备了世界地图，并从网上下载了1620年第一艘英国移民船“五月花”号来到北美洲这段历史的文字、图片、视频，有助于学生理解感恩节的由来及意义。

（2）风土人情（local customs，manners and feelings）。风土人情指一个地方特有的自然环境、风俗、礼节等，学生对这些很感兴趣。八年级下册 Unit 9中介绍了新加坡，除文中提及的地理位置、人口、语言、食物、景点、气候，教师可以拓展一些背景，如华人南下的历史、前华人总统李光耀的简介、当地良好的社会秩序和道德水平等。又如介绍复活节的由来、各种庆祝方式等，甚至带领学生过一个真实的复活节（染彩蛋、寻彩蛋、要糖果等），让学生在直观感受中，增加对节日的理解。

（3）生活方式（the ways of life）。生活方式指人们的衣食住行、劳动工作、休息娱乐、社会交往、待人接物等。中西方人的生活方式差异明显，如九年级Unit 10中，说到时间观念，哥伦比亚的特雷莎（Teresa）说：“We are pretty relaxed about time. We don’t like to rush around，so we don’t mind if people are a little late sometimes.”瑞士的马克（Marc）说：“In Switzerland，it’s very important to be on time.”了解各地人们的生活方式，有助于学生更好地沟通和相处。

（4）文学艺术（literature and art）。文学艺术包括小说、诗歌、散文、戏剧、书法、绘画、雕塑、建筑、音乐、舞蹈、戏剧、电影等。教师要充分利用各种资源，提高学生的文学艺术修养和鉴赏力。八年级下册“Unit 8 literature and music”可设计成一顿丰盛的“大餐”，借助各种资源，进行一次精彩之旅，驰骋在名著的奇思世界，徜徉在音乐的美妙海洋中。在教九年级 Unit 7、Unit 14 时，教师可介绍一些著名诗人，让学生欣赏、感受多种诗歌的风格。

（5）行为规范 （behavior rules）。行为规范是社会成员在社会活动中应遵循的标准或原则，如在公共场所大声喧哗、吸烟、穿拖鞋等是不礼貌的，进入别人的房间不敲门是不礼貌的，等 等。教师要关注并帮助学生树立规则意识，培养他们形成良好的行为规范。

（6）思维方式 （ways of thinking）。思维方式是看待事物的角度、方式和方法。不同国籍、文化背景的人思维方式有差异，如西方人直线思维，喜欢开门见山，观点鲜明，喜欢“求异”等，而中国人喜欢曲线思维，迂回曲折，喜欢“求同”等。

（7）价值观念 （value）。价值观是一种对事情做出评价或判断的标准，贯穿在生活的方方面面。勤劳、诚实、善良、勇敢、公平、正义、互助等是各国各民族都推崇的优良品质如八年级下册Unit 1，美国人Aron 独自登山遇险，右臂被巨石压住，坚持5天获救无望，他强忍剧痛，用小刀切断右臂自救的真实事件，体现了他的崇尚冒险精神（spirit of adventure）和勇敢顽强（bravery）。

总之，无论是以话题为中心的英语复习，还是话题下的英语课堂教学，教师应多角度、多层次地运用听、说、读、写、看的教学手段，使学生有机会把已学的知识与本话题的学习任务结合起来，使新旧知识在头脑中形成网状记忆，使中考英语复习更有趣味，效率更高。我们知道，学生综合能力的培养是多维的、立体交叉的，偏重哪一个或废弃哪一个都不会达到预期的教学目标。只有坚持听、说、读、写、看“五步并举”，以话题为中心展开复习，才能实现真正意义上的英语综合能力的提高。当然，我们教师还应该在探索中不断地反思和总结，不断地完善我们的复习策略与方法，对学生精雕细琢，才能取得好的成绩。

第九章

探索实践话题教学的思考

新课程改革下新的教材、新的教法，对英语教师和英语课堂效率自然也有新的要求。我们和很多教师一样，在这种新形势下积极应对，寻求新的教学方式以进行更加有效的教学效果。新的尝试自然也会困难重重，面对单元话题教学中的听说、语法、语篇及写作，在缺乏辅导材料的情况下，我们整合教材，以本单元的话题为主线，改编原文，或自编文章来补充教学材料及教学资源，举步维艰。在话题整合下教学的实践中我们意识到了自己的诸多不足，同时痛苦的磨炼也让我们收获了很多，最突出的感受有以下两点。

一、教师、学生的角色转变

《新课程标准》要求教师要转变在教学中的角色，不仅仅是知识的传授者，还应成为学生学习的促进者、指导者、组织者、帮助者、参与者和合作者。教学的过程是教师与学生交流的互动过程，教师要有意识地引导学生发展自主学习的能力，使学生真正成为学习的主体。

别利雅也夫认为，从心理学的观点看，词就是一个复合刺激（在感知和理解，说和写的过程中），又是人的同等结构复杂的反应（在口关头或书面表达自己思想时）。就是因为词的这些特点，所以在教学中要想方设法调动学生对外语的积极学习，只有这样学生才不会觉得学习英语很单调、枯燥，只有这样才会积极参与解决学习中所产生的多种心理障碍，达到预期的学习效果。

以往的英语课堂是教师在主宰，甚至是教师“一言堂”，而话题下英语教学则通过话题呈现，学生体验，学生探究，学生之间互助合作，自评或他评完成对本单元话题的学习。整节课学生活动占了4/5，成为真正的学习活动的主体。而教师的作用则体现在：①学习活动的设计者和组织者。将词汇呈现—

词汇运用—句型支持和口头练习—形成文章—自评、他评等各个学习环节加以设计并组织在课上实施。②话题学习的导航者。教师在课前要做大量材料收集查阅工作，选取一些适合初中学生阅读的语篇，并将话题词汇融入语篇之中。③学习过程中的促进者和帮助者。学生在自主学习或合作学习的时候，肯定会遇到一些知识上或者语言运用上的问题和障碍，教师要为学生提供及时有效的帮助。学生的学习方式发生了显著变化，他们不是被动地充当教师知识灌输的对象，而是变为学习活动的主动参与者，所有活动均由学生独自或协同完成。学生在明确任务的指引下，充分发挥各自的积极性，充分运用已有的语言知识，在完成文章的同时，既完成了任务又提高了英语的综合运用能力。

二、话题下初中英语教学提高了学生对英语学习的信心和兴趣

《新课程标准》明确指出，中学阶段是学生人生发展的重要阶段，教师要在教学中通过多种教学方式，使学生有机会通过联想、推理和归纳等思维活动用英语分析问题和解决问题，获得经验，增强自信，提高个人素质和综合能力。

我们首先要抑制“丧失学习动机的因素”。最常见且破坏性最大的是焦虑（anxiety）。焦虑指心理异常或过度渴望，它是个体由于不能达到目标或不能克服障碍的威胁，使自尊心和自信心受挫，增加了失败感和内疚感，从而形成一种紧张不安、带有恐惧的情绪状态。学生在学习英语时，常常会出现这样的情况。因此，在学习的过程中，首先必须激发认知主体（学生）的学习兴趣，才能充分调动学生参与的积极性，增强他们的主体意识。一般来说，决心越大，信心就越足，恒心也就越持久。同时，教师更应该在平时注意观察和引导学生，使他们相信，只要自己努力去做，是可以掌握英语词汇学习的策略和技巧，最终学好英语的。

在话题下的课堂中，学生活动遍布各个任务环节，通过参与、体验、协作、自评或他评，最后成功完成了对本堂课的英语学习，每一步成功都是对学生英语学习能力的褒奖，尤其是对于学困生而言，用一堂课换来其对英语学习的信心恐怕比学到什么更重要。重拾信心的学生也会以加倍的热情投入到英语学习中，而优生的话题篇章每每被学生和教师作为美文加以评判，自然更添了

自豪，而这种优越感也是这个课堂带给学生的。

作为新课程改革下的英语教学工作者，一定要不断地学习、不断地探索，提高自身的素养和教学水平，适应新课程的要求。由于时间尚短，笔者对于话题下的教材整合及话题下英语教学的探索才刚刚起步，自己也深知尚有很多不成熟之处，但笔者期望能在话题下的教学上帮助更多的学生重塑信心，奋勇前行。

参考文献

[1] 秦小惠. 多元智能理论与英语课堂教学 [J]. 现代交际，2010（8）：110-111.

[2] 刘道义. 试论中小学英语教师的专业发展 [Z]. 人教网，2010.

[3] 杨建宁. 浅谈初中英语教材的单元整合 [J]. 课程教育研究，2013（34）.

[4] 梁承锋，张丹. 初中英语新课程教学法 [M]. 北京：首都师范大学出版社，2010.

[5] 中华人民共和国教育部. 义务教育英语课程标准 [M]. 北京：北京师范大学出版社，2011.